THE STRIFE
OF THE SPIRIT

THE STRIFE
OF THE SPIRIT

ADIN STEINSALTZ

Selected and with a Foreword

by

Arthur Kurzweil

Jason Aronson Inc.
Northvale, New Jersey
London

The author gratefully acknowledges permission to reprint the following material from:

Ariel: "Remembering Jerusalem," vol. 27, Autumn 1970; *Aura:* "The Test of Jewishness," 1984; *Contemporary Jewish Religious Thought,* edited by Arthur Cohen and Paul Mendes-Flohr and used with the permission of Charles Scribner's Sons (copyright © 1987 Charles Scribner's Sons), "Sin" and "Talmud"; *De Yiddishe Heim:* "Dissonance in the Book of Psalms," vol. 38, 3 Kislev 5729 (1969); *Judaism:* "Religion in the State of Israel," vol. 22, September 1973, and "Hasidism and Psychoanalysis," vol. 9, no. 3, Summer 1960; *Parabola:* "Abraham," vol. 3, no. 2, "The Private Gate," vol. 3, no. 2, "The Strife of the Spirit," vol. 7 no. 4, "Becoming Unstable," vol. 9, no. 1, and "The Vertical Adventure," vol. 10, no. 1; *Shefa:* "Repentance," vol. 1, no. 1, "A Time for Joy," vol. 1, no. 2, "Death Shall Be Defeated," vol. 1, no. 3, "The Imagery Concept in Jewish Thought," vol. 1, no. 3, "Worlds, Angels, and Men," vol. 1, no. 4, and "The Psychology of the Soul," vol. 2, no. 4.

Library of Congress Cataloging-in-Publication Data

Steinsaltz, Adin.
   [Selections. English. 1988]
   The strife of the spirit / Adin Steinsaltz; selected and with a
foreword by Arthur Kurzweil.
     p.   cm.
   Translations from the Hebrew.
   ISBN 0-87668-986-1
    1. Judaism. 2. Spiritual life—Judaism. 3. Tradition (Judaism)
4. Judaism—Israel. I. Kurzweil, Arthur. II. Title.
BM45.S798213 1988   87-32173
296—dc19   CIP

Manufactured in the United States of America.

Contents

PART II

THE GIVING AND THE RECEIVING OF THE TORAH

PART III

TESHUVAH

PART IV
SOURCES

PART V
THREADS

PART VI

CONVERSATIONS WITH
RABBI ADIN STEINSALTZ

Foreword

A legendary Chasidic personality, Aryeh Leib, the son of Sarah, is known to have returned from a meeting with his mentor, Dov Baer, the Maggid of Mezhirich, at which time Aryeh Leib said, "I did not go to the Maggid of Mezhirich to hear his words but to watch him tie his shoelaces."

Of the many impressions this episode has made over the decades, a popular one is the notion that the Jewish student must not only learn from his teacher the words of wisdom handed down through the generations, but must also learn the practical wisdom, ways of doing and approaching things, appropriate perspectives, orders of priorities, down-to-earth information. This, too, is Torah.

An encounter with an authentic teacher of Torah is therefore an opportunity to learn many things on many levels. At times, the transfer involves sublime wisdom, blinding in its luminousness. At other times, the lessons learned consist of fresh and original approaches to old, familiar questions. Sometimes the master teacher is the bearer of secrets of esoteric insights into the complex nature of reality; at other times, the student is satisfied with simple procedures for the commonplace.

It is in the spirit of Aryeh Leib, son of Sarah, that I have collected these pieces. They were surely not written with this collection in mind. Rather, I have searched for these pieces, with the cooperation of their author, for the sole purpose of bringing them together—for myself, for other students of the rabbi, and for those who might want to get acquainted with some of Rabbi Adin Steinsaltz's work.

This collection of essays, discourses, and interviews is an opportunity to encounter an authentic teacher of Torah. Rabbi Steinsaltz himself has become a legendary figure in his own time; his wisdom, understanding, and knowledge have nourished many in seemingly diverse sectors, both within the Jewish world and without.

Adin Steinsaltz is perhaps best known for his own new edition of the Babylonian Talmud; its potential impact is being compared to that of Rashi. Today's most learned sages, among them the late Rabbi Moshe Feinstein and the Lubavitcher Rebbe—as well as the absolute beginners of Talmud study—all sing praises for Rabbi Steinsaltz's edition. He has also made a considerable impact with his books, which have been translated into English, foremost among them, his "discourse on the essence of Jewish existence and belief," *The Thirteen Petalled Rose*.[1]

The Thirteen Petalled Rose, whose publishing history includes a translation into Russian, known to be circulating in the Soviet Union, is a brief, 181-page introduction to Judaism, but unlike any primer on Judaism heretofore written or made available in English. Rooted firmly in the teachings of the kabbalistic masters, *The Thirteen Petalled Rose* presents a vision of reality that is a sophisticated analysis by a modern teacher, and at the same time offers a description of a series of worlds within worlds, populated by seraphs and angels, multileveled human souls, Divine commandments countless in number, and the process of reincarnation. (Its publication prompted a full-page article in *Newsweek*; indeed the rabbi has been the subject of articles in the *New York Times*, *Washington Post*, *Time*, and the press worldwide.)

Rabbi Steinsaltz has also written an introduction to the Talmud,[2] a collection of commentaries on several tales by the Chasidic

---

[1] *The Thirteen Petalled Rose*. New York: Basic Books, 1985.
[2] *The Essential Talmud*. New York: Basic Books, 1985.

master, Rabbi Nachman of Bratslav,[3] a Passover Haggadah,[4] a guidebook for individuals who are returning to Judaism,[5] and a series of brief, penetrating portraits of biblical personalities.[6] Simultaneous to the publication of this present collection is the rabbi's most recent book, *The Long Shorter Way*, an extraordinary series of discourses on Chasidic thought.[7]

In Israel, where the author has lived all his life, his public lectures, radio and television appearances, and prolific writings have attracted a wide following. In the United States and Europe, Rabbi Steinsaltz has also inspired a significant and growing group of students through his writings and public lectures. Representative of the esteem in which he is held in academic circles are the invitations he has received from Princeton's Institute for Advanced Research and Yale's illustrious Terry Lectures.

This volume, *The Strife of the Spirit*, is an eclectic collection of samples of the thinking of Adin Steinsaltz, written or spoken in varied circumstances during a long span of time. Their audiences were, moreover, quite diverse, as are the lengths, styles, and formats of these selections. While they all have, to one degree or another, a shared concern for the spirituality of human existence, the primary common thread is the author himself. Students of Rabbi Steinsaltz have long awaited this collection, which brings together writings that otherwise might never have become readily available.

Some of the chapters in *The Strife of the Spirit* are fragments of larger works in progress, some are occasional journalistic pieces, and some others are self-contained explorations of age-old theological questions. Neither the selections nor their order are the work of the author himself but rather that of one of his devoted students.

Part I, containing the title essay, "The Strife of the Spirit," consists of six essays that, in one way or another, are concerned with in-

---

[3] *Beggars and Prayers.* New York: Basic Books, 1985.
[4] *The Steinsaltz Haggadah.* Jerusalem: Karta, 1983.
[5] *Teshuvah.* New York: Free Press, 1987.
[6] *Biblical Images: Men and Women of the Book.* New York: Basic Books, 1985.
[7] *The Long Shorter Way.* Northvale, N J : Jason Aronson, 1988.

ner aspects of human existence. Particularly noteworthy in this section are the original, longer version of Rabbi Steinsaltz's essay, "Soul-Searching" (the shorter version having originally appeared in *Contemporary Jewish Religious Thought*), and a slightly different version of the first chapter of *The Thirteen Petalled Rose*, "Worlds, Angels, and Men." Also in this section is a discourse on the paradox as expressed by Rabbi Akiva: "All is foreseen and free will is given."

Part II is comprised of essays that focus on the Torah. "The Imagery Concept in Jewish Thought" is a concise statement that was more fully explored when the rabbi delivered the Terry Lectures at Yale University. In this section we also have a brief response to a biblical passage, offering the student an opportunity to see how a master teacher approaches an ancient text.

Part III gathers pieces of special interest for the newcomer to traditional Judaism. Rabbi Steinsaltz, having been born into a secular family, has himself experienced the trials and challenges that confront the returnee, the *baal teshuvah*. Each of these selections speaks powerfully to the individual working his or her way back to Jewish tradition.

Part IV brings together a few samples of original pieces of a unique nature. In a form that most resembles fiction, Rabbi Steinsaltz retells stories found in our classical religious texts. The results are narratives that are simultaneously rooted in tradition yet highly original.

Part V, "Threads," has no related themes or forms and perhaps best illustrates the usefulness of such a varied collection as the present one. These pieces give the student an opportunity to see how basic Jewish approaches apply in varied contexts. What the student often needs most desperately from his or her teacher are examples of "applied" Torah—not abstract, theological notions alone, but the application of these notions to real-life situations or events.

The volume concludes with a remarkable collection of interviews with Adin Steinsaltz, all originally appearing in *Parabola*, a quarterly journal that is a forum, from time to time, for the rabbi. Although the contents of these interviews are in and of themselves highly informative, the special aspect of these dialogues is found in the way in which Rabbi Steinsaltz receives questions, restructures them, and sheds light on the topics at hand by challenging basic assumptions that are frequently hidden in the questions themselves.

I am grateful and honored that Rabbi Steinsaltz responded positively to one loving student's request for access to some of his work. In making these chapters available, I only hope this volume can become a vessel through which the light of Torah nourishes and sustains us.

Arthur Kurzweil

Acknowledgments

W arm gratitude is due to those who devoted their time and energies to the translations of the articles in this collection. First among them was the late Dr. Aryeh Toeg, friend of my youth, who was killed in the first days of the Yom Kippur War. Amongst the others who are now scattered in various places in Israel and the United States are Jonathan Omer-Man and Michael Swirsky. In particular, Yehuda Hanegbi translated most of the essays and literary pieces. There are still others whose names have escaped me but who are no less deserving of my thanks.

Adin Steinsaltz

THE STRIFE
OF THE SPIRIT

PART I

SOUL-SEARCHING

1

The Strife of the Spirit

Peace of mind has come to be regarded in our time as one of life's highest ideals. Clergymen, leaders of cults, psychologists, advertisers—all seem to agree that this is the thing most to be desired. And of course all of them are in some measure prepared to provide it. Rest and relaxation are no longer the exclusive province of resorts and sanitariums. Peace of mind is regarded not merely as something pleasant and desirable but as a spiritual ideal and significant life goal, the final achievement to which various schools of thought and meditation aspire.

The reasons for this longing for tranquillity are not hard to find. Modern life, particularly in its characteristic urban form, is beset by political and economic upheaval, insecurity and fear. It is an unquiet life. Global tensions impinge not only on the body politic and its functionaries but on each individual citizen. People in general, even those most concerned with peace of mind—be it for themselves or as a "commodity" to be sold to others—have very high *material* expectations, which in turn necessitate ceaseless striving. The shattering of accepted values and the distrust of established frameworks create confusion and changed, sometimes contradictory, expectations. All this makes modern man tense, pressured, discontented. Hardly anyone escapes this stress or the measure of difficulty it adds to life. Home, family, friends, and good works all gradually disappear or are drastically altered in form, and to the extent that they survive at all they tend themselves to become sources of tension and competition. Thus, beyond all the internal and external turbulence, what man seeks is tranquillity, relaxation, and peace, at least with himself. The almost physical need for quiet and surcease quickly received legitimation and even reinforcement from psychology, philosophy, and religion. Tension and stress of all kinds have come to be seen not only as discomfiting and harmful but as morally invalid. Peace and quiet have become the great motive forces of all striving, including the spiritual.

Of course, the quest for peace in all its forms is quite ancient, as old as mankind itself. So, too, is the elevation of peace as a supreme value. Nevertheless, there is still room to question the notion of peace of mind and its place in the hierarchy of human needs. What, first of all, does it really mean? One important definition is provided by the Jewish sages in the context of a lengthy discussion of the many virtues of peace: "The Holy One, blessed be He, found no vessel but peace which could contain all blessing." This beautiful passage, which makes peace the very basis of all good things, goes on to make a telling distinction: peace is a vessel that can contain blessing, but it can also contain nothing at all, can be an *empty* vessel. Here is a truth with wide applicability, be it in the international or the interpersonal realm, or in the life of the individual soul. Peace with no content, meaningless tranquillity, rest without sanctity—all are empty vessels. At best, the emptiness is soon filled with positive content. In all too many cases, however, the empty vessel becomes a repository for whatever comes along. In the absence of anything else, rubbish and abomination can fill the void. It is the same with empty peace of mind: the tension and pressure seem to be gone, but nothing positive comes to take their place. A vacuum results, an existence devoid of effort or thought, which is in no sense better than what preceded it. A life of vain struggle can be relieved of pressure and anxiety and yet remain as vacuous and meaningless as before. Furthermore, while stress is likely (particularly when unremitting) to be unpleasant, it has the potential of achieving meaningful, valuable change. An equilibrium from which stress has been eliminated can be a terminal state, a condition from which all further development is likewise excluded—in short, the peace of death.

The notion of peace of mind as a supreme value, as a standard by which to judge all other aspects of life, is worse than inadequate. It carries with it the real danger of apotheosizing emptiness and negation—negation of good as well as evil, release from achievement as well as from stress. The Torah's identification of life with good and death with evil (Deuteronomy 30:15) is cast in different, less exalted and more down-to-earth imagery in the Book of Ecclesiastes: "Better off the living dog than the dead lion" (9:4). And the reason given has to do with the potential for change, however bitterly expressed: "For the living know that they shall die, while the dead know nothing at all" (9:5). In other words, as long as there is activity, as long as there is struggle—however lowly, however reduced to the level of the "dog's" struggle for bare existence—it is better than the empty tranquillity of death, the peace which contains nothing and points nowhere beyond itself.

The underlying issue here has to do with the positioning of a scale of values. As soon as there is some kind of ordering leading to a final goal—be it material, spiritual in a broad sense (knowledge, truth, love), or specifically religious (divine enlightenment, etc.)—one must judge each situation and each action, not according to its "comfortableness" but according to whether or not it is likely to bring one nearer to that goal. In our case, peace of mind may come as pleasant relief to one sorely pressed by the exigencies of life; but as long as he aspires to more in life than escape, such peace cannot be for him an end in itself. Inner tranquillity and turmoil, relaxation and tension, must be judged in light of the ultimate goal. And there are goals that cannot be attained except through struggle waged within the soul.

The path of inner conflict is neither easy nor pleasant. Every struggle, first of all, carries the risk of an undesirable outcome. Every attempt to reach a higher level of existence, to break out and ascend, entails not only the possibility of failure to rise but also the possibility of falling even lower than the point where one began. Then too, no spiritual ladder can be ascended without constant effort, tension, and anguish. In many ways, this struggle is between different and often opposing values. But in a much broader sense, it is an ongoing struggle between the given, present reality and that which has not yet come into existence but waits to be created. The inertia of what already exists is always the great enemy and can never be fully overcome. The never-ending conflict between the existent and not-yet-existent is at the root of man's whole inner struggle.

In fact, it is in the nature of inward, as opposed to outward, political or economic struggle, that it knows no termination, no clear-cut end point at which victory or defeat can be pronounced. There may be brief pauses for rest or changes of pace along the way, alternations between stretches of acute, violent exertion and stretches of slower, more measured progress, but there is no real conclusion. Not only are the goals of spiritual struggle loftier and more difficult to attain than other kinds of goals, they are enlarged by the very process of achieving them, by the inward growth of the struggler himself. Thus, when quiet overtakes the spiritual struggle, it is in itself a sign of backsliding and descent. There can be no greater danger to one laboring to reach a higher spiritual and moral plane than the feeling that he has achieved it. Such feelings of self-satisfaction generally indicate a blurring of the vision of the goal itself.

In every serious discussion of spiritual matters there arises from time to time the question of whether man is capable of reaching any goal whatsoever except through such protracted inner conflict. This is not just a theoretical question. In fact, everyone whose life is oriented toward goals beyond his present reality, goals that are not simply the direct and natural outcome of his present way of life, is already involved in such a conflict. Is there no alternative? For most of us, the answer is no. There does not appear to be any magical way, without deception, to resolve, conclude, and thus dispense with the inner struggle.

True, there are in this world people with extraordinary gifts who are able to bring the opposed forces in their own souls into genuine harmony with each other, harmony that these forces energize rather than undermine. But such abilities result not from following any particular teaching or path but from rare inborn attributes. The latter are not unlike other sorts of native endowments—natural beauty, for example, which radiates from every movement and gesture and needs no artificial enhancement; or genius in a particular discipline, which is reflected in nearly total mastery. People with such endowments do need to make a certain effort, but it is mainly to avoid spoiling what they already possess. There are, likewise, rare cases of people especially gifted in the moral realm, and here too, the quality is not one that can be achieved by any sort of exertion. Of course, many who are not particularly gifted are responsible for significant and even decisive achievements in this realm, but never without effort or by taking an easy way. The extraordinarily talented are like rare works of nature—orchids or birds-of-paradise—whose character is something to marvel at and enjoy but not imitate. Nor do such people usually reach the same heights or depths as others in their grasp of truth. For there are certain precious insights that cannot be acquired except through tribulation, things born of struggle and effort that can never be harmonized, and it is the pursuit of these that makes for the highest levels of aspiration. It is, in any case, the unavoidable lot of most men to choose, not between turmoil and tranquil perfection, but rather between a harsh struggle to find themselves and a degeneration that in the last analysis offers no peace of mind either. Instead of waiting for a miraculous rescue, let a man take the other path, the only meaningful one, and prepare himself to do battle within.

Part of the preparation lies in this very recognition, that without inward strife there can be no life, that what a man endures is no mere "punishment" being exacted of him as an individual but the way of all men. And in a wider perspective, man's inner struggle is part of the larger process of life itself. On one level, the struggle within the human soul is likely to be between good and evil, while on another level it is between the natural (animal, biological) and supernatural (divine) elements in the human makeup. Taking yet a broader view—and one that does not contradict but complements the picture already presented—it is a struggle in cosmic terms between chaos and Creation, or, in physical terms, between entropy and life. In a sense, all physical existence represents the struggle of mute form to preserve itself, its weight, its volume, its component elements; and the same is especially true of life forms whose very being is a perpetual process not only of maintenance but of metabolic transformation, not only of self-preservation but of growth. This ceaseless tension between being and nothingness is no mere epiphenomenon or superstructure but part of existence itself, at all levels and in all manifestations. It is thus impossible for man to escape this tension or negate it entirely. It can be ignored or not recognized, but there is no release from it.

Indeed, man's question should not be how to escape the perpetual struggle but rather what form to give it, at what level to wage it. The tension of existence is to be found even in a molecule of inarticulate matter; in man, as in all living creatures, there are the tensions of biological growth and change. He can live his life and carry on his struggle entirely on that plane. If he does, that, too, will be the plane on which his spiritual life is lived, for even at its basest, human life cannot be lived without consciousness. At whatever level man struggles, there will his consciousness be involved. What differentiates the saint from the lowly creature of instinct, cunning, and cruelty is not the life-tension within him but the level at which his conscious being joins the struggle he must wage for survival. The choice between good and evil is preceded by an even more fundamental choice: whether to give spiritual or moral expression to the contradiction inherent in one's humanness or to try to ignore that contradiction. Difficulty and tension, bitterness and pain, are to be found as much in the ash heap as in the heavens. Each human being must decide where to take his stand and fight his battle.

2

Soul-Searching

Although the term *soul-searching* is relatively new—its use dating only from the Middle Ages onwards—the concept of a spiritual reckoning is as old as Jewish culture itself. The forms of this reckoning and the issues it encompasses may have changed from generation to generation, but it has remained a principal element in Jewish life and thought of all periods.

The forms of soul-searching are determined by the spiritual and existential background of the seeker, whether this is an individual or a whole community. Furthermore, there are certain criteria that are fundamental to the essence of such introspective review and that must be present in order for the process to take place.

The sages have called soul-searching "world-reckoning," in accordance with the concept that it is really a reckoning of broad generalities and of major principles, an audit encompassing a whole world. Of course, there are those accounts that focus on small sums or are even squandered on pennies, but true soul-searching is basically all-embracing, penetrating every aspect of one's world. Even when it begins or ends with small things, it always arises out of a feeling of the importance of those small things. Where this feeling of importance, of significance, is absent, we do not have a true searching of the soul, even where the objects of review are very great. True soul-searching must always be subjective, substantive, thorough, and fundamental.

Obviously, no soul-searching or world-reckoning can be carried out without some basic assumptions regarding its viability. In the absence of basic criteria that define its parameters, there is no substance to evaluation and reckoning. The criteria need not necessarily be religious or moral (in the usual sense of the word), but they must be acceptable to the seeker as a yardstick against which he can measure his spiritual state. In fact, every reckoning, of whatever kind, can only be carried out on the basis of established criteria and standards. Where these are absent, there is no reckoning and no account. For this reason, soul-searching can only be carried out against a specific cultural background that recognizes certain given values and rules as fundamental and essential. Their absence, or "relativization," denies a society (and the individuals making up that society) the basis from which such a reckoning might be made. More than this, in order for introspection to be a true exploration of the soul—a reckoning in which the individual or the community judges and weighs deeds, acts, and thoughts—that culture must possess a tradition of introspection. That is, the criteria in question must be consciously integrated and not remain merely external. Obviously, an extrovert society can also take stock of itself or of its relations with other societies, but such a stock-taking is of quite a different kind, a relatively superficial experience. A society whose laws and regulations are all social–behavioral may stand or fall on whatever merits it possesses, but it will never have the opportunity for true spiritual introspection because it has no criteria against which to measure itself and nothing to serve as a standard of comparison between what is and what should be.

In Jewish culture, which is basically a culture of values grounded in the belief in good and evil as definable and substantive values, "thou shalt" and "thou shalt not" are not merely social conventions, rules of social behavior. It naturally provides the background against which effective soul-searching may take place. What is more, the Jewish world view, with its exacting standards and qualities, actually requires this accounting, both of the community (the world community or the community of Israel), and of the individual within that community. In the Bible as a whole, and in particular in the Torah, soul-searching is primarily on a large scale, whether it is the weighing of a nation or of the whole world. This is in keeping with the scope of the Bible, which tends to relate to the Jewish people as a whole and in which the individual is not an independent entity but part of a society, of a wider public. Perhaps it is not surprising, therefore, that the first example of true soul-searching in the Scriptures is one made on a universal scale and apparently by God himself: "The Lord saw that the wickedness of man was great on the earth and that every imagination of his heart was only evil continually. And the Lord was sorry that He had made man on the earth, and it grieved Him to His heart. So the Lord said, "I will blot out men whom I have created from the face of the ground. . .for I am sorry that I have made [them]" (Genesis 6:5–7).

In spite of the theological problems inherent in this passage, it is still a classic example of soul-searching, a general reckoning in which deeds are assessed and the decision is in accordance with the conclusion reached during that assessment. Like any significant accounting, soul-searching must draw some conclusion, whether negative or positive. The fact that this particular reckoning is being made by the Almighty not only does not detract from its fundamental significance but can also serve as a model, as an example, to men to do likewise. This great principle of *imitatio Dei*, the imitation of God, is an explicit motif throughout the Bible: "You shall be holy, for I, the Lord your God, am holy" (Leviticus 19:2). Sabbath observance, itself one of the central commandments of Judaism, is another expression of this imitation: As God rested on the seventh day, so, too, do we. Thus, this first instance of soul-searching—and its aftermath, the Flood—contains all the elements essential to the process: review, recognition of offense, regret (or, in the case of man, repentance), and remedy.

Elsewhere in the Scriptures we find other examples, no less powerful, as in the stern admonitions of Leviticus 26:3 and that of Deuteronomy 28–30. In all these exhortations, one element is outstanding: Whenever man errs and sins, whenever the prevalent notions appear impervious to reproof and new ideas, there is nothing like calamity and disaster to bring the nation to its senses, to encourage soul-searching. This is something that is emphasized again and again by all the prophets, both in the historical books of the Bible and later, in explicit calls to repentance.

In general, it seems that the Books of the Prophets only relate to one or another aspect of repentance and soul-searching. Yet, there is little similarity between the prophets who foretell the future in order to give practical advice and guidance to the nation, and those whose dominant message—in the visions of disaster as in those of consolation—is one of admonition and reproof intended to bring the individual and the community to an examination of self, soul, and actions.

The dramatic instance of Ezekiel 3:16, 17, and the even more dramatic Chapter 33, describe the prophet's role as the "watchman of Israel." The watchman on his lookout post is not only meant to observe events—his ability to do so is, of course, the *raison d'etre* for his appointment to the task—he is primarily expected to give warning of approaching danger, to arouse attention to forthcoming attack by all the means at his disposal. In the same way, the role of the prophet is not merely to warn of approaching catastrophe. (Paradoxically, a "successful" prophet is one whose prophecy of disaster does not come to pass, because his warning has been heeded and people have altered their ways accordingly.) In many ways, it is the task of the ruler of a state to prepare for danger. It is he who must observe events and anticipate their possible outcome. This anticipation is not prophetic, although certain political figures have tended to see themselves as having prophetic authority, even when neither their personality nor their vision afforded a basis for such pretension.

The paradoxical position of the prophet—and this paradox is integral to his true role—is vividly expressed throughout the Book of Jonah. Jonah himself is very much aware that the more he himself succeeds, the more his prophecy is confuted. Jeremiah, all of whose prophecies of disaster are fulfilled, is unhappy in his role just because his words do come true, precisely because he himself would have wished it otherwise. The more important role of the prophet is to stimulate change, to provide alternatives, and to awaken the dormant strength and potential of the nation. "Let us search and try our ways and turn again to the Lord" (Lamentations 3:40) is the call; everything else is but an elaboration of this.

In postbiblical literature, spiritual introspection also has a prominent place, whether this is manifested in general admonitions or whether in an emphasis on, and encouragement to, soul-searching. "Come, let us reckon the world's account," or "Come, let us make our reckoning with the world," figure prominently, whether tacitly or overtly, in homilies and exegeses. However, there is a marked change between the biblical calls to introspection and those found in the Talmud and later literature. While the approach in the Bible is public and national, it later acquires a more individual, private character.

In the Bible, the kings of Israel and Judah are exhorted to repent not because of their importance as individuals but because their behavior (including their most private actions) has a significance that affects the whole nation. It is possible to discern an occasional duality of attitude in that the prophets regarded private sin, even a grave sin, with less severity than they did a minor public transgression. There are many examples of this distinction, notably in relation to the sins of Saul and David. Saul's sin—his disobedience of the Prophet Samuel—was punished by the cessation of his dynastic line. David's sin, in the episode of Uriah and Bathsheva, was forgiven, even though at the personal level he was severely punished. The sages comment that this striking difference lies in the very essence of those sins. Saul's transgressions, great and small, were in the national sphere: He sinned as a king and as a leader. David's sin was private and personal, so that his punishment, as it were, fitted the crime and did not imply a total rejection of his line. Thus we see that the prophetic admonitions are directed mainly toward the nation, the community of Israel, in which individuals are only part of the whole. In the Talmud, on the other hand, the admonition, the call to repentance and to soul-searching, is more likely to be addressed to the individual. It appears that this difference is not one of principle but is rather a matter of social outlook and has two distinct aspects: the nation as a spiritual entity and the nation as a political organization.

The prophets did not address themselves to specific individuals but to the nation as a whole, because individuals tend to act not only of their own volition but in accordance with, and in response to, the general consensus. The prophets themselves were not representative of their generation, but outsiders to it, struggling against the tide, against the conventions of their society. The need for revision, which they preached, did not therefore relate to the individual level; it was a call for national change and was aimed at those very sectors of society that had the power to bring about such changes and to introduce innovations. "Hearken ye this, O priests, and hearken ye house of Israel, and give ear, O house of the king, for judgment is yours" (Hosea 5:1). In other words, "you" have the power to change things.

From Second Temple times on, however, matters changed considerably. Not that people suddenly became paragons of virtue, but the general world view had altered and the national consensus had changed, formed as it was by the leadership of the day, by the scholars. Individuals and whole groups, including the leadership itself, might sin—willfully or in error—but a general consensus existed as to what in fact constituted transgression or sin, and certain norms and rules were common to the Jewish people as a whole.

From this point in history, soul-searching, world-reckoning, was no longer a call to drastic change, for a different perspective of the world, for renewed national awareness. Rather, it became a detailed examination of the exceptional, of correction at the individual level. To be sure, even in talmudic times and thereafter we find criticisms of the community, sharp reproofs against large sectors of Jewry (and even against the nation as a whole), but the point of departure was now a widespread acceptance of those same fundamental principles. In most cases, the preacher and the exegist of the Second Temple period, the scholar expounding in the synagogue in mishnaic and talmudic times, the preachers of the Middle Ages and thereafter, acted as representatives of the community. True, they were critical of defects and failings, calling for soul-searching in relation to both personal and communal issues. Yet preacher and community were no longer opponents but rather partners. More than they came to renew, these teachers came to remind and recall. They preached continuity rather than revolution and, to the extent that there was a call for change, it seems to have come as an expression of a fundamental consensus within the community as a whole.

Over the course of centuries the political structure of the Jewish nation had altered and developed. At the time of the First Temple it was a geographically and socially compact unit, and for a very long period of time the authority of the central government was not only unchallenged but also extended to the most fundamental national issues. Even when there was no centralization, there were other significant, partly autonomous political constellations, as, for example, the tribal units or the great families of premonarchical times. During the Second Temple period this "national consensus," or cohesiveness, gradually weakened and it became clear that, *de facto* if not *de jure*, the nation no longer functioned as one unit. Those same, largely autonomous congregations still lacked the sociopolitical power to make decisions that would be binding on the nation as a whole. Even the head of the Babylonian exile, despite far-reaching authority and official backing, had far less control over his own community, let alone others, than did, for instance, a tribal leader in the time of the Judges.

Thus, a basic change took place in determining decision-making centers at different periods. At first a centralized and structured society was activated by its elected or hereditary leader as a single body, in which individuals had only a limited degree of influence on communal decisions, while later societies were in fact more "democratic" (that is, they were based on the voluntary cooperation of the individual with the community in which he lived). Certainly the Jewish leadership often acted as if this was not so, even though they knew very well the limitations of their power and of their ability to impose drastic change from above, even in those cases where official government support was great. Through the ages, it can be shown that in each place where powerfully attractive movements arose, the Jewish leadership of the day was unable to counteract them to any significant degree. Thus, many undesirable religious and political phenomena, such as the deep-rooted vestiges of Sabbateanism, were finally eliminated, less by official edict than by a prolonged process of admonition and persuasion.

It is obvious that the way in which the "guardian" approached the nation in post-talmudic times differed from the days of the Prophets. There was no longer a call for overall substantive change but for conceptual, attitudinal revision on the part of the individual. Historical modifications came about as the result of accumulated individual variations in thought and behavior, which gradually affected the whole community. For example, let us examine the immense spiritual shift that took place in the Jewish nation, in particular with Spanish Jewry, at the end of the Middle Ages. The admonitions sounded in those days are indicative of the spiritual vices that existed in the nation. Many have pointed out that perhaps the majority of those Jews who, under duress, adopted Christianity were from the educated upper classes—a fact that points to a deep, long-standing internal weakness in Spanish Jewish society of those days. The changes that subsequently took place, however, did not result from national decision, nor even from a large-scale communal one, but from changes within individuals, by people at all levels of society, each one of whom actually acted as an independent entity.

The call to soul-searching, that admonitory call that appears so often in literature, was also for many generations an essential part of Jewish practice. For generations, both the *maggidim* in the cities and the itinerant preachers who visited the outlying hamlets and villages preached repentance and soul-searching. Several days of the year were set aside for this purpose, such as the entire period from the beginning of the month of *Elul* (August/September) until the Day of Atonement itself. What's more, it was for centuries the accepted custom among all the communities of Israel to set aside the eve of every new month as a day of repentance and fasting known as a "minor Day of Atonement." On these days, the central theme of sermons and study was the soul-searching incumbent on the individual vis-à-vis the Creator and the reckoning that same individual must make with himself. Many people dedicated several hours daily to studying *musar* literature, which dealt with ways of improving and correcting the soul.

This kind of introspection was intended not for outstanding scholars and the pious but for the ordinary Jew—the Jew who throughout the year was absorbed with the problems of livelihood and business and all the other cares of daily life. Needless to say, soul-searching was more refined and developed (and even became the central issue) in those circles and groups that devoted themselves to an intense spiritual life, such as the kabbalists among Sephardic Jewry and the *Chasidim* among the Ashkenazic Jews. For such people, soul-searching was a matter of profound, daily significance, and whether they were Torah scholars or not, they set aside some time for reviewing the deeds, words, and thoughts of each day. The long version of the *Shema* recited on retiring at night, containing as it does a passage of repentance and regret, was considered by many as particularly appropriate to this purpose.

Yet, despite these instances of soul-searching as part of the routine of life, as something consciously present at all times, for the community as a whole, such introspection usually occurs only in times of trouble and distress. This is true both of imminent and anticipated catastrophe and of events that have already taken place, leaving a deep and tragic impression. In this context, the Torah itself expresses a constant, unequivocal call to reconsider, to reflect, *before* it is too late. "Only take heed and keep your soul diligently" (Deuteronomy 4:9). This call is frequently repeated in a variety of different ways. Nevertheless, it seems that we also come across another, more pessimistic yet more realistic attitude: "And when all these things have come upon you, the blessing and the curse, which I have set before you, and you call them to mind among all the nations where the Lord, your God, has driven them, and return to the Lord, your God . . ." (Deuteronomy 30:1, 2). That is to say, the hour of reckoning, when not only the few undertake to search their souls, is the hour of catastrophe and its aftermath. It is disaster that motivates self-scrutiny and self-examination. This assertion, which appears many times in all the prophetic books, has time and again been historically verified. Thus, it appears that catastrophe is the spur, the great stimulus that brings both the individual and the community to reconsider their spiritual state.

One of the reasons for this may lie in the very nature of man: One tends not to make an extensive spiritual reckoning over trivial matters, and the round of daily life offers little opportunity, or at least little time, for this. Catastrophe, on the other hand, destroying as it does the continuity of routine, creates leisure. Yet, although soul-searching is often complex and requires time and profound attention, this is not always the case. Such a reckoning can, in fact, be swift and brief. Many scholars have commented, half-jokingly, that the higher the level of individuals (or nations)—the better they are—the harder it is to carry out this spiritual accounting; but where things are plain and obvious, there is no need for very extensive searching or for great profundity in order to reveal what is amiss, at least superficially. People usually have no "leisure," however; they cannot set aside the required period of time to make this reckoning and to draw even a temporary solution to the situation in which they find themselves. Under normal circumstances they are involved in their own affairs, in the flow of words and actions around them, so that they have no natural opportunity to pause, to stand and wonder at things, to balance accounts.

A catastrophe, by its very nature, brings a halt to the flow, a break in the routine of life. This break gives one the time to take stock and review. Another effect of catastrophe is shock—the confusion that seizes individuals and communities in times of disaster. Normally, routine is the common element of daily life everywhere, the element that prevents man from reexamining his circumstances, because human beings are creatures of habit. People become accustomed to, and learn to live with, not only good things but also those that are—even in their own eyes—undesirable. The sages have pointed out that if a man commits a transgression and "sleeps on it," then that transgression is, as it were, sanctioned. In other words, when one sins knowingly and then repeats the same sin or error, it becomes part of one's routine and one no longer pays attention to it as something requiring correction. Shock jolts man out of his rut and enables him to look at things anew, to reexamine his life. What is more, catastrophe usually forces one to admit mistakes and to recognize that things are not all they should be, since in normal times man devises all manner of means to avoid the unpleasant recognition of failing and error. To be sure, a little enlightened foresight before a crisis occurs might have revealed that all was not as it should be and that there was a need for change. Such awareness, however, is not common, and in most cases not even desired by the people concerned. For this reason, it is only when things cannot be denied, at the moment of truth, that one is forced to admit that one did not act as one should have. Yet even then, even at this hour of greatest need, the defense mechanisms that prevent us from searching our souls in the first place may persist.

In Leviticus 26:14–24 we find the admonition: "Then if you will walk contrary to Me and will not hearken to Me, I will bring more plagues upon you." The sages interpret this to mean that although people see disaster approaching, they tend to pass it off as "chance," as a coincidence, having no connection with them and with their acts (or their omissions). Only when the misery intensifies and when things become unavoidably obvious, "Then will their hearts surrender" (Leviticus 26:41). Sometimes the wish not to be stopped, not to change, not to admit error is so deep and so strong that not even a whole series of disasters can avail. The sages say this is because of that very factor operating when one attempts to alert people to impending troubles: They try to isolate the events, to view them as random and unconnected, to destroy all traces of causality between the past and the future, between actions, deeds, and their outcomes. Thus, it is sometimes necessary for shock to be intensified and sharpened until it permeates the general consciousness. Because of the existence of these defense mechanisms, warnings of forthcoming catastrophe and disaster are seldom effective. This is usually not because of a lack of belief in, or the credibility of, he who warns, but is rather the result of an unwillingness or inability to make some kind of spiritual reckoning. Since the will is lacking, only profound shock can change things. Commenting on the psalmists' description of the exiles from Jerusalem ("By the waters of Babylon, there we sat and wept as we remembered Zion" [Psalms 137:1]) the Prophet Jeremiah is said to have retorted, "If you had only wept for one hour in Jerusalem, you would not be here to weep over her [destruction] today." Total destruction, exile, were necessary in order to make people aware of the truth of the warnings they had heard so often before the Fall.

Soul-searching is a long and complex process, requiring a certain amount of preparation, or at least a tacit assumption of doubt, insecurity, the need for review and revision, and the need to reassess one's life. This awareness of the need for review is an essential condition of soul-reckoning. Even within the normal routine of daily life, most people do make some kind of accounting, which, as often as not, contains a basic defect that reveals itself only under the most scrupulous examination. Soul-searching carried out in the rough-and-tumble of active life, without pausing or leaving room for reciprocity, may be fundamentally incorrect. The summing-up may be accurate, the calculations precise, but what is considered as credit is actually debit, and what the arithmetic books define as profit proves in reality to be loss; that which seems clear and straightforward is revealed as a futile dream. Errors of this sort, which are, of course, more than mere errors of arithmetic, are not revealed by a routine accounting process.

In other words, as long as the matter in question is assessed on the basis of the same fundamental assumptions with which one started out, the errors in the account will remain standing until some disaster occurs to reveal the defect. People do not make mistakes over "petty cash," the adding up of the pennies of the daily round. Here, a reasonable degree of accuracy is maintained. What is more, the very fact of routine, of methods and systems used in this kind of accounting, makes it possible for it to function regardless of the existence of some fundamental error. Whereas small mistakes are quickly discovered, and as quickly rectified, the fundamental error produces a whole complex, interdependent structure, which in its own confined sphere becomes a law unto itself. The fundamental error thus contains its own feedback mechanism, which serves to reinforce and verify it. Soul-searching, on the other hand, obliges one to look afresh at those things that seem to be whole, good, and beautiful. A certain *tzadik* is reported to have said, "When I think of repentance, I don't review those deeds I know to have been sins but rather those *mitzvot* that might give cause for concern." Soul-searching is therefore much more than a profit-and-loss accounting. Regardless of the kind of problem it deals with—moral, economic, or political—it is an overall reckoning that includes in it a presupposition of the possibility of error, of a great and fundamental mistake.

There is a well-known fable about the animals who decided to repent because their sins had brought disaster on them. The tiger and the wolf confess that they prey on other creatures, and are vindicated. After all, it is in their nature as predators to hunt and kill. So all the animals in turn confess their sins and, for one reason or another, all are exonerated. Finally, the sheep admits that she once ate the straw lining from her master's boots; here at last is obviously the true cause of their misfortune. All fall on the evil sheep and slaughter it, and everything is in order again.

This fable is usually taken to point out the hypocrisy of the animals, who ignore the sins of the strong and attack those of the weak. The basic issue, however, is something rather more profound: This is an example of the kind of soul-searching that merely confirms the status quo. The wolf may hunt and the tiger may savage because it is in their nature to do so. As long as soul-searching does not address itself to such basic and fundamental issues, as long as it does not question even the most obvious assumptions, then the sin singled out for correction will be trivial and no overall change will be forthcoming.

True soul-searching is based on quite a different premise, one that assumes that those matters we take for granted, the status quo, the general consensus, are all the very things that require review and revision. In the Bible this is expressed in Leviticus 26:40—"And you shall confess your sins and those of your fathers"—an exhortation that finds its echo in the confession in the daily prayer book: "But we and our fathers have sinned" (Jeremiah 3:25). This inclusion of the fathers in the confession is not accidental. Rather, it is an attempt not only to examine oneself at the level of present being, but also to penetrate to the very roots of one's existence.

The old cliché, "That's the way it's always been," or the even more common "Everybody does it" are no excuse for sinfulness. There is a story of a man who comes to a rabbi and, after recounting a long catalogue of misdeeds, excuses himself by saying, "But everybody does it," to which the rabbi retorts, "Hell is big enough for everybody." This excuse of "sanctioned by habit/custom" continually evoked, reveals the perennial lack of spiritual strength that might encourage thorough review and that prevents us from penetrating to the root of things, to the ancient, primal sin and its source.

All this, which relates to soul-searching at the individual level, is even more true at the communal level. It takes infinitely more effort for a whole community, or a nation, to carry out soul-searching than it does for the lone man or woman. First, in the context of the community, although individual deviations may be condemned, the errors or shortcomings common to the society as a whole are usually reinforced. Second, the conscious effort of will required to put a halt to the ongoing process of daily life is very great—as is the inertia of a large group, sect, community, or nation—so that a great deal of strength is required in the one case, and very great shock or upheaval in the other.

When an entire nation is headed for disaster, not only are its citizens to some extent inured to what is happening to them, because the whole society is subject to the same conditions (which thus become to some degree "normal"), but there is also no opportunity in the rush of events to stand back and assess what is going on, much less devise an effective means of response. Thus, every individual within the whole falls victim to the general inertia. The dash of the lemmings to their death is not only a funcion of the urge of each little creature but is also a product of mass inertia, the fact of being physically dragged along by the mass of its fellows traveling along the same route. At the national level, shock must therefore be more intense and drastic to reach a point at which the individual realizes where he has gone wrong.

There is another aspect to the problem of the nation as a whole. Individuals have their own thoughts and ideas, but these are not always common to the national entity. Indeed, the course of a nation is never the sum of the life experiences of the individuals who make up that entity, just as the body is not the sum of the nervous impulses of its limbs and organs. The overall condition of the body is determined by a few organs, each with a specially defined function. So, too, within every nation there is a particular class or group that determines and decides, that sets the pace, direction, and tone. Sometimes this class or group is very able and broadly representative, and sometimes it is quite unsuited to its role. Be that as it may, it is this leadership, whether political or spiritual, which for good or ill, determines the path of a nation.

In the Bible, the leaders are called the "eyes" of the community, an assumption that they are to be the "receivers" of coming events, instruments for orientation and control, for sensing danger and anticipating developments long before these become manifest. A nation whose eyes are not beautiful is one whose whole body requires examination, because the failure of the eyes almost always signifies the failure of the whole. This is true even in those cases where a nation appears to be finer and better than its leadership.

Our sages used a folk saying to explain how great disasters might befall a nation: "When the shepherd is angry with the flock, he blinds the eyes of the leading ewe" (*Baba Kama* 52a)—and woe to the flock whose leaders are blind! These things hold true in all ages, because even in times of peace and plenty we must check things out, be aware of dangers to come. How much more true is this in times of soul-searching, at a time when there is a need for a fundamental examination of our lives, when the very roots of existing reality must be explored. Such exploration must be made not only in terms of existing assumptions, but on a review of the most fundamental values, and at such times it is essential that the eyes of the community see far and clear and penetratingly. In ancient Israel, the prophet was defined as the "Scout of the House of Israel," the one who saw from afar and who, in simple speech, was called "the shepherd." A nation needs its guides and shepherds, its scouts and leaders of the flock, who will carry out the function of leadership: the ability to feel and the power to think.

⸻ 3 ⸻

Fate, Destiny, and Free Will

Man's struggle—every man's struggle—with his fate is one of humanity's most ancient problems. Like most fundamental issues, it is universal: pondered and argued everywhere, in all periods of history. Countless solutions to this problem have been proposed, yet no final answer has been found, either at the individual or at the cultural level. Sometimes, some kind of satisfactory conclusion is reached in this regard; more often than not, the problem is left unresolved in a kind of eternal "deuce."

In almost every religion, this struggle with fate appears in the context of a preordained decree, and although this decree, this "sentence," is divinely determined, the question still remains: What, if anything, can man do to commute this? Does he, in fact, have any free will, or is his whole life—in this world and the next—determined by a supreme ordinance that can be neither revoked nor altered?

A parallel to this question is raised in scientific thinking, both ancient and modern: If one assumes a causal universe, one has to accept a deterministic system of reality, which assumes that from the first impetus of movement in the universe (whether we speak of the big bang theory or some other), the world is at the mercy of a blind, immutable sequence of cause and effect in which all that happens is predetermined from the very beginning of time until the end of days. Others see history as being determined by great historicoeconomic forces, while exponents of various psychological methodologies have tried to produce models of behavioristic reaction, which have questioned the very freedom of human thought. Thus, although precise formulations of this problem have appeared in each and every age, and in accordance with the given attitudes of time and place, the factor common to them all is whether, within this predetermined reality, it is possible to bring about any meaningful change.

Fate is not only an intellectual challenge of the first order, dealt with by every known philosophical system, it is also a human challenge in which the individual's willingness—and ability—to confront his destiny plays an important part. Is there in fact any point in striving, struggling for one's own place in the world and for universal redemption? If everything is already irrevocably determined and resolved in advance (whether by some intelligent power or by blind natural forces), is there any point in trying to resist? The fatalistic view tends to lead to a deep conservatism, to an acceptance of events as an inevitable sentence from which there is no reprieve, to a failure to even try to bring about changes in existing patterns. This attitude, which has characterized many cultures in the past, can lead, in extreme instances, to the justification of every urge, every action, and every behavioral eccentricity, since it assumes that if an event has already taken place or a deed has been perpetrated, it is for the best and there is no point in considering the outcome, and certainly no room for regret. Even the dictates of the heart are seen to be an inevitable part of one's destiny, and follow them one must, with all that this implies.

Even those cultures that have not taken this fatalistic view but have created a scale of values by which confrontation with natural law and historical determinism is of the highest order, have had to overcome intellectual and emotional resistance to the chances of acting against the apparently preordained. Philosophers of history, such as Spengler and, in his wake, Toynbee, have postulated that every human culture passes through a cycle of organic growth and development, decline and death. After reaching its zenith, a culture begins to degenerate. No amount of endeavor can alter this ruling and indeed, cannot even significantly temper it. In this way, the intellectual problem, which is perhaps the problem of the few, becomes an existential problem for the many—for the community and for each individual.

As an academic and philosophic question, man's freedom in the face of environmental determinants belongs to those problems classed by Kant as the antinomies: fundamental issues that logically compel us to accept two contradictory solutions. Kant then constructed a magnificent system of thought to deal with this problem in rational terms. Long before, Moses Maimonides had grappled with the question in a searching discussion of basic Jewish laws in his compilation *Mishneh Torah*. Dealing with the supposedly inevitable contradiction between divine omniscience and free will, he asserts that this problem cannot be solved by human reason alone but is among those things that can only be understood by a recognition of that same divine omniscience and omnipotence.

Rabbi Abraham ben David (the Ravad) in a critical commentary on Maimonides' code, comments that there is no point in asking a question when one can only offer the solution that there is no answer. Although this comment may have some educational significance, it could be countered by the reply that a negative solution also has validity. More than this, there is a theoretical as well as a practical importance to the conclusion that a given problem cannot be solved within a certain area of cognition, and that its solution has to be found elsewhere by using a different mode of reasoning, as in mathematics, where negative proofs of this kind are well known.

The nature of man's freedom and his capacity to resist his preordained sentence is discussed in different ways in all Jewish thinking since biblical times, even if the philosophical formulations rarely reached the same degree of discernment and complexity as Maimonides. The sages hint at the problem in veiled or obscure form; various exegesis have resulted in some clarifications and, although areas of uncertainty still exist, the main trends of thought on this question are fairly clear.

A basic and unchanging principle, persisting through the whole spectrum of Jewish thought, is the awareness that man has the freedom to choose between good and evil. This is one of the fixed and secure elements in Scriptures and in the writings of the sages, even those who were influenced by Greek and Arab philosophy. It is also found in the Kabbalah. What is more, one can say that this essential recognition of free will is so fundamental to Jewish thinking that it has come to be a test of the authenticity of the Jewish approach. Almost without exception, a philosophical or religious system of thought that does not accept the axiom of man's free will does not properly belong to the truly Jewish sphere—even if it is totally orthodox in every other respect. Thus, in the case of the Dead Sea sect, the Pauline Christians, and others, the acceptance of a preordained fate was one of the fundamental issues that marked their separation from the community of Israel as a whole, and although the principle of free will does not appear in all the formal "lists" of the essentials of Judaism (and certainly not in Maimonides' "Thirteen Principles of Faith"), it is of crucial importance. One of the great minds of the Chasidic movement, Rabbi Baruch of Kossov, asserted this idea in his book, *Sod HaEmunah* (*The Secret of Faith*), when he wrote that, essentially, man should accept the apparently contradictory aspects of the problem of free will and recognize the existence of choice, while at the same time believing that the Hand of the Creator guides him in making that choice. If, however, a person cannot accept both Divine providence and free will, he had better opt for the latter. This recognition is an important guideline to the way a man lives his life, forms his thinking habits, and functions in the world.

The problems of predestiny and retribution (and thus by implication, free will) are expressed in the prophetic polemics as: "The fathers have eaten sour grapes and the teeth of the sons are set on edge" (Jeremiah 31:29). On superficial reading, it is possible to see this as the despair of those who feel, "Our fathers have sinned and are no more, and we have borne their iniquities" (Lamentations 5:7)—that the "pain of inheritance," inevitably, remorselessly, burdens the descendants. A more analytic examination of this argument reveals that its importance lies not in the abstract discussion of whether we do, or do not, suffer the sins of the fathers; rather, the crux of this statement lies one stage beyond—in the issue of the relationship between men and their deeds. We have in the aforementioned quotation from the Book of Jeremiah not only a tendency to fatalism but a recognition that human freedom, even if it exists, has no significance:

Everything has been predetermined and cannot be corrected or changed. Ezekiel's words of prophecy and admonition, on the other hand, alert us against this approach both in the abstract and in practical application. There is no binding predestiny that compels one to take a certain route and determines one's fate in advance, regardless of one's deeds and actions.

Man has always had the ability to change, whether this change lies in a deviation from ancestral ways or in some revolution in the life of the individual himself. It is the emphasis on this ability to change that proves that the emphasis on man's freedom is the subject of Ezekiel's contentions. Righteousness and evil are not character traits determined in advance or by heredity, but lie rather in the hand of each one of us. We can all carry on with "the deeds of the fathers"— or we can radically change them.

Maimonides himself points out that the Bible assumes the individual has it in his power to decide, to forge a way of life of his own, and to choose between good and evil. Although the Book of Job raises the question of Divine justice of a fate that determines the reward or punishment of man regardless of his deeds, the Scriptures as a whole, with their admonitions, their call to repent and to choose between good and evil, repeatedly testify to this basic assumption of man's power to choose. The aforementioned reference to the Book of Ezekiel merely raises the issue to the level of theoretical, theological discussion, that people may say, "The way of the Lord is impossible" (Ezekiel 33:20) when He grants man an absolute freedom of choice.

The sages also discussed the problem of free will and differed widely in the conclusions they reached. Rabbi Akiva expressed some of the subtle complexity of these answers in his famous saying: "Everything is foreseen, yet free will is granted." Rabbi Akiva then continues: "All the good of the world has been decided, and it is all according to man's deeds," which makes the original interpretation not at all clear. Naturally, this was one of the hotly debated issues of the day. It has already been said that "Everything is foreseen" does not necessarily mean "foreseen in advance," and this saying is less a theological paradox than a simple statement of fact. Everything is foreseen in the sense that God knows and sees the deeds of each individual; at the same time, that individual is permitted to choose for himself the path he will take in life. Yet it is clear that the problem of predestination versus free will, even if it is not clearly manifest in this saying, has not been solved and continues in other discussions of the same issue.

The well-known dictum "Israel has no star of fortune" is not an assertion of misfortune nor the denial of a degree of predestination (natural or supernatural) but simply an indication that for Israel—the Jewish people—not fortune, nor historical determinism, nor any other fatal factor is totally limiting, and that man is granted a certain freedom of choice in affecting his own destiny. However, it has also been said: "Follow fortune, and fortune brings riches," a saying that, in its simplest sense, relates to the belief in astrology, a belief in the stars as controlling man's destiny. Incidentally, a significant change has taken place over the generations in the use of the Hebrew word *goral* (fate), which originally meant quite simply a chance of winning in a lottery and which today has come to have implications for man's whole life. The word *mazal*, meaning luck or fortune, on the other hand, which originally had a much broader meaning, now has the much more limited application of chance success or failure.

Maimonides, one of the few people in the Middle Ages to deny the validity of astrology, quoted the phrase "Israel has no star of fortune" in support of his argument, while others produced opposing opinions to back their views. The controversy over the effect of the stars on human life and history, however, is not relevant to a discussion of free will. It is an incidental behind which lies an assumption of predestination, no matter how this causality or determinism manifests itself. A certain acknowledgment of predestination is to be found in several writings of the sages, even if this is formulated in such a way that it bears no relation to "fortune" in its limited sense. One may even generalize and say that in the Middle Ages the sages—like most scholars of their time, including the kabbalists—assumed the existence of a certain preordained framework, within the confines of which each generation was permitted a certain amount of freedom. Even those who passionately asserted their belief in Divine providence (and that includes most of the kabbalists and the Chasidic groups, some of whom held that this providence extended not only to human beings and all living creatures, but also to every object and particle of matter) held to this notion. Yet, even if everything is foreseen, the freedom and the ability to bring about changes is granted. The controversy lay in determining the degree of freedom allowed. In contradistinction to this view, Maimonides held that Divine providence was reserved only for certain exceptional individuals.

An assumption common to every Jewish philosophical system is that expressed by Rabbi Hanania: "Everything is in the hands of Heaven—except the veneration of Heaven." Even if the course of life, down to its most minute particulars, is in the hands of God, the relation to God is still in the hands of man. This saying has its parallels in all the literature of the sages and is the essence of the Divine command in Deuteronomy 30:19: "I call Heaven and Earth to witness against you this day that I have set before you life and death, blessing and curse; therefore choose life." The problem raised by this is, if everything is in the hands of Heaven, if the events of a man's life (as well as his temperament and character) are not determined by him but by a superior force, how can he still have the capacity to choose between good and evil? How can the individual—and much more so, a large group of individuals, a community—be free to choose its response in any given situation if the eventual outcome is in any case preordained? The answers to this vexing question are many and various. Broadly speaking, in the context of Jewish thinking we may suggest that predestination, when it is dependent on the causality of natural laws and their processes, works in a very general way and applies only to the macrocosm. In relation to the microcosm, the individual has a certain leeway to act as he chooses. His actions may not alter the general, overall picture, but within the confines of the fixed ordinances, matters can to some degree be redirected. Over a generation ago, the scientist Heisenberg defined this principle in his "Law of Uncertainty," which states that in nature there is no underlying causality, beyond a certain large-scale order, and that in the subatomic reality, there is no certainty at all.

To be sure, this uncertainty does not alter the overall statistical probabilities, although it does alter the existence of certainty and causality in each separate system. Parallel to this scientific concept, the causal pattern of the world must be seen as a whole when it relates to the problem of freedom. The question of macrocosm and microcosm are then broken down into different aspects of the problem, the larger the dimensions dealt with, the greater the degree of determinism and stability of the relevant laws. Thus, laws governing the relationships between events and society at large are much more rigid than those touching on the personal decisions of individuals. More precisely, in the general course of fairly fixed occurrences, a certain freedom of action still exists in relation to individuals or small groups.

Another element that is more important to an understanding of the controversy of predestination versus free will is significance. Events in general—even those immediately affecting individuals—are in themselves meaningless. In terms of the laws of nature, there is no difference between the force that attracts galaxies to each other and that which sends a falling child hurtling from a rooftop to his death. In both cases the same basic equation of movement and acceleration operate. In terms of the significance of each event, however, there is a great, fundamental difference between them that is not found in the natural order of things. That difference is the human contribution, the thought, the feeling and the wonder at events. Significance is what gives otherwise random occurrences their specific values in man's life and being. In other words, events are like absolute numbers, with specific sizes but no positive or negative value. It is the human response that gives the "plus" or "minus" quality. When we examine this fact closely, we will see that our ability to attribute value to things, even those things predetermined in the smallest detail, not only affects our assessment of and reaction to them, but also the good or evil that we perceive in them. This attribution of value also defines the nature of the miracle.

Contrary to popular convention, it is not the wonderful in an event that determines its "miraculousness" but the value and significance that that event holds for us. A given occurrence can be most wondrous and still not be considered a miracle, but merely a natural "curiosity." The fact that somewhere out there in a barren wilderness, a stone has rolled to the foot of a mountain, remaining upright all the while, is strange and astonishing, a wonder in itself. In the absence of significance, however, it is not a miracle. On the other hand, a perfectly natural occurrence can, under certain circumstances, be considered a miracle because of its significance to the human condition. An outstanding example of such a "natural" miracle may be found in the biblical story of Esther. Although the sequence of events described therein proceeds with an inner causality that explains the motivation and actions of each protagonist, it is the historical and personal significance of events that lends this very sequence its miraculous nature. In the same way, one can, to a great extent, measure the moral value of an action—or an omission. It is not the deed that determines value so much as the intent on the part of its perpetrator. The same physical action may be performed legitimately or illicitly, willingly or by coercion, knowingly or in ignorance, accidentally or wantonly, with good intentions or maliciously. In every evaluation of a deed as good or evil, it is the underlying attitude that determines significance in each case. Let us say that even where circumstances dictate a given action, the choice of how to relate to that action is free, and its significance follows accordingly.

This change in attitude, in attributing significance to an occurrence even when one cannot prevent or alter the great course of events, still has a certain capacity to effect changes—possibly inconsequential in absolute terms but nevertheless ultimately meaningful even in the context of a much larger system. For example, if we take two people who are in every respect similar to each other and give each of them equal opportunities to choose between good and evil (and to assess events and their own relationship to them), even the small differences between the two would bring about cumulative changes in their immediate environment and would affect their whole lives. The implications of this are indicated by the sages in the saying, "Everything is in the hands of Heaven except for thorns and snares." "Thorns" and "snares" are those obstacles and events that, in themselves, belong neither to the realm of good nor to that of evil but lie within the individual himself. With care and reflection, they may be avoided.

Our sages have said that a person is sometimes saved from stumbling, not by his own restraint, but by Divine intervention, causing him to be protected from an immediate and known difficulty without actually changing the overall picture of his life. Thorns and snares exist or lie in wait for every human being, and there is no doubt that only the smallest can be avoided. In relation to greater, more all-encompassing events, man's ability to avoid or change these is much more limited. Of course, snares may also be elements within the larger social structure (the community or nation), which may be able to deal with small problems but be quite unable to cope with disaster on a large scale. Small occurrences have a cumulative value that influences subsequent events. The man who breaks his leg because of carelessness, or one who chooses evil over good—both enter a vicious circle in which whatever happens to them "afterwards" takes on a different significance. As a result, their reaction to subsequent events will no longer be the same, and what is a matter of indifference for one can be a powerful impetus for good or ill for another.

According to this concept, a situation is therefore created in which freedom of movement in a small, inner world changes the meaning and significance of events, even though the world at large goes its way unaltered. Decisions apparently irrelevant to the larger order of things become a matter of principle and are fateful for those who have some means of evaluating those same events. Under normal conditions, one very general pattern can, given an average degree of probability, determine the way of life for an individual almost from birth. Two such lives may be identical in form; their content may well be totally different.

As an interesting version of this viewpoint, according to the kabbalists, every year in which the coming of the Messiah is reckoned as possible is a difficult one. Events of great importance are anticipated, sweeping changes are awaited, and yet the substance and value of these changes, their significance, is dependent on man's freedom to choose how he will act. Thus, if redemption does not come as forecast, the year in which it was anticipated, will, on the contrary, be a year of tribulation. One the one hand, we have the assumption that there is a definite order of events and phenomena, a predetermined and fixed destiny. On the other hand, the measure and meaning of this destiny is seen as being open to significant changes in accordance with the degree of freedom granted to mankind. Consequently, even if everything is indeed foreseen, the degree of freedom granted within the proscribed framework is very great indeed—as great, in fact, as the concomitant human responsibility and obligation.

4

Human Holiness

Our sages said, "Six things were said about man:
in regard to three, he is like the ministering
angels, and in regard to three, he is like beasts."

—*Babylonian Talmud, Chagigah 16a*

This combination of angel and beast is only one of the strange and
various combinations forming man. Angel and beast are incompatible contrasts, but in man they are created into a many-faced unity.
The combining of the material, bestial body with the angelic, Divine
soul, is characteristic of man's combination of contrasts. Flesh and soul,
good and evil, are different names for the same things. Within their
existence in man, there is no possibility of clearly defining the relation between them, although each of them has for itself a very clear
and defined essentiality.

The same combination occurs in many forms and always in this
indefinite way: the highest strivings and desires, and with these—with
the same force—bad, bestial wants. Reason on one side, and on the
other, imagination and emotion quite independent of each other. And

so, many desires of the most various kinds, innumerable wants and wills, simple and strange—all these are found in man.

Thus, we come to the great question: What is man? What is the true essence of this unity of angel and beast, body and soul, reason and emotion, good and bad? Truly, of all these, there is not one that can give a satisfactory definition of man's real self; only the combination of all these is man—this is the *human* in him. Man is not an angel, nor is he a beast; he is the combination of both: *a man*. And he is so with all the many combinations and links of these contradictory facets; there is no place for one of them without the others. Their unification into *one* creates the true being of the man.

Although it is agreed by everyone that man is complex and that this is characteristic of him, there have been continuous attempts to define this multicolored compound in terms of some simple unity. True, the mere wish to find unity in multiplicity is by no means a negative wish. The basis of every kind of philosophical or scientific thinking is this uniting of many facts into principles. The attempt to find such central points about man is in itself positive, but it involves some danger; for after finding the focal point of man's being, it is very natural to mistake one point for the whole.

It is not difficult to show that man is a rational creature, in which reason determines much of the nature, behavior, and mind. After accepting the accurate statement that reason is a factor in man's being, it is very easy to come to the erroneous conclusion that reason is *the whole man*. Indeed, in the first stage, the realization that this is not *all* of man is still remembered, and there are some details that are not included in this generalization. But afterwards, the habit of thought and the building up of a complete system on one basis only causes one to forget the true nature of things. After a time, such an artificial construction *becomes* the real man.

This way of thinking is common because it is natural and easily understood, but it must be remembered that it is always untrue. A mistake of this nature was made by Freud. His method, which began with seeing the great importance of sex in our lives, brought him to the conclusion that man is in essence purely sexual, and all other parts are secondary and unimportant. And so Freud built a system in which man, his deeds and thoughts, are merely results of the only basis of spirit: sex. The same happened with Marxism as well. From the acknowledgment of the importance of economic factors within society, there issued the inevitable mistake in ascribing these factors as the sole basis of all human actions—social life, culture, and thought.

Processes of this kind usually end in an artificial construction that is based on one thing and builds within it and of it a whole, complicated figure, which has to represent man. The degree of likeness between such a representation and reality depends on the creator's talents. If he is talented and consistent, it can be made very like a living man, but there will always be some human part "forgotten" and left behind, without notice. Perhaps this last part is of secondary importance, but there is no possibility of being man without it, so this construction, with all its speculative success, is not the structure of man.

This new, schematic creature is perhaps more perfect than the man known to us, and is always much more logical. Nevertheless, this is not *man*—he will always lack *humanity*. And without humanity, the construction remains cold and dry. This is a logical structure of a creature resembling man, which remains, with all its human likeness, a lifeless being, a fabulous monster.

Not only in the realm of secular theories is there some wish to understand man on the basis of only one aspect of his being. There are such mistakes in religious life as well, and their results are parallel to the artificial secular constructions. In Judaism, under the influence of foreign philosophy, a conception of man was frequently erected on the sole basis of reason, which was thought to be the center of man's world and spiritual being, while other parts of the soul were abandoned and thought unimportant, and sometimes even harmful. Of course, in religious life as well, there were unsatisfactory results. Here also, man as exclusively rational is an artificial creation who cannot live a real religious life, just as the religious man who is only emotional cannot live so.

These constructions, the basis of which is reason or emotion, are not typical of religious life; they are only secular forms in a religious philosophy. But there are also, in religious life, parallel endeavors that are really typical. It is known that man is a combination that includes angel and beast, and religion strives to tame the inner beast and to bring it nearer to the angelic element in him. From this correct educational wish there came, in some inner evolutionary way, a quite different wish: *to make of man an angel.*

The fulfillment of this wish was not possible, of course, because man is by nature not an angel. But in time, something much worse occurred—this pseudoeducational wish to make an angel of man became more than that: an assumption that man *is already* an angel. All other nonangelic facets of man's nature were therefore thought to be mere transient and unimportant defects, which, with some strength of will, everyone could conquer and change into angelic perfections.

Of course, no one had ever defined things so; it was never said openly that man is an angel, with some bad parts that could be removed by a conditioned education. But even without saying it, such a thought influences a large world of thinking, albeit on a somewhat unconscious level. It is reflected in the way the Jew is perceived as one who wants only to study the Bible and whose life is wholly spent in doing good, praying, and studying. It could not be ignored that a Jew also had a body, and therefore certain wishes and desires—but these were considered of no value; man's will and wishes were not his real wishes, and man's thoughts were but foolish and unworthy ones. All that was of any importance was directly related to religion; everything else was considered superfluous.

In many books that reflect the understanding of generations, it was implicit that a Jew could not have any real interests in this world. His object of love was supposed to be just the one of doing good deeds. Wishes and desires, eyes seeing the world and hands feeling it—all these did not exist in that angelic perfection called a Jew. Of course, it does not mean that Jews in any period, even in the darkest of the Middle Ages, did not live in our world, did not love, hate, and think about other subjects. But all these facts were "formally" unknown. For religious Jewry, man remained forever an angel.

Many generations have wanted to make an angel of man. These experiments, although they did not succeed (there being no satisfactory way of doing so), were successful in pretending that man is by nature an angel. Such an opinion, held in reverence by generations, is worth some thought: Man is really comprised of beast and angel, and the angelic part is the more important one. But must this belief lead to the conclusion that man has to be changed into an angel? The essence of man's being is in just this combining of angel and beast. When this combination is destroyed, man ceases to be human; he becomes some other sort of humanoid—but surely not man!

Converting man into an angel does not mean any exaltation for him. If God had wanted man to become an angel and to do everything as such, He would simply have created more angels. But His wish was to create *man*. "We shall make *man* in our form and image," and not, "make an angel in our form."

Of course, a man must not stay forever in the same meaningless state of angel–beast; man must try to become better. But whatever the manner of his exaltation, it must not be by forcing man to the angelic. Because man's way—that in which he has to go—is a special way for him alone. Forcing man into a life of mere learning and doing good deeds cannot create an angel; it can, at best, only move him toward being what he has to be. The religious man of today is not a perfect religious man. Orthodox religion pretends that man is only made for prayer and devotion, and therefore a religious man who has another attitude cannot identify himself with his religion. He feels that his religion is manifested only in that part of him that is concerned with learning and praying. The man who is praying is not a whole man, but only part of a man. Perhaps this part is the better part, but it is not man.

A man cannot enter into such a closed circle of angelic religion. A perfect man has within himself a whole world—heaven and earth, the highest and the lowest—and is not compressed in the little space of such doubtful religion. Such a man cannot pray wholeheartedly. because the synagogue is too narrow for containing all his inner world. Making man an angel is creating a dry, petty, and partial being.

A good example of this dryness and constraint can be found in many books on morals written during certain periods. However, these books, which are masterpieces in themselves, lack the elements of true humanism. The greatness of these books is lost because the average man, full of every human feeling, cannot relate such books to his life; they often do not even hint at certain moral questions. You could study a classic book on morals and not find anything about love, social relations, work, physical life, et cetera. True, these books are good books, but they are good only for that part of man engaged in religious issues. These books are *textbooks for angels*; they cannot teach people. It was this contraction of religion into purely religious problems that caused the freezing of every human emotion and led to conservatism and, to some extent, self-deception and hypocrisy, for, if all religious subjects were so detached from everyday life, they would become merely frozen conservative forms that did not have any true meaning for anyone.

It is told that once the Rabbi of Kotzk asked one of his pupils to tell him what he thinks of while praying. The man began to tell the Rabbi about his thoughts during prayers—a very learned lecture about the unity of God in the higher world and in our world. The Rabbi, who was a volcano of God-seeking and truth-seeking, and one of the greatest teachers in those subjects, could not suppress his anger any longer and cried: "And where is your stomach?"—meaning: "Where is your own prosaic self in all this high philosophy? Where are *you* in this strange, cold, distant and impersonal exaltation?"

In Chasidism we can find many sayings criticizing the conversion of man into an angel and ignoring the other, nondevotional facets of man. Of course, Chasidism is a strictly religious movement, but the way of Chasidism was not to ignore those facets of man's being, but to sublimate them into a higher state. Chasidism itself was a protest against the conventional frozen religion, and that is why we can find in it so much life. Every problem of those times can be found in Chasidic books, and dealt with in a plain, straightforward way.

This multiformity is very typical of Judaism, and in most classic books we can see plainly both life and humanity. In the dark Middle Ages (which did not exist in the Jewish nation at all), in that strangulation of every Jewish attempt to live normal human lives, we find a classic moral book, *Sefer Chasidim*, which is full of deep piety and also full of life. Almost every facet of human existence—the inner problems as well as all sorts of social problems—is thoroughly examined. It is all very pious, but it is a live and human piety that touches the soul of a whole man.

So, too, does the Talmud. In "the sea of the Talmud" (as it is called by some) all can be found: farfetched and very abstract legal forms of thought, lively, fanciful fables, advice about commerce and agriculture, medical treatments, popular proverbs. There is not—even in the most legal or circumlocutionary pages—a dry or "nonhuman" paragraph in the Talmud. The personalities there are always *human*, people of whose lives we know the most intimate and prosaic details. We know about their quarrels and sins as we know about their great qualities, and they are so close to us because they were fully men, because the Talmud is a human book.

To an even greater degree do we find it so in the Bible. Every verse in the Bible is so full of life and humanity that one can say the Bible is a complete picture of man. Studying the Bible we find that all of it—the stories and the religious commandments—are equally intended for a living people, full of wishes and desires, for the average man who is liable to sin, showing him the way to repentance and reelevation.

Just the collection of the various books of the Bible is a demonstration in itself of full humanity. He who does not understand this essentiality of the Bible will never understand why it contains a book like Ecclesiastes, which seems so unsuitable to the general character of the Bible. But man, who is not perfectly angelic, has within himself the same questions, doubts, and skepticism that are contained in the book of Ecclesiastes. These "heretic" questions are not ignored, and the entire book remains in the Bible.

The true Jewish way is that of human exaltation. From the Pentateuch to the Last Prophets, from the Talmud to the great rabbis of Chasidism, there is an attempt to deal with a whole man, a man in whom part of the wholeness is his being combined of body and soul, bad and good. All the duties of Judaism are for a *man*, a physical and restricted creature. And for this reason there are also certain laws that are only for the satisfaction of the bestial desires of man. That is not negative in any sense because, since man is imperfect, there must be a real relation to sin. "You must stoop to him if you want to elevate him."

This way is not a necessary evil but an ideal way in itself. In a more general sense, the aim of man is not to do holy duties and to be an angel on earth. Man's task is to "reveal God's being in the lower world"—and this is done by elevating the base and low elements and exalting them. The lowest elements in the world are, essentially and originally, of the highest sources, because only very holy and great souls can enliven mean creations, and the task of man is to bring these souls back to their exalted origin.

And so man has not to elevate his soul, because it is already high without man's efforts; his task is to elevate his body, his intellect, his desires. The human being is to give all his essence to God, but not by elevating his mind to higher subjects and converting his desires into a desire for God. The real way is higher: to find God in all these thoughts and desires, to be a whole man—but to a higher degree.

5

Worlds, Angels, and Men

The physical world in which we live, the cosmos which we can observe objectively, is one part in a vast system of worlds. The other worlds are for the most part ethereal, that is, nonmaterial. They can be envisaged as different dimensions of being. They do not exist elsewhere, in different sets of spatial coordinates, but rather in another order or plane of being. Furthermore, as we shall see, these various worlds interpenetrate and interact with each other. In a certain sense it can be said that each of the worlds is a replication, by means of transformation, change, or even distortion, of that immediately above it. World after world is reflected in that which lies below it, and finally all the worlds—with their complex interrelated influences—are projected into the world we know and experience.

The terms higher and lower do not indicate a physical relationship of altitude, which does not obtain in the spiritual realm, but rather relative positions on the scale of causality. A higher world is more primary, elemental, concentrated; a lower world is secondary, more remote from the primal source, and thus a replication. However, such a replication is not simply a coarser version, but is in itself a total system with a life and existence of its own, and with its own specific properties and characteristics.

42

The totality of the world in which we live is known as the World of Action. It is the world of our sensual and nonsensual apprehension. It is not, however, homogenous. The lower part is subdivided into an ethereal realm (to be described later), and what is known as the material World of Action, which is of a physical nature, and is governed by the laws of nature; the upper part, known as the spiritual World of Action, is the realm of spiritual activity. Common to both parts of the World of Action is man; situated between them, he partakes of both. Insofar as he exists in the lower part, man is governed by the physical, chemical, and biological laws of nature; from the standpoint of his consciousness, even when it is totally concerned with physical or base matters, he belongs to the spiritual part of the World of Action. The ideas of the World of Action are for the most part bound up with the physical world, indeed, they are functions of it. This obtains both for the most exalted speculations of a philosopher and the cruder thought processes of the ignorant savage or the child.

Human existence is thus dual in nature, partaking of both matter and spirit. Furthermore, in the Word of Action, the spiritual is largely subordinate to the material, to the extent that physical objects and the laws of nature are the basis of reality and determine its nature. The spiritual life almost exclusively derives from and acts upon this substrate.

However, the World of Action is but one in a general system consisting of four fundamental worlds, each of which is a complete cosmos in itself, with its own essences and nature. In the literature of the Kabbalah, these worlds, from higher to lower, are called Emanation, Creation, Formation, and Action (in Hebrew, *Atzilut, Beriah, Yetzirah,* and *Assiyah*). The world above our own is thus the World of Formation. The differences between those worlds can be understood if we examine the manifestations in each of them of three traditional dimensions of existence known as "world," "year," and "soul." In modern language these would be termed space, time, and being. For example, in our world, space is a basic system that is necessary for any object to exist; it is the matrix within which, upon which, and from which all living creatures operate. In the higher worlds, this dimension is manifest in what is known as the "mansions" (*Heichalot*). It is not space as we know it, but a framework of existence within which all forms and beings are related. A useful comparison to this concept is that of a self-contained system, known in mathematics as a group or a field, in which each unit member is related in a specific and fixed manner to all the other members and to the totality. Such systems may be inhabited, partially or to capacity, or sparsely to empty.

Time, too, is manifest in a totally different fashion in the higher worlds. In our experience, time operates and is measured by the movement of objects in space. More abstractly, it is perceived as the process of change, the transition from state to state, from form to form; it is an essential feature of our concept of causality, which establishes the limitations of transitions within certain laws. In the higher worlds, the system of time becomes increasingly abstract, and its connection with the measurement or perception of change is diminished. It becomes no more than the essence of change, or the potentiality of change.

In the World of Action, the dimension called "soul" is manifest in the totality of living creatures functioning in time and space. Although they are essentially part of this world, they are distinguished from it by their faculty of consciousness of self and of other. In the higher worlds, too, souls are self-conscious beings acting within the framework of their respective "mansions" and "years."

The World of Formation is a world of sentience. The beings that populate it are pure, abstract manifestations of what we, in our world, would call emotions or feelings. These beings, or creatures, operate in a similar fashion to the way we do in the World of Action. They are called "angels."

There are millions of angels, and each of them possesses its own unique character. No two are alike. The distinctive personality of a particular angel is a function of two features, which can be termed "content" and "degree." The content is the specific feeling or emotion, of which the angel is a pure manifestation, and the degree is its position on the scale of fundamental causality. An angel may thus be an inclination, or impulse, toward love, fear, pity, and so on, at this or that degree. However, each of these contents is subdivided into an almost infinite number of related feelings (no two loves are the same), and angels thus fall into large groups. Such a group is called a "camp of angels."

Another characteristic feature of angels, one that distinguishes them from humans, is the fact that they are unchanging. Circumstance, time, place, and even mood alter the content and the intensity of most human emotions. However, whereas emotion is ultimately secondary to our existence, it is primary and essential to angels. An angel is by definition the constant, unchanging manifestation of a single emotion or feeling.

It would be quite misleading, however, to regard angels as abstractions, as hypothetical conceptualizations of emotions that have no real existence. Each angel is a complete being that possesses consciousness of itself and awareness of its surroundings. It is able to act and create within the framework of its existence, the World of Formation. A characteristic feature of angels is implicit in their Hebrew name, which means "messenger." In fact, the task of angels is mediation, to maintain two-way communications between our world, the World of Action, and the higher worlds. They serve as emissaries of God in bringing divine plenty down into the world, and of men, in raising up certain consequences of our actions.

Men and angels belong to separate categories of existence. Even if we ignore the human body and look only at our apparently more angelic aspect, the soul, the differences are great. The human soul is a heterogeneous, complex entity composed of distinct elements, whereas an angel is homogeneous, a single essence, and thus ultimately unidimensional. Furthermore, the human being, by virtue of the multiplicity of facets in his personality, with the implicit capacity for internal contradictions and conflicts, and by virtue of his soul, which contains a spark of the divine, possesses the power of discrimination, in particular between good and evil. As a consequence, man has the potential to reach great heights, and also to fall to abysmal depths. Not so the angels, which are always the same. Whether an angel is ephemeral or eternal, it is static, and remains fixed in the coordinates of content and degree in which it was created.

Some angels have existed since the beginning of time, and are the channels through which divine plenty flows into the world. There is, however, another kind of angel, those that are constantly being created. This process of the creation of new angels takes place as a consequence of actions and phenomena that are performed and occur in all worlds, but especially in our world, the World of Action.

It is said that with every *mitzvah*, every good deed that he performs, a man creates an angel. In order to understand this, it is necessary to envisage each such act, or prayer, as being an operation on two levels. The first level is behavioral; it is the initiating or bringing about or completing of a transformation—no matter how small—in the physical world. The other level is spiritual and involves the thoughts, feelings, emotions, and mystical meditations that should accompany the performance of the external act. These spiritual actions coalesce and form a discrete spiritual entity, which possesses objective reality, and which, in turn, creates an angel in the World of Formation. Thus, by means of the *mitzvot* he performs, man extends the realm in which his activity is effective from the lower to the upper worlds. He creates angels, which are, in a manner of speaking, his messengers in the higher worlds. Whereas a newly created angel retains its essential bond with its human originator in the World of Action, it acquires reality only in the World of Formation. In this way, the spiritual content of the holy deed, by becoming an angel, rises and initiates changes in the upper worlds, and especially in the World of Formation, the world immediately superior to our own. In fact, the nature of the World of Formation is determined by the relationships between the angels and between them and the worlds above them, and they, in turn, influence these higher worlds too.

The angels who serve as emissaries of God and the upper worlds down to our world are apprehended by men in a wide and sometimes strange variety of forms. The reason for this is that as the angels derive from a totally foreign world of being, they are invisible to man in their "true" forms, for the human sense organs, and faculties of comprehension, are incapable of grasping them. Some kind of "translation" is necessary before they can be seen. A useful analogy is that of a television transmission. The electromagnetic carrier waves are of a frequency that is totally invisible to the human nervous system, which in fact is incapable even of detecting their existence. However, when these waves are processed by the television receiver, the information and signals they bear are translated and become visible on the screen. There is, of course, no resemblance between the electromagnetic waves and the picture, as there is none between the true form of the angel and what is perceived. The Kabbalah describes such a process as "clothing in garments" or "containing in vessels." The garments and the vessels are remote perceptible manifestations of the unknowable essence. This is the form in which angels appear to men.

Such manifestations generally take place in one of two situations: one is the vision of a man who has attained a high level of holiness, such as a prophet; the other is in an isolated incident of enlightenment or revelation from the higher worlds experienced by a more ordinary person. In either case, the person involved experiences the reality of the angel as it is clothed in garments. Even so, frequently the form of this manifestation is of a degree of existence that is not easily processed by the human mind, and especially by that part that involves verbal communication, and the descriptions offered are occasionally strange and fantastic. Given the cultural limitations of our linguistic skills, it is natural that many such images will be, to some degree or another, anthropomorphic. The visionary images one finds in the prophetic works, such as winged animals or eyed chariots, are secondary human translations of undescribable phenomena. When Ezekiel describes the angel that he saw as possessing the face of an ox, it does not mean that the angel had a face at all, let alone a bovine one, but that one aspect of its inner essence, when translated and projected into our physical reality, is expressed in a form that shows a conceptual likeness to the face of an ox.

All articulated prophetic visions are, in fact, depictions in comprehensible human language of abstract, formless, spiritual realities. There are, notwithstanding, cases in which angels are manifest in "ordinary" form, are clothed in familiar material garments, and appear to be natural phenomena; on such occasions, the viewer will encounter difficulties in deciding whether an apparition or a natural object stands before him, whether the pillar of fire or the man he perceives belongs to this world, with its own system of natural causality, or to another. Furthermore, the angel, that is, the force sent from a higher world, may not only be manifest in the physical world, but may also appear to act according to, and be governed by, the laws of nature, either totally or to a limited degree. In such cases, only prophetic insight can determine whether, and to what extent, higher forces are active.

The fact that a man can create an angel, which is instantaneously transposed to another world, is not, in itself, a supernatural event;

it is a part of a day-to-day way of life that can on occasion seem ordinary and commonplace—the life of *mitzvot*. When we perform an action that results in the creation of an angel, we are generally aware of no more than that we are acting on, and within, the physical world. Similarly, the appearance of an angel does not necessarily involve a deviation from the normal laws of physical nature. Man is thus in close contact with the upper worlds, and though the actual route, the nature of the link, is hidden, the fact of the relationship is as axiomatic as the duality of his body and soul, of matter and spirit. Man does not pause to wonder every time he moves from the physical to the spiritual part of the World of Action, and takes for granted the occasional penetration of higher worlds into our world. When we use the word "natural" in its widest possible meaning, that is, comprehending everything that we experience and know, the appearance and creation of angels are not "supernatural" phenomena.

The world immediately above the World of Formation is known as the World of Creation, and also as the World of the Chariot, and the Throne. In an image derived from the vision of Ezekiel, it is the Throne above that stands for "the likeness of the Glory of the Lord." This Glory, which is the aspect of divinity revealed to prophets, belongs to the highest world, the World of Emanation. The World of Creation is its Throne, and our world is its footstool. The World of Creation is the matrix through which passes all the divine plenty that descends to the lower worlds, and all things that are raised up to God. It is a sort of crossroads of all modes of existence. A central element of the Jewish esoteric, mystical tradition, called the "Study of the Chariot," deals with this world. It is the highest level to which the mystic can aspire, the limit beyond which even the holiest of visionaries can apprehend only the vaguest impressions. Of course, not even this world can be comprehended in any more than a fragmentary fashion. Deep study of this world places the spiritually developed person at the point of intersection of all worlds, and gives him knowledge of all modes of existence and of change—past, present, and future—and an awareness of God as prime cause and first mover of all forces acting in every direction.

The World of Creation, like the other worlds, is structured according to the manifestations of the dimensions of space, time, and being. The "mansions" of this world are metaphysical realms of existence in which past, present, and future, cause and effect, are related, and time is a genus of rhythm. This world, too, is populated by beings, called "seraphs." Whereas angels are manifestations of feeling or emotion, the beings of the World of Creation are the pure essence of intellect. The word "intellect" has many connotations in modern English, but here its significance is closer to the older philosophical meaning. Seraphs are the potentiality of the ability to grasp the inner content of phenomena, in both creative and perceptive aspects. Like the angels, they are unchanging and characterized only by content and degree. Seraphs of different levels reflect the relative planes of consciousness and comprehension. Like angels, they serve as messengers between the worlds.

The superiority of the World of Creation over the World of Formation is not merely a feature of the relative positions of intellect and emotion on the scale of fundamental causality. It is also a function of another aspect of "highness": the higher worlds are more transparent to the divine light, which is their vitality and being. As one descends in the system of worlds, there is more and more matter. Another way of stating this is that the beings of the lower worlds have a greater awareness of their independent, progressively separate selves, of their private "I." This consciousness of self obscures the divine light, and dims the true, unchanging "I" that exists within each individual being. Nevertheless, this opacity is a prerequisite for existence of any kind. Each of the worlds can only come into and remain in being by virtue of the concealment of divine light. They can only exist when God conceals himself. Were the divine plenty to be manifest in its fullness, there would be no room for anything else. A world can exist only by virtue of the withdrawal of its creator. However, as one descends to the lower worlds, the concealment becomes overwhelming and the divine plenty scant. In our world, the World of Action, this trend has reached such proportions that the inhabitants may, and frequently do, reach a situation in which not only can they no longer perceive the divine plenty, but they deny that it exists.

Whereas the inhabitants of our world must be equipped with prophetic insight, or vision, or faith in order to be able to discern the divine plenty in its various forms, the higher worlds are much more lucid, and there is little impedance to the flow of light. The World of Creation is the highest of the three lower worlds, and so its creatures, the seraphs, possess a very high degree of awareness of the divine light. Nevertheless, it is a separate world, and the seraphs are characterized by individual, separate selves. They are capable of experiencing the divine light, and they accept its sovereignty in everything, but they know that they are separate from it. Consequently, even the seraphs are consumed by a great yearning to approach God.

The highest of the four worlds, the World of Emanation, is of a totally different nature. It is a mode of existence characterized by absolute clarity, no concealment, and no separate beings. There is no individuation, and no "screens" or filters separate God from that which is not God. In fact, the World of Emanation is not a world in the sense that the other three are: in a certain sense, it is the Godhead itself. The gulf between this world and that which lies below it is immeasurably greater than those that separate the other worlds; it is substantial, and not a matter of degree. It marks the border between the realms of differentiated individual beings—each of which is separated from the others and from the source of all by screens of varying degrees of density—and the Godhead, where there are no screens, and unqualified unity prevails.

Before the created, differentiated world could exist, God had to withdraw something of His divine essence and wisdom. This voluntary absence or concealment is depicted as the archetypal screen. It is the critical point of Creation, "the darkness on the face of the deep," on the one side of which is God, and the other, the template, which is the basis for the coming-into-being of the world.

In addition to the physical and spiritual parts just described, the World of Action contains many other ethereal or spiritual realms, which differ widely from each other in both their content and their spiritual significance. On the one hand, there are the realms of the various manifestations of human wisdom and creativity, such as philosophy, mathematics, poetry, and art, which are all ultimately "neutral" as regards their spiritual orientation. On the other hand, there are realms that possess a distinct spiritual charge, which may be either positive or negative. Furthermore, just as man can relate to various physical and spiritual features of the World of Action and thereby raise himself in the direction of holiness, so can he tie himself to the realms of the unholy, and move and act in them. These are the realms of evil, in the most general sense of the word, and are known by their Hebrew name, *Kelippot* (singular, *Kelippah*), which means husks.

The *Kelippot*, like the worlds of holiness, have their own "mansions," and are arranged in an inverted hierarchy, with the evil becoming more intense and distinct as one descends. They are, in their own way, all related to the World of Action. In fact, it can be said that our world, to the extent that it is neutral in its spiritual orientation, belongs to the realm of the *Kelippot*, more specifically to the one known as *Kelippat Noga*. This is a level of existence that contains all things that are not intrinsically directed either to the holy or the evil. Although it is neutral, when a man sinks into it entirely and does not, or cannot, disentangle himself from it, he fails to fulfill his specific human destiny and is wanting at the core of his being.

The relationships between the realms of the *Kelippot* are to a certain degree similar to those obtaining in the higher worlds. Thus, between each successive level, there are translations and replications of the mode of existence, and the manifestations of each are expressed in the same three dimensions: space, time, and being. The *Kelippot* are inhabited by ethereal beings, a species of angels known as destructive, or subversive, angels, or alternatively as devils, demons, or evil spirits. Like the holy angels, they all have their own individual personalities, which are defined in terms of their particular unchanging content and their degree. Corresponding to the angels of love-in-holiness and awe-in-holiness are the destructive angels of love-in-wickedness and awe-in-wickedness. Furthermore, some of these destructive angels are ephemeral; that is, they are created by man's actions, whereas others are eternal, or rather, they came into existence with the world and will continue to exist until evil is finally vanquished. Each evil deed that a man performs brings into being a destructive angel, which, in turn, has its effect in the deeper realms of the *Kelippot*. Nevertheless, there is a substantial difference between the two systems. There is obviously no equivalent in the *Kelippot* to the World of Emanation. Evil has no independent, ontological existence, and its direct source of nourishment is the World of Action; indirectly, it is sustained from the higher worlds. By performing an evil deed, a man not only creates a destructive angel that will accompany him and be bound to him as part of his ambience, but he actually diverts the divine plenty into the upper realms of evil, whence it is dragged down to the deepest *Kelippot*.

The eternal destructive angels are the messengers that mediate between the various realms of evil, just as the holy angels move up and down in the upper worlds. Destructive angels are manifest in our world by means of "clothing in garments," and they appear in ethereal or material forms that are sometimes as bizarre and strange as those of the holy angels. These destructive angels are the tempters who try to incite man to evil by bringing the idea of wickedness to our realm of existence; in return, they receive the diverted divine plenty. They also serve as the instruments by which a sinner is punished. Just as the reward received by the righteous man or the saint is an extension of his good deeds, so the retribution for shortcomings is part and parcel of the sin itself. In this life, punishment is no more than to be held in close contact with the evil one has created, in a variety of manifestations and translations—bodily and mental torment, despair and anguish, and failure.

One of the most severe forms of punishment is the "mansion" of the *Kelippot* known as Hell. When a man dies, his soul is separated from his body and relates only to the ethereal beings, which he created and with which he was associated in his lifetime. The soul finds its level. In the case of a great sinner, this will be in the company of the destructive angels he created, who will punish him for bringing them into existence, until the full measure of remorse is exhausted. But even this extreme retribution is not extrinsic, for it is an organic continuation of the actual sins committed.

Though the destructive angels are manifestations and the messengers of evil, they are also part of the totality of existence. Like the entire system of *Kelippot*, to which they belong, they are not optimal, but they do fulfill an essential role in maintaining a certain balance in the cosmos, by deterring men from slipping deeper into evil. Were evil to be banished from the world, they would disappear, for ultimately they are parasites on men and cannot exist without his wickedness. But as long as man uses his power of choice to do evil, they feed off, incite, and punish him. In this sense, the existence of destructive angels is conditional, rather like a police force, which is necessary only as long as there is crime.

The fact remains, however, that far from disappearing, the destructive angels are growing stronger and more powerful, as evil waxes in the world. Their ontological status is no longer clear, and far from being mere instruments of deterrence within the total system of existence, they appear to be independent beings acting in their own terms of reference, subjects of a sovereign realm of evil.

The significance of man's role in Creation is thus immense. When the day comes that we free ourselves from the overwhelming temptations to sin, the entire system of evil will fall back into its proper dimensions. Those aspects of it that came into being as a consequence of man's deeds—the ephemeral destructive angels—will disappear, while the eternal structural elements, which now serve as deterrents, will assume a new, entirely different role. That which now appears to be evil will be reintegrated into holiness.

6

The Psychology of the Soul

What is the relationship between the external manifestation of the human soul (its "aspects," or forces) and the essence of the soul itself? This question lies at the center of much Chasidic speculation concerning human psychology, and is central in the doctrines of the *Chabad* school.

The founder of *Chabad*, Rabbi Shneur Zalman of Liadi, made apparently contradictory statements concerning the nature of this relationship. In his major work, the *Tanya*, we read: "The soul...consists of ten aspects (*bechinot*), which correspond to the ten Divine Manifestations (*sefirot*) from which they are descended...and are subdivided into Intellect (*sechel*) and Attributes (*middot*)" (Chapter 3). Later in the same book he writes: "The essence and the being of the soul...are its ten aspects" (Chapter 12). These are clear statements in favor of the position that the soul's essence is identical with its manifestations. Elsewhere, however, Rabbi Shneur Zalman modifies this stand. In his *Yalkutei Torah (Vayikra 4)* he writes that his statements in the *Tanya* were not accurate, and that even the highest of the ten aspects is not identical with the essence and the being of the soul. All the forces and the aspects of the soul are no more than modes in which the essence of the soul is manifest. The reason underlying this reservation is also made clear. Understanding the soul to be made up of separate parts would be to deny its unique nature. Seen in this way, it would no longer be a single entity, but a package of different qualities or aspects.

Observation of life and of human development buttressed the Chasidic view that the manifestations and the essence of the soul are not identical. The soul, the vital force of the body, exists within a human being by virtue of the fact that he was created. In its essence, it is a unique, single, stable, and unchanging entity, but as a person grows and develops, his intellect, attributes, and feelings, which are all manifestations of the soul, do change. Life, in fact, can be perceived as an ongoing process of change in the manifestations of the soul. Thus, although the manifestations are ultimately derived from the essence, they are in fact separate and discrete.

If the soul is not identical with its manifestations, what is it? The traditional Chasidic response to this question is that we do not know, nor can we know. Whereas the manifestations of the soul are knowable, the essence is beyond the limits of our comprehension. The essence of the soul, like the being of God, is inaccessible to the human mind, and is not a subject for human inquiry. The questions that may be asked concerning the soul, then, concern the various manifestations, their relation to the essence, and the relationships between them.

The manifestations of the soul are, as we have seen, separate from the essence, but this does not imply that they are simply vehicles by means of which it is revealed. There is a wide range of fundamentally different manifestations of the soul, including Intellect, feelings, cognitive powers, speech, and action. In order to understand their nature, we shall have to clarify what is involved in the process of revealing.

The image used in earlier kabbalistic and Chasidic works to describe revealing is that of "garbing." The distinction between the two concepts, "garbing" and "revealing," is extremely important. The implication of "revealing" in the sense in which it is normally used is that the entity itself, in its essence, is made apparent, is uncovered, and that there is no intermediary between it and the perceiver. "Garbing," on the other hand, refers to a situation in which there is precisely such an intermediary, a "garment." The garment is a separate entity, although it generally possesses no character or personality of its own: it serves as an instrument, whose function is to reveal the nature and the goal of another entity.

The use of the two linked images, garbing and garment, highlights the two-sided nature of revealing—it is both a covering and an uncovering. A person does not appear in company undressed; without his garments, he is not seen. The garment is an instrument by means of which the entity is revealed, but, on the other hand, it hides the true essence and nature of that which it garbs: from without, we can see only the garment. Speech, for example, is frequently described in the *Tanya* as a "garment for thought." Thought is an inner, spiritual process that cannot be transmitted to others. For it to be communicated, it must be garbed in the garment of speech (from this point of view, writing is considered to be a special case of speech). What is revealed, that which is made manifest, is not the thought itself, which remains hidden and concealed, but a kind of projection, a shadow of the reality. Speech is incapable of transmitting thought perfectly; it can convey the content of thought, but not its essence.

Another aspect of the garbing and garment symbolism is the close connection between that which is garbed and the garment. The garment is an external entity, but it does reproduce or copy the essence of that which is garbed. This is an important characteristic, and it marks the difference between garments and other instruments. For the most part, an instrument does not reproduce the content of the entity that employs it. The garment, even though it conceals, does provide background material that will help us to understand the inner essence. Thus, speech can be considered a garment for thought only because the "alphabet of speech" is a kind of transcript, a translation, of the "alphabet of thought."

There are various kinds of garments. A particular essence can be revealed or made apparent in numerous ways, and each of these modes of garbing is different. It is possible to analyze these forms in great detail, but two broad categories can be distinguished: that of inner garments and that of outer garments.

In a certain sense an outer garment is the simplest form of

revealing—the making apparent of concealed content to others. Nevertheless, such a garment is generally relatively far-removed from that which is garbed, both in its essence and in the accuracy of the reproduction. Speech is an example of an outer garment. An inner garment, on the other hand, does not reveal to the external world, to others; it is more of an inner revealing, to oneself. It is the bringing to light, making manifest, of something previously either not understood or not present in the realm of consciousness. An example of such an inner garment is thought, when it is seen as garbing the soul; thought reveals to the subject something of his own soul, and yet is never seen on the outside.

A characteristic common to all garments is that they possess no intrinsic connection with what is garbed, and always remain as separate entities. Nevertheless, in certain circumstances they may affect the entities that they garb. Thus, what a person says may provoke his thoughts, but such stimulation is not a function of the garment as a garment but as a new entity, which may or may not have such an effect.

There is another mode of manifestation, that known symbolically as an "adornment." Its connection with the essence that it reveals is much closer than that of even an inner garment. To a limited degree, the adornment does unite with the essence; from the perspective of the external world, the inner essence and the adornment appear to be identical. The adornment is thus more than a garment, for it is intrinsically connected with the essence it garbs; it is not a totally separate entity, but assumes part of the personality of the essence. There are, however, two aspects of the adornment. In terms of its own primary being, it remains separate and discrete, and is never one with the essence. As seen from the outside, however, there is no way of distinguishing between the two. The essence does not merely use the adornment as a medium to establish a connection with the outer world; the bond is much more profound. When the essence is revealed by an adornment, it becomes, in a way, a sort of adornment itself, for it is totally identifiable with the particular mode of manifestation operating at that time. Even though the adornments may change, for whatever period of time the connection exists, the identity with it is complete.

Let us now apply the distinction we have made between garment and adornment to what is knowable of the soul. Thought, speech, and action are among the garments of the soul, whereas Intellect and Attributes are its adornments. As we have noted, the function of the garment is to reveal the essence to the exterior. In other words, thought, speech, and action are the means by which the soul is manifest, by which its Will is revealed. Nevertheless, the soul is not identified with any of these garments. Even thought, which is an inner garment, is not to be identified with the soul itself. Thought does no more than convey or express a particular content, desire, idea, or impulse that arises in the soul. Thought transcribes that which it receives from the soul into its own alphabet—words. This is not the case with the adornments, the so-called powers of the soul. Let us take, for example, Will, one of the highest of these powers. Will is more than just a means of expressing the soul. Although it does serve as a medium through which the soul is manifest, when it is operative, Will is united with the essence of the soul, and from the perspective of the external world, it is the soul.

A characteristic of garments, both inner and outer, is that they may be imperfect or flawed. When this occurs, as it does to some degree in every individual, the manifestations of the soul are likely to be distorted. This can impair the establishment of a connection between the soul and the exterior, or result in a faulty connection. Thus, thought may be unable to express fully the true essence of the soul, when it is limited by defective methods of reasoning or by erroneous concepts that are not compatible with the essence of the soul. Such distortion does not occur with the adornments, the powers of the soul: in a sense they are the soul, and they do express the soul correctly.

These differences are of far-reaching significance when we wish to understand the distinction between Intellect and thought. As noted, the two are not identical. Thought is only a garment, and, as such, its basis is the revealing of a particular content. The fact that thought, word, and action are connected in a kind of permanent bond shows that they are all modes of manifestation of more inner essences, and that the differences between them are only of degree. Although thought is an inner garment, close to and almost inseparable from the soul, it is still in the same category as speech and action. Like the other garments, thought is a function of the physical body, to which the soul gives life and the ability to exist. The difference between the activities of the various garments is ultimately a function of the instruments with which they express themselves. Thus, the differences between action (the hands) and speech (the mouth) and between speech and thought (the brain) are functions of the sensitivity and subtlety of the instruments. Thought is an activity of the physical body, but at a more spiritual, refined level.

Intellect is the *capacity* of the soul to comprehend, the basic essence of the soul's power to understand. It is the soul's intrinsic ability to attain holistic intellectual understanding. Comprehension by the Intellect (as opposed to that by thought) is of the totality of whole entities, and to a certain degree, of things-in-themselves. At this level, the concepts and words of thought are not manifest. When, however, thought emerges from this general state of potentiality and enters the instrument of thought—the brain—there is a transformation from potential content to actual content, a translation of the abstract capacity for comprehension into words and concepts, which, in turn, are expressed in the alphabet of thought, and are garments. Thought, a physiological–mental activity, serves as a performing instrument, carrying out the directives of the Intellect.

The relationship between the Attributes of the soul and the emotions is similar to that between the Intellect and thought. The Attributes are the first sparks, the forces that activate the emotions in their development; they are simple essences, the primary impulses. When such an impulse reaches the brain, it unites with the capacity of thought, and an emotion can take form, in all its mental and sentimental complexity.

In the *Tanya*, the relation between the Intellect and the Attributes is usually described as that of cause and effect. The primacy of the Intellect over the Attributes is supported by observation of human life and of the changes that take place in Attributes. Special attention is paid to the objects of the Attributes in children, "whose affections are for little, unworthy objects, because they have not the knowledge to love that which is worthy of love, love being according to Knowledge (Chapter 8)." This statement of the ontological primacy of Intellect is subsequently modified, and it seems that the Intellect does not create the Attributes, but rather provides the objects for them. Even if the

Intellect alone can activate the Attributes and bring them out of latency, it cannot be that it brings them into being. Furthermore, because of the basic differences in the nature and essence of the Intellect and the Attributes, Intellect cannot in itself relate to them. At most it can be said that the Intellect is the midwife of the Attributes.

We would seem to be moving in the direction of an unexpected rationalism: even though the emotions are not created by the Intellect, nevertheless their coming into existence is conditioned by it. In fact, further examination of the distinction between Intellect and thought shows us that the relationship is more complex. Intellect is essentially the capacity to comprehend and to absorb reality—whether this is outer or inner; Attributes, on the other hand, are the impulses inherent in man, although only in potential, as first sparks. What they contain is the possibility to love or to hate (or more precisely, to be drawn to or repelled by), to respond to beauty, and so on. But such impulses are blind as long as there is no object upon which their particular energy can be focused. Without the background of mental contents provided by thought, they cannot make contact with reality, and remain in potential. It is the Intellect that chooses the objects to which human impulses can relate. Only after such an initial selection of objects, and a complex process, during which the primary attitude of the Intellect toward them is fixed in thoughts and words, can the inner impulses begin to be manifest and to act as genuine human emotions.

It cannot be said that a child loves or hates less than an adult. His primary impulses (Attributes) exist within him to the same extent, and they are certainly very active. The difference is that the child's Intellect is less developed than that of an adult, and it selects different objects for love or for hate, from a more restricted range of possibilities. By generalizing the comparison of child and adult, we can see that the smaller the guiding, directing power of the Intellect, the greater the relative influence of the Attributes-as-impulse on thought and behavior.

The Chasidic theory of moral growth was based on what may be called a species of sublimation. In the *Chabad* doctrine, this was developed into a system that prescribed the way in which the individual could become a more complete human being—by directing the Intellect toward more noble objects.

PART II

THE GIVING
AND THE RECEIVING
OF THE TORAH

7

The Imagery Concept
in Jewish Thought

Modern Western thought is characterized by an extensive use of abstract concepts that exist and operate within a more general abstract system. Jewish thought, on the other hand, has, with very few exceptions, done without them. Abstract concepts are not to be found in the Bible, the Talmud, or even in relatively modern Chasidic texts. Indeed, with such a small number of abstract concepts, it would appear to be almost impossible for Jewish writings to express anything profound. This, of course, is not true, and although they employ few abstract concepts, Jewish writings do deal with abstractions. Furthermore, Jewish literature is distinguished by a progressive abstraction of ideas, and thus the absence of abstract concepts cannot be attributed to the antiquity of the texts.

It is, of course, quite impossible to manipulate complex and abstract ideas without concepts, and Jewish sources do employ them. The concepts used, however, are not abstract but rather plastic and depictive, and they communicate their meaning rather like a metaphor or a visual representation. In other words, Jewish thought uses pictorial or imagery concepts instead of abstract concepts. The imagery concepts used are frequently derived from the commonplace, from everyday life and work; for example, legal texts frequently use words and phrases like "horn," "tooth," "foot," "warned," and "the blow of a hammer." The latter phrase, for example, encompasses the entire range of activities, that, using abstract concepts, we would call "the completion of a task." It may seem strange to us, but Jewish legal texts will say of a man who makes a collar for a garment on the Sabbath that he is culpable because of "the blow of the hammer." Furthermore, a wealth of such phrases and imagery concepts are used in the Kabbalah and the Aggadah to express abstractions that would be described in other systems by means of abstract concepts. Once one has become accustomed to these imagery concepts, they can be seen to be no less effective in expressing abstractions than the abstract concepts with which we are familiar.

The imagery concept is the product of a specifically Jewish mode of thought, and as such defies definition in other terms. It is not a symbol, a circumscription or a metaphor, nor is it merely a Jewish substitute for an abstract concept. It is something unique, with a nature of its own. Attempts have been made to explain its usage as a function of semantic development, that is, that certain expressions possessed in antiquity specific meanings, which in the course of time underwent a process of abstraction, until eventually they embraced something much broader and more complex. Although this theory seems quite logical, it does not stand up to the facts. Thus, while talmudic literature does employ generalizations that are derived from terms in the Bible, most such usages are independent of earlier sources and were coined at a later date for the specific purpose of expressing abstractions by means of imagery concepts.

For example, when we see how frequently the concept *regel* (foot) is used in talmudic discussions of the laws of torts (*regel* is the damage caused by a domestic animal while walking, during its customary activities), it is plain that the Jewish thinkers of the past simply had a strong reluctance to coin obvious abstract concepts. Imagery concepts were used, then, as a matter of deliberate and conscious choice. They do not reflect a weak or primitive mode of thought. They are rather a special form of expression, marked by its own advantages and disadvantages. This Jewish conceptual structure is neither better nor worse, neither more advanced nor more backward than Western abstract conceptual thinking: it is a parallel development.

As we have noted, the imagery concept is neither symbol nor metaphor; it does not seek to compress a wide range of phenomena into a single term, nor to find a suitable comprehensive linguistic equivalent. Let us return to our previous example, the expression "the blow of a hammer." This phrase has been described as meaning the completion of a task, but this does not exhaust its meaning, nor is this imagery concept, or any other, a symbolic abstraction of the essence of the idea or situation. The imagery concept, nevertheless, does have a distinct meaning. Its particular, detailed representation is included within, and is part of, the generalized abstraction or category it is expressing. Perhaps the best definition is that the imagery concept is a special case, a concrete and characteristic example, of a certain category of abstraction.

When a scholar of *halachah*, who is discussing the activities forbidden on the Sabbath, wishes to specify those connected with the extraction of food from that within which it is held, he calls them "threshing." He selects one characteristic activity from the totality, a highly concrete and specific item, and makes it the key imagery word for the concept, so that a person who milks a cow on the Sabbath can be said to have transgressed the law against "threshing."

In all imagery concepts, the image depicted is never remote from the abstraction, and it is therefore always possible to make the transformation from the general to the particular and back with facility. A remarkable example of this is to be found in kabbalistic literature. Each of the various *sefirot* or Divine manifestations is depicted by a number of different images, all of which bear a relationship to each other, and to the other *sefirot*. These images may be functions of physical, anatomical features, of psychological entities, or of cosmic forces. Thus, "love" and "fear," which are two opposing but symmetrical powers operating in the world, are represented as the right and left hands, the limbs that perform the work of the soul.

The use of imagery concepts to formulate and communicate abstractions possesses some advantages, though it is also fraught with dangers. It permits the construction of a complete edifice of interrelated concepts, the building units being a very wide variety of significant depictive expressions. In contrast to systems based on abstract concepts, which can be highly intricate and present difficulties to comprehension, the Jewish method is on the whole relatively easy to grasp, because it generally involves a simple story about real situations.

Its great disadvantage, which hampers both beginners and scholars, lies in the fact that the representations of concrete objects and actions are always associated with a fixed time and a certain place. The imagery concept is a specific detail that has been extracted from the flow of life and inserted, together with its connotations, into a conceptual framework. Such a detail, even after it has been removed from the organic unity of life, still retains something of the temporal and local essence of its parent organism. It still bears many of the contextual elements of its origin. So long as life conditions are relatively stable and concepts unchanging, this does not matter; all the connotations are understood, and the significance of the image is unchanged. When life conditions change, however, as a result of either major cultural upheavals or the simple intergeneration gap, the significance of a story or an image may be lost. With the passage of time, the multiplicity of details becomes a source of confusion, and it is difficult to distinguish between the main idea and the insignificant features. Let us take as an example a passage from the Bible (Exodus 13:13): "And every firstling of an ass thou shalt redeem with a lamb; and if thou wilt not redeem it, then thou shalt break his neck: and all the firstborn of man among thy children shalt thou redeem." What is permanent and eternal here, and what is temporary and incidental? Is the ass really an ass, or is it an imagery concept representing the entire category of domestic animals? Is the lamb really a lamb, or is it a special case illustrating the general principle of making an offering? In many places in the Bible there are such problems, and it is the task of the *halachah* to elucidate them, to determine in which cases the scriptural text is literal and precise, and elsewhere, when it is an imagery concept, to elucidate it, to understand it, and to extract its essential meaning. This aspect of halachic activity—the understanding of what is limited and restricted and what is general in the Bible—is to be found in the *Midrashei Halachah* and the Mishnah. Later generations found it necessary to elucidate these sources too, and thus, much of the Talmud is concerned with establishing the significance of the imagery concepts found in Mishnah, which itself is frequently not a logical presentation, much of it being composed of anecdotes, fables, and examples. The entire course of halachic literature since the Talmud has continued in the same direction, namely, the mapping out of the vast system of imagery concepts within the coordinates of the concrete realities of every generation. The number of cases has grown, as each historical stage divided and subdivided the imagery concepts of its predecessors, each new accretion becoming part of the tradition.

As we have seen, halachic sages were compelled by circumstances to decode and abstract the imagery concepts and the realistic examples found in older texts, to develop them and provide a new meaning suited to each generation. In the field of *halachah*, this was quite essential, for it is impermissible to leave such matters obscure. It was necessary, in fact, to establish as a basic principle that the meaning of each statement in the Torah exceeds the simple meaning conveyed in the words. Thus it is written in the Talmud: "He who translates a passage as it seems to be, is a deceiver." Direct renderings of the formal content do not present the true significance, only a reduced aspect of the imagery concept.

The circumstances that made it necessary to elucidate imagery concepts in the *halachah* did not apply to philosophical and aggadic texts. As a result, the original imagery concepts in these fields of thought were on the whole not clarified or interpreted, and, furthermore, additional images were added. This explains to a large extent the highly variegated and even diverse nature of the various trends of Jewish thought, especially in later periods. They were all based on the sources, in which one can find everything, and nothing. Perhaps the only development that will lead to the elucidation of this immense body of obscure material will be the advent of a generation that will urgently need to understand the Torah in order to apply it to its problems and doubts.

The attempts to reach such an understanding, however, will encounter a number of basic difficulties. It will be necessary to go beyond the literal to the abstraction or the generalization by discarding the components of fixed time and place, just as one removes the shell to get to the nut. An image used in Hebrew to describe this process is *hafshatah*, which means both undressing (that is, removing the outer garments) and abstraction. In so doing, we will discover that imagery concepts are not all of the same value, and that no one method of abstraction can be applied in all cases. The imagery concepts in the sources (or, in fact, all concepts found in the Scriptures) must be treated in the knowledge that their literal meaning does not exhaust their ideational content, and that each form of expression is characterized by a special mode of symbolization. There is thus a special significance concealed behind even corporeal images and expressions.

The imagery concepts found in the Zohar (and in all kabbalist literature) are to a large extent also symbols: each image has a parallel and, as it were, synonymous abstract concept. If "right arm" signifies "*chesed*" (kindness) in one place, it will mean the same in every context in which it appears.

However, in contrast to the consistency of meaning of imagery concepts used in the Kabbalah, which, as we have seen, resemble symbols, the situation in the Bible and the Talmud is quite different. There, the significance of any given concept is not uniform, and even in those cases where there is no doubt that such a covert meaning is intended, no standard key exists for its interpretation. Furthermore, there may well be more than one key for different aspects of its meaning.

Some modes of interpretation attribute hidden meanings or strange symbolic connotations that the literal reading of the texts cannot possibly support. These are esoteric interpretations (known in Hebrew as *sod*, secret, in contrast to *drash*, simple exegesis), and though they are perfectly legitimate in their right place, they are not really part of the process of the simple, direct elucidation of the material.

In order to comprehend what a particular sage, kabbalist, or prophet meant, it is necessary to be familiar with the historic context within which he wrote and lived, with his personality, point of view, and even the manners and customs implicit in the text. Only then will it be possible to extract its more universal, human message. Although the words were originally intended for the writer's contemporaries, all generations of Jewish sages expressed themselves by means of imagery conceptualization of abstractions. If we approach the task in the proper way, we, too, shall be able to find the general meaning. Once we grasp what they were saying for their own time, we shall be able to understand what they are still telling us today.

The search to discover the timeless content and meaning of scriptural sources should therefore be conducted in the same way that the *halachah* is approached. First, a careful inquiry must be made to establish the exact meaning of the passage as it is expressed in the original text, and then the general meaning must be extracted. Let us take as an example of the halachic approach the treatment of the biblical precept, "And if an ox gores a man..." The idea here is straightforward, and the meaning is clear. A simple, concrete situation is described. Nevertheless, it is necessary to ask whether the animal involved is necessarily only an ox. Could it not also be a donkey, a dog, or a bird? And is "to gore" only one, specific type of injury, or could it also be applied to biting or kicking? After such questions are posed, and the text is carefully analyzed, both intrinsically and by comparison with parallel passages, all according to the techniques of traditional hermeneutics, halachic conclusions are drawn, and it is seen that this particular case of an ox goring a man can be expressed in the abstract, in terms of "animals" that attack and "injure" people.

The same technique can be used in interpreting a nonlegal text—for example, Chapter 44 of Jeremiah. After the disaster in Jerusalem, many Jews fled to Egypt, and the prophet berated them for offering sacrifices to the "queen of heaven." Though he was relating to something very specific, and restricted in time and space, his words are just as applicable to those who sacrifice to the queen of heaven in a wide range of modern ways—whether they call her "money," "socialism," or anything else. This extension of significance is very much more than a forced comparison between two rather remote phenomena or a moralistic recourse to an ancient example. The modern idea is in fact embodied in the biblical passage. Jeremiah's deeper intention, the fundamental theme that was evoked in his restricted and limited example, is a general, eternal idea that is certainly valid today. This can be easily confirmed by replacing the name "queen of heaven" with another—Bel or Ashtoret. The idea remains the same. The queen of heaven was a special case, according to the Jewish mode of imagery concepts we have just described. Jeremiah was not speaking only to specific persons who had offered sacrifices to one particular pagan goddess; rather, he was delivering a fundamental message that would have the same validity in other circumstances, and concerning any other object of worship.

A second nonlegal illustration, taken from the Talmud, is of a completely different nature. The saying "Life, sons, and livelihood, these do not depend on a man's worth, but on the stars" appears not only to be remote from our experience, but also simply not correct. It seems to be based on the assumption, which we reject, that the arrangement of the stars at a man's birth determines the course of his life. Since we do not believe in astrology, the saying is apparently lacking in significance for us. In fact, however, it is a special case, an imagery concept that possesses far more content than is apparent in its literal meaning. In terms of contemporary culture, this particular saying would probably be expressed thus: "Sons, life, and livelihood [or, in more abstract terms, the ups and downs of life] are not contingent on a man's worth or virtue, but are dependent on the laws of nature [or on the same general causality that operates throughout the world]." Thus, when the abstract content of the imagery concept is extracted, it is revealed as neither strange nor remote, but familiar and pertinent.

The examples presented are relatively easy to interpret and understand. Jewish writings abound with far more complex images, the inner meaning of which is extracted with difficulty, as they are expressed even more graphically, and involve specific incidents and circumstances. circumstances.

Nevertheless, by aspiring to deeper comprehension, by trying to apprehend the basic ideas and not just the irrelevant appendages of the imagery, we shall be able to observe that the source books of Jewish thought are—with all their so-called outmoded ideas and images—new and vitally meaningful.

8

The Image of Isaac

At the very beginning of Genesis 25 there is the seemingly unnecessary repetition, "And these are the generations of Isaac, Abraham's son: Abraham begat Isaac and Isaac was forty years old when he took Rebecca to wife." As Rashi mentions in his commentary, it is apparently a fact to be emphasized—that Abraham was the father and the true beginning, and Isaac was the one who carries on, who continues. This is indeed insinuated in Genesis 28:4, when Isaac blesses Jacob with "the blessings of Abraham." Also, this introductory sentence to the annals of Isaac tells us that he was forty years old when he took a wife; there is no mention of the *Akedah* (the sacrifice of Isaac) which is the more unique and specific fact defining him. Isaac remains, forever, the sacrifice, the one who is offered up, who is acted upon. Essentially, he plays the submissive and passive role and is known as *Olah Temimah*, the innocent, pure offering. Even his wife, Rebecca, is brought to him; he doesn't have to do anything to win her or even to decide his destiny or the destiny of his sons. There doesn't seem to be anything personally significant about his actions, even in the few that the Scriptures tell us about. In this and in other matters, he is unlike his father, Abraham, or his son, Jacob, who were much more dynamic, well-defined personalities.

And yet in Kabbalah symbolism, Isaac is the prototype of *Gevurah* (courage, firmness), which is also called *Pachad Yitzchak* (Isaac's fear), whereas Abraham is *Chesed*, the one who loves God and exemplifies Divine grace, and Jacob is the combination of, or balance between, the two, *Tiferet* (harmony, beauty). The fact that Isaac personifies a certain strength coming from fear of God, a sense of justice, and a steady courage is not necessarily a contradiction to his passivity. For there are two basic movements in relation to existence: one is an outward movement, a movement of expansion and of giving, that which is interpreted as love (*Chesed*); the other is an inward movement, a more centripetal action, of concentration or withdrawal (*Gevurah*). It may therefore be said that *Gevurah* is not really power; for power is *Gedulah* (greatness), which is another name for *Chesed*. Nevertheless, there is a certain force in *Gevurah*, a capacity to focus power, to concentrate it to a point. Indeed, this is the real meaning of *Gevurah*—that heroic action depends on the focusing of power. In any struggle, physical or spiritual, the one who can concentrate energy or force to a single sharp point of effectiveness is stronger than the one who diffuses largeness (power), or abundance, in all directions. So that even though fear and courage, which make up *Gevurah*, are not the same in emotional terms, and may even be considered opposites, they are similar and intimately related in that they hold back and require control. As the proverb says, "Who is the hero? The one who conquers his impulse [passions, or instincts]."

Chesed, on the other hand, expands and gives bounty in all directions and all the time, without limits and without necessarily choosing the recipients. So that *Midat HaDin*, the quality of justice, has to belong to *Gevurah* and not to *Chesed*. It demands a holding back, a control, of mercy and love. And in the chart of the *sefirot*, it is Jacob, the synthesis of Abraham and Isaac, who represents *Tiferet*, which is pity and mercy as well as harmony and beauty.

Isaac is therefore limited to a narrow range of action, his passivity is that of restraint, of *Gevurah*, rather than of the feminine quality of softness. Nevertheless, he is receptive; his task is to receive and pass on the blessing and as even modern psychology has not failed to observe about such men, his wife, Rebecca, tends to be a dominant and dominating figure. She is an archetype, one of the four Mothers. She is described not only as the daughter of such and such a family, but as the sister of her brother, Laban. This has later consequences and deeper meanings. Incidentally, when we examine these original patriarchal families, we may observe that there are patterns, curious brother–sister combinations and uncle–nephew relationships. Also, for example, Nahor has twelve sons, Abraham has twelve sons, Isaac has only the twins, and Jacob, of course, bears the famous progenitors of the tribes, the Children of Israel.

Throughout the story of this larger family, or clan, we are confronted with the problem of choosing the one who is to carry the blessing. Rebecca is selected to be the wife of the chosen one, Isaac; and it is important for both Jacob and Esau to obtain wives from the family (Esau does so as a second choice). When they consider the choice between the twin brothers, there is some uncertainly, with Isaac showing a preference for Esau, and Rebecca convinced that Jacob shall be the one to receive the blessing. Truth to tell, it may not have been so easy to decide between them; both appear to have resembled their maternal uncle, Laban, in many ways. Jacob (Yaacov), which also means the devious, the one who circumvents as well as he who goes at the heel, is not as straight as his later name Yisrael would imply. Indeed, he only gradually takes on the quality of directness and forthrightness. At first he is very much a subtle character, more complicated than any of the others, except perhaps for his son Joseph, who also has to go through a long, devious route to become straight. Esau remains a part of the Laban tradition and is considered an untrustworthy character to the end, whereas Jacob, as stated, changes; he becomes straight and is eventually called Yeshurun as well as Yisrael. Once the choice is made, he grows to become the father of the nation. (The Jews are not called the children of Abraham or of Isaac, but of Jacob, *B'nai Yisrael*.)

One of the interesting indications of this change of personality may be gathered from the short exchange between Rachel and Jacob, when, after years of marriage and true love, she comes to him demanding children, and he answers, "Am I in God's stead that I did not give you children?" To be sure, Jacob already has children by his other wives, so that his relying on Divine providence is not merely a matter of submission and piety. And one should remember that there was always a certain dread of *chutzpah*, of daring, to force God's decisions in one's favor. Though to be sure, Isaac seems to have done precisely that, when he prays for his wife, barren for twenty years—and it is clearly stated that it is for her sake—to become pregnant. It is one of his few decisive acts and elucidates the Isaac personality: *Gevurah*. He does not, for instance, take any other wife; he loves his only, rightful wife, and only by her does he want to have children. And his prayer is indeed a play on the word *vayiater*—derived from an uncommon verb that can also mean "more" (*yoter*) or abundance. In other words, he is even overinsistent—doing that which perhaps Rachel wanted Jacob to do—and gaining his desired end.

In terms of Jewish prayer, such insistence is uncommon, not only because of the wrong attitude implied, but also because of the danger involved in getting precisely what you demand. In the Talmud for instance, it is written, one should not pray too much and too persistently for the possession of a certain woman, or one may be likely to get her, and that could turn out badly—either in divorce or in untimely death, either the woman's or one's own because of her. In any case, it is not at all clear whether praying for the satisfaction of a personal wish is right, so that Rebecca seems to have certain apprehensions when her womb troubles her with its own inner strife, and she seeks reassurance from God. She is afraid they have overdone it in their insistence on having children. Her asking God to learn the fate of her unborn child is a unique instance—not Sara nor Leah nor Rachel nor any of the other mothers in the Bible ever do it. Perhaps she is afraid of giving birth to a monster. And the answer she receives does indeed have the tragic overtones that dominate the rest of her life: "Two nations are in thy belly," and they will be locked in conflict for all time.

=9=

Dissonance
in the Book of Psalms

All who have ever read the Book of Psalms—be it out of sheer interest, or be it as prayer, making the verses sing their song—will in all probability have found strange dissonance in several of its chapters.

Let us take Psalm 104 as an example. The exultation of the spirit and wonderment at the work of creation, making one feel the beauty of its harmony, steadily build up to ever greater excitement over the perfection in God's works. Suddenly the idyllic mood into which this psalm puts us is disturbed by a passage that jars our senses. We have just read, "May my meditation be pleasing to Him, for I rejoice in the Lord," and without any preparation whatsoever and out of context, follows the verse, "Let sinners be consumed from the earth, and let the wicked be no more!" Having accompanied the psalmist in his emotion, we must feel that the latter passage is nothing short of forced. In the description of the beautiful order in the world, what place is there for mention of the sinner and the wicked?

This is not the only passage that leaves us with such a disturbing impression. We see a similar phenomenon at the end of Psalm 63. Here, David, having gone through the ordeals of the desert, gives expression to his thirsting for God and the need to cling to Him. Rather than end on a note that is the main theme of this psalm, we read, again without warning, "But those who seek to destroy my life shall go down into the depths of the earth." Here also we ask ourselves, what purpose does the mention of evil doers serve at a point where they seemingly have no relation whatsoever to the theme of the psalm? Similarly, in Psalm 139, the deep feeling of attachment to God, of seeing His Presence fill the universe and of the great thirst for coming closer to Him, all stand in sharp contrast to the strange and surprising ending: "Do I not hate them that hate thee, O Lord?"

In many similar cases we find that a truly idyllic picture is suddenly disturbed by mention of sinners, evil doers, or other negative influences. Does this all not seem as if, in the middle of the impassioned description of the mystery and harmony in God's work, the psalmist comes purposely to distort this beautiful impression and spoil the sweet melody with a grating dissonance?

An answer to this problem (which is more a question of feeling than of reason) may be attained by further study. Here, as in many other cases, the answer is contained in the question, and the more we attempt to penetrate the problem itself the closer we come to its solution. For instance, when in Psalm 104 we read the idyllic description of nature and are permitted to share in the joy the psalmist finds in its beauty, the sudden mention of sinners and evil doers serves only to destroy the impression of inner peace. Of course, we can find justification for the attack on evil doers. Nevertheless, they seem terribly out of place in this context, and the one or two verses that refer to them are bound to destroy the beautiful impression created by the whole chapter. Let us attempt to penetrate this question from the psalmist's point of view and present it in a drastic form: Did not the psalmist himself discern this lack of accord, did he not also feel the grating of the senses?

The psalmist wrote his words with deep emotion; how can it be, then, that he was not conscious of the extent that these conflicting elements disturbed the inner melody? Let us, therefore, assume that the psalmist was not indifferent to the apparent contradiction. But then, we must ask, why did he write it? Because he felt that this is how things actually were, and this realization gave rise to the grating feeling in his soul.

Characteristic of the Bible is the unwillingness to shut its eyes to any of life's aspects. On studying the world and life, we must admit one looks away from the unpleasant aspects in an attempt to keep the beautiful illusion from being disturbed. Indeed, when the psalmist looks upon the wonderful harmony in the world, when he examines all of God's works, he is moved and impassioned by the mystical unity and by the order and perfection found everywhere. Nevertheless, in this peaceful melody that encompasses the whole world, we do hear a grating sound—those people who do not live by His supreme and holy order, the evil doers. The psalmist would have liked to end on a note of inner peacefulness, but he could not ignore these humans who are a blemish on the perfect beauty of this picture that is creation. For that reason, out of a feeling of deep pain at seeing the conflict between the world in its perfect state and those who seek to disturb this perfection, the psalmist's reaction is natural. He curses and cries out against the evil doers, feeling that were only that blot erased, everything would return to its original state of perfection.

This dissonance in the Book of Psalms, we conclude, is neither an accident nor does it reflect lack of taste. It is, rather, an expression of that grating of the feeling caused by those who disrupt the peacefulness of Creation. When given over to the loftiest emotions, the psalmist sees those who seek to mark the world with their blemishes, and expresses his reaction in the words: "Let the sinners be consumed from the earth, and let the wicked be no more." Then, and only then, will he truly be able to say, "Bless the Lord, O my soul."

10

Talmud

The Talmud is the main (though not the only) work of the oral Torah (*Torah shebe'al peh*). It is second only to the written Torah, that is, the Bible, in its sanctity, and its impact upon the life of the Jewish people throughout the centuries has been no less than that of the Bible—if not greater.

The Talmud, in the broad sense of the word, incorporates two different works: the Mishnah and the Talmud (or Gemara, literally, completion) proper. The Mishnah is a comprehensive collection of laws and regulations touching upon nearly every area of Jewish life. Its final redaction was made about 200 C.E., in the Galilee region of Palestine, by Rabbi Judah HaNasi. Even though its final editing took place at this time, it includes a great deal of earlier material, part of which was already set in its literary form during the last few centuries B.C.E. The Mishnah is the fullest crystallization of the oral Torah up to the date of its editing. Its language is the Hebrew of that generation, which differs somewhat in syntax, grammar, and vocabulary from biblical Hebrew.

The Mishnah is divided into six main divisions, or *sedarim* (literally, orders), each of which deals with a specific group of subjects, and these in turn are divided into a total of sixty-three tractates (*masechtot*) of different sizes, each of which treats one central subject. Each tractate is further divided into a number of chapters, and each chapter into individual sections (*mishnayot*).

Generally speaking, the Mishnah is arranged as a code of law, each *mishnah* constituting an individual point of law, expressed either in an abstract manner or, more typically, as an instruction on how to behave under given circumstances. Frequently, a number of different opinions are cited regarding the *halachah*, without any clear conclusion; likewise, various opinions may be cited in the name of specific sages. Less frequently, there is also discussion of the different opinions cited, albeit in abbreviated form. While most of the material found in the Mishnah consists of normative statements of law, there are also occasional historical descriptions as well as ethical exhortations (such as the tractate *Avot*, which deals entirely with the field of ethics). The language of the Mishnah is one of very exact, but concise, legal terminology, which generally gives neither sources nor reasons for its decisions.

The Talmud, in the narrow sense of the word, is the corpus of commentaries, discussions, and theoretical analyses of the teachings of the mishnaic sages, but it goes far beyond the exegetical realm, both in the development of the legal system itself and in its penetrating analysis of the foundations and the principles of that system.

The Talmud itself consists of two different works: the Jerusalem Talmud, composed primarily of the teachings of the Palestinian sages and edited by a number of scholars in Tiberias and Caesarea around 400 C.E.; and the more important and influential Babylonian Talmud, which contains the teachings of the sages of Babylonia (that is, Mesopotamia), compiled by Rav Ashi and his disciples in Sura around the year 500 C.E. Even though the Talmud is arranged as a commentary to the Mishnah, it does not encompass all tractates of the Mishnah; for some tractates no Talmud was ever compiled, while for others the Talmud has been lost. The language of the Talmud is an Aramaic jargon, reflecting the dialects spoken by the Jews of Palestine and Babylonia over the course of many generations, mixed with many words and idioms taken from Hebrew, as well as a considerable number of Hebrew quotations from the teaching of the sages of the Mishnah.

At first glance the Talmud appears to be an expanded commentary to the Mishnah; the sages of the Talmud are referred to as *amoraim*, a term literally meaning "translators." Indeed, a considerable portion of the Talmud does consist of textual and other exegeses of the Mishnah. In reality, however, the Talmud is as old as the Mishnah itself, constituting the theoretical framework underlying the final rulings formulated in the Mishnah. Moreover, unlike the Mishnah, which is primarily a code of law whose primary purpose is to instruct the individual or the Jewish community how to act, the talmudic discussions are essentially theoretical and are directed toward clarifying the basic principles of the law and the different schools of thought therein; practical inferences are considered essentially derivative, secondary conclusions drawn, for the most part, from the abstract discussion.

Discussion in the Talmud generally begins with the text of the *mishnah* and follows one of several fixed forms: elucidation of the origins of the mishnaic law in the biblical text; examination of the relationship of the *mishnah*, which generally appears anonymously, to the system of a given sage; or the resolution of contradictions between the *mishnah* under discussion and another *mishnah* or other legal source from the mishnaic period. The talmudic interpretation of the Mishnah may also include textual criticism, both linguistic and comparative, as well as harmonization of various different approaches.

Talmudic discussion seldom has recourse to abstract terms; instead, it constructs various hypothetical situations, from the analysis of which the inherent abstract principle comes to the fore. Since these situations do not necessarily stem from real life, these cases may deal with unrealistic or nearly impossible problems; as we have already observed, however, the main function of the Talmud is to serve not as a compendium of practical law but as a vehicle of theoretical explication. The theoretical character of the Talmud also influenced the method of discussion and of proof. Even though the axiomatic framework of the discussion is not explicit in the Talmud itself, such a framework, which bears considerable similarity to that used in mathematics, nevertheless does exist. The statements of the mishnaic sages are discussed as though they were geometrical theorems, both in terms of the precision and compactness of their expression and in the search for convincing arguments by which they may be proven or disproven. At times, the law may be decided in practice on the basis of inadequate or incomplete proofs, but this is never the case in the theoretical discussion. Even though there was a need to rule in practice among different options within the *halachah*, on the theoretical plane (which constitutes the bulk of the Talmud) the *halachah* is best understood by comparison to a complex equation with a number of possible solutions. From this follows the talmudic saying, "Both of these are the words of the living God, and the *halachah* follows so-and-so" (Babylonian Talmud, Eruvin 13b). Each solution is deserving of full clarification in its own right. The fact that a given approach is not accepted for purposes of halachic decision-making does not deny its truth value or its importance in principle. The determination of the *halachah* is understood primarily as the application of one of the true solutions to a given actual situation, and not as an absolute statement concerning the truth of the argument per se or the validity of an approach that has not been accepted in practice.

Most of the material in the Talmud is structured as a kind of précis of the discussions held in the study house (*bet midrash*) among different individuals. The problems discussed there were similar, despite the geographic and historical distance between different schools and different generations. While each school approached issues somewhat differently, in keeping with the outlook and personalities of the sages involved, the essential elements were transmitted from one place to another (sometimes via special emissaries) and from one generation to another. Despite the historical layering and the variations between different places and approaches, the essential discussion, from many times and places, was thus known everywhere. For this reason, the Babylonian Talmud not only reflects the school of Rav Ashi, but serves as an ahistoric platform for discussion in which the sages of all the generations participate.

Although the arrangement of the Talmud follows the sequence of the Mishnah, it glides into many other subjects related to one another in an associative manner—sometimes through similarity of subject matter, sometimes through stylistic or linguistic similarity, and sometimes through authorship by a particular sage. Subjects mentioned in passing may become a central subject, which in turn may lead to other, more remote subjects. The associative flexibility of the interconnections notwithstanding, the work is precisely arranged in terms of its stylistic details. There are exact and fixed formulas and meanings in the internal order of each discussion and in the usage of words within the discussions.

A certain portion of the Talmud (which is not fixed, and is greater in the Babylonian than in the Jerusalem Talmud) deals not with *halachah*, that is, problems of law and legal norms, but with the area known as *aggadah* (literally, sayings). The *aggadah* of the Talmud is not all of a piece; it includes biblical homiletics and exegesis, discussions of theology and ethics, stories and parables, historical descriptions, and practical advice dealing with all aspects of life. Although there was always a certain distinction between the realms of *halachah* and of *aggadah*, and there were sages who dealt primarily with one or the other area, there is no clear dividing line between the two, and they are intertwined with one another without any clear demarcation. Sometimes there are practical conclusions drawn from the *aggadah*, while on other occasions a halachic discussion may bear theological or other nonlegal implications. Speaking generally, aggadic discussions are less precise and more poetic in their form of expression. Moreover, much of the *aggadah* is symbolic, though there are no clear, uniform keys to the understanding of its symbolism, leaving room, both at the time they were composed and in later generations, for many different schools of interpretation. To an even greater degree than in the halachic realm, we find a multitude of parallel schools of interpretation without any felt need to reach an unequivocal consensus.

The impact of the Talmud upon the Jewish people has been immeasurable. Throughout the generations, Jewish education demanded considerable knowledge of the Talmud, which functioned as the basic text of study for all. Indeed, much of post-talmudic Jewish literature consists of commentaries, reworkings, and new presentations of the Talmud. Even those areas that were not directly related to the Talmud drew upon it and were sustained by it, and there is hardly a work in any area of Judaism that does not relate to it.

Of even greater significance than this was the methodological influence of the study of the Talmud. In the opinion of virtually every modern scholar, "the Talmud was never closed"—not only in the historical-factual sense, but also with regard to the manner of its understanding and study. The method of Talmud study was an extension of the Talmud itself; its interpretation and analysis required the student continually to involve himself in the discussion, to evaluate its questions and argumentation. As a result, abstract reasoning and the dialectic method became an integral part of the Jewish culture.

The open-ended character of talmudic discussion did not detract from the reverence felt toward the Talmud as a text with religious sanctity. The methods of study, like the conclusions of the work itself, became the undisputed basis for religious legislation in all subsequent generations. Both medieval Jewish philosophy and Jewish mysticism, despite an ambivalent attitude toward the exclusive study of Talmud, treated the Talmud with great respect, and later kabbalistic literature even found in it concealed allusions to mystical truths. In the final analysis, the Talmud was understood as, and in fact created, the unique phenomenon of "sacred intellectualism."

═ 11 ═

The Giving and the Receiving
of the Torah

The day celebrated as *Shavuot*, the day of the giving of the Torah by God, is sometimes also called the day of the receiving of the Ten Commandments by Israel. And it would seem to be a natural pairing of concepts—the giving and the receiving being the two sides of the same action and apparently interchangeable as descriptions of the event.

Nevertheless, they are not identical. Each has its own particular meaning, in terms of ideas as well as in historic actuality. As the Kabbalah puts it, the giving of the Torah is a movement from the above to that which is below, while the receiving is a movement from below reaching upward. And in the dimension of time, the giving of the Torah is essentially a single act, while the receiving of the Torah is a diversified and continuing process in history.

Before expanding on this point, it may be helpful to clarify what is meant by the word "Torah." In the past, it was a wholly religious concept; in more recent times, it has undergone a considerable amount of secularization, and today, like so much else, this also means profanation. In modern Hebrew, one can use the word "Torah" to express the law or knowledge of something, like the Torah of Einsteinian physics or the Torah of physical exercise, whereas the Scriptures are called the Torah of Moses. To translate Torah as "law" evidently misses the mark, even though the Bible may be seen as a book containing laws and moral instruction for living. On the other hand, this aspect of instruction—the teaching—is certainly basic to Torah; without it the Torah would be just a monumental work of literature.

Moreover, Torah that is not a living framework for action is no longer Torah. Therefore, the giving and the receiving of Torah is more than just the transmission of a certain body of information. It is the communication of a message that causes a profound change in the thought and behavior of those who receive it. It is clear, too, that Torah constitutes a bridge between the Divine essence and man. As the sages said, quoting a phrase from the Bible itself: "A *tzadik* shall live by his faith." The Torah answers the question of how to live by faith.

The actual giving of the Torah at Mt. Sinai is reported to have been a most dramatic and awesome event, with heavenly voices and trumpets, lightning and thunder. One may wonder a little at all the fuss, considering that the Ten Commandments—which are supposed to contain all the other commandments—are no more than fundamental rules for the conduct of any society. In part, at least, they are already to be found in the older codes of Babylon and Egypt, India and China; and there are traces of similar rules in most primitive societies.

Hence, it must be admitted that the full weight and power of the Ten Commandments is not only in their content, but in the special way they were given. After all, the prohibitions against murder, theft, rape, and giving false witness are basic elements of the social contract; they are formal commitments necessary for a society to exist. In the Ten Commandments, however, "Thou shalt not murder" is not a ruling set by some local chief or council to avoid vengeful blood feuds. It is the command of an Almighty God, and this is what gives it power and meaning. To transgress against any of the commands of the Torah is primarily to defy God, and only after that is it an offense against society.

This, however, is only a relatively external, formalistic aspect of the giving of the Torah. More significant, it is an act from above to below, the crossing of the infinite gap between God and the world. Whether one conceives the gap logically/philosophically, or whether it is felt in terms of the sublime, there is no way man can cross it.

One can only cry out in despair, "What has He to do with us dwellers of the dust?"

To be sure, this is not just a modern thought; it is repeated often enough in the Bible and is probably a basic experience in all religions. Indeed, the inner message of the Ten Commandments is in answer to this feeling of man's insignificance. It is a central aspect of the confrontation at Sinai, as it is written: "Behold, the Lord our God hath showed us His glory and His greatness, and we have heard His voice out of the midst of the fire: we have seen this day that God doth talk with man, and He liveth" (Deuteronomy 5:21). The importance of this encounter is not in the actual words spoken but that God appeared before man and told him what to do, that God established some sort of contact with man. And this is the meaning of the whole Torah; all the rest is commentary and expansion.

Consequently, the giving of the Torah is essentially this crossing of the abyss between the human and the Divine, and the establishing of a permanent bridge. Its lasting impact on the soul lies in the wondrous generosity of that action from above, and in its uniqueness: It happened only once.

The giving of the Torah is thus a single historic event in which the Divine is the decisive factor. The receiving of the Torah, by contrast, is an enduring process in time, with man as the decisive factor. The paradox is resolved when the two movements with their contradictory directions and rhythms meet.

This was succinctly expressed by the sages, who, in commenting on a passage in Isaiah that reads, "You are my witnesses, saith the Lord, and I am God," said that it may therefore be inferred that when you are not my witnesses, I am not God. In other words, Israel has to be ready to bear witness to the Divine presence, and on this ground the encounter, which is the Revelation of Torah, can take place. And again, let us recollect that it is not the content, not that which the Torah says, that is being considered. It is that someone is ready to receive it even before knowing what it is. This becomes the decisive factor.

The receiving itself is therefore not just a matter of passively listening to the message of Torah; it is an act of committing oneself to absorbing the poetry and the principles, and carrying out the commandments all the days of one's life. To begin with, there had to be a certain receptive state of mind—as expressed by the cry, *"Na'aseh V'nishma"* ("We shall do and we shall hear")—in order for the Torah to be given. On the other hand, the inner meaning of this formulation of readiness only became evident later, as expressed by the words of Moses forty years later when, in taking leave of the people, he said, "And God did not give you a heart to know and eyes to see and ears to hear until this very day" (Deuteronomy 29:3). And indeed, only many generations later could it be said that the people of Israel had developed a heart able to know the Torah designated for them.

As the Rabbi of Kotzk, in his blunt fashion, put it:"The feast of *Shavuot* celebrates the day of the giving of the Torah, because on that day the Torah was given to Israel. But every person of Israel receives the Torah in his own way and in his own time." The receiving of the Torah, however, is not just a capacity to grasp a certain body of knowledge; it is an act of breaking the limits of time and of contacting the infinite. It is enough for a person to be reminded of it ("Remember this day . . .") in order for its meaning to be perpetuated for thousands of years.

This idea—that the receiving of the Torah took place at a time different from the giving of the Torah—is not merely a metaphorical way of saying something; it is a recurring theme in the Bible itself. Indeed, it may be said that the Bible as a whole is a detailed account of the conflicts, the rises and falls, the deviations, the errors, and the reconciliations in the process of receiving the Torah. And this is true not only of the time the Torah was being absorbed but even prior to Sinai, the long period of inner preparation.

Time is needed for any truly revolutionary teaching to be understood, and there are any number of intermediate stages. In the history of Israel, it may be assumed, on the basis of what the sages have written, that only during the time of the Second Temple did the people of Israel as a whole accept the Torah as an obligatory way of life. From that time until recent generations, there has no longer been any serious division between the Jews and Torah. They have been one consistent entity.

More than a thousand years elapsed, then, between the giving of the Torah and some sort of total receiving of the Torah. And even to this day, it remains an "open question." Of course, it is not simply a matter of the spiritual and intellectual capacities of one generation or another. So long as men are possessed of free will, the problem of receiving the Torah will be posed anew for every individual in every generation, as one can learn from the words spoken by Joshua to the elders of Israel after the conquest of the Promised Land. He lists the favors of God granted to Israel since their exodus from Egypt, and concludes by putting everything in terms of free choice: "And now therefore fear the Lord, and serve him in sincerity and in truth. . . . And if it seem evil unto you to serve the Lord, choose you this day whom ye will serve; whether the gods which your fathers served that were on the other side of the flood, or the gods of the Amorites, in whose land ye dwell: but as for me and my house, we will serve the Lord" (Joshua 24:15).

In other words, the problem of free will on the part of the individual, and even the public body, is not solved by the single historic decision. Of course, this decision creates its own process of coercion, as vividly described in the Book of Ezekiel and other writings of the Bible. Nevertheless, it never reaches the point of forcing the actual receiving of the Torah. Even in terms of the original enthusiasm ("We shall do and we shall hear") the acceptance of the practical details remains the province of each and every individual. It is a continuity; there can be no forcing of the issue at any point, and there can be no final point of completion.

To what extent is the time gap necessary—between the giving and the receiving of Torah? Sometimes the absorption of a new and complicated culture can be accomplished in a relatively short time, like the adaptation of the Japanese to modern technology. Nevertheless, it is true that the more profound the change in ideas and consciousness, the more time is generally required. There is the initial lag (to decide that one wants to learn the new ways and concepts), and often there is the tendency to adopt external forms long before the inner content and meaning are absorbed. Backward societies put on the garments of democracy or communist collectivism before they are ready to comprehend them. These intermediate forms arise to fill the vacuum, but the external copying of a model very often blocks the chances of internalizing the original idea on a higher level. One becomes lulled by satisfactory external action into thinking that one has realized the ideal.

The receiving of the Torah by Israel has always continued to be a rather trying ordeal as well as a source of inspiration. The difficulties have been not only a matter of trying to grasp the essence of the message but of being obedient to the externals. There have been serious alterations in the very structure of consciousness and in the nature of the social body. For instance, the offering of sacrifices by ancient Jewry in order to establish a complex harmony of inner relations with the Divine evolved into the work of study and prayer in order to achieve a similar end. There is a historic development, then, which is extremely demanding of mind and heart.

The process of receiving the Torah has thus been continuing—from the incident of the Golden Calf to the present day. It is a process of training the Jew to genuinely absorb what is being offered to him. And, as we have seen, it cannot be a straightforward learning process. It is always being obstructed and delayed, not only by the diverse kinds of rejection, but also by the many forms of inadequate or premature acceptance. After thousands of years and countless good intentions and incessant struggle on the part of generation after generation of devout Jews, we can only be sure of one thing: The Torah once given at Sinai continues to be received by Israel.

PART III

TESHUVAH

12

A Time for Joy

The festival of *Sukkot* (Tabernacles) is referred to by a number of names in the Jewish sources, but no epithet seems to reflect its essence as much as that given in the prayerbook: "The time of our rejoicing." Such a definition, however, raises some fundamental questions: How can a specific date in the calendar be set aside for rejoicing? How can one obey an injunction to rejoice on a certain day, irrespective of one's mood or condition?

The fact that this is possible is abundantly clear in the way that *Simchat Torah*, the final culminating day of the eight-day festival, is celebrated. Not only do believers rejoice, but they frequently manage to draw others into their dancing and gaiety. It is difficult to distinguish between this obligatory happiness and purely spontaneous manifestations of individual and communal joy.

The commandment to rejoice on *Sukkot* is in fact just one of a number of such obligations that concern one's mood. The Jewish calendar designates days of contemplation, of mourning, and of joy. Though at first sight it may seem to be a paradox, it can be said that only he who has the strength to mourn on *Tishah b'Av* (the anniversary of the destruction of the Temple and of other disasters in Jewish history) is capable of rejoicing on *Simchat Torah*. In spite of the apparent polar differences between the two activities, there is a profound bond between them, for both draw upon the same inner strength.

The ability to rejoice on a preassigned day derives from self-discipline, which is an integral part of the religious life and an essential characteristic of the religious Jew. Even when the *mitzvot* are observed on a superficial level, there is still a need for the internalization of values and demands. External pressure to conform can never be totally effective, even in the most coercive society. No policeman could possibly supervise every single activity of each person, to make certain that he keeps all the *mitzvot*. One thus needs inner strength to perform the *mitzvot* in general and to make the particular decisions associated with their performance in various situations and states of mind. The observant Jew derives such strength from a standing commitment to assume certain responsibilities, which is called "the yoke of heaven." The depth of this commitment clearly differs from one person to another, and it cannot be denied that the shallow religiosity of the man who unthinkingly does as he was taught as a child is not uncommon. However, even when an individual's level of commitment is no higher than this—and we may justifiably hold such a person in some disdain—he does possess, to a considerable extent, the capacity to live according to his conscience, no matter how weak and undeveloped it may be. This "simple" observant person may well be the product of an indoctrinating education; he may be ignorant and lacking in spiritual courage, and in possession of little understanding of the significance and implications of what he affirms and practices. Nevertheless, he still lives at a certain spiritual level, and his life is determined by values.

All this may seem to be self-evident, and the emphasis with which it has been stated quite unnecessary. Today's observant Jew, however, is frequently no longer religious in the full sense of the term, and his personality is fashioned largely by habit and by membership in a certain group or sector of the community. Despite this, the inner strength of discipline that makes possible a truly religious life can be achieved, because of the "heavenly yoke."

Every person who keeps the *mitzvot* bears the heavenly yoke, at least to some degree. Even the religious philosopher or mystic who has undergone the most profound, authentic spiritual experience cannot do without it, for he cannot identify totally with all the *mitzvot* at all times. Though he may understand and feel their significance and be able to perform them without reservation, it is simply not possible for him to do so with spontaneous and natural willingness on every occasion. Although there are some human activities that are performed spontaneously, they are generally associated with specific physiological functions such as hunger, thirst, or the sexual drive. There can be no such reflex performance of the *mitzvot*, for they are not generated spontaneously from an individual's needs but are a response to a higher law that man cannot totally identify with or comprehend. The believer cannot expect them to flow from within, for he knows that their source is above and beyond him. Accordingly, he must construct and develop a unique orientation toward his spiritual life, one that involves preparation. It is necessary for him to bring himself to a kind of empathy with *mitzvot*, both as a totality and with each individual act on each particular occasion.

This formulation is not the one generally given, but in fact it is the basis of a large body of Jewish contemplative literature, which addresses itself to the question of intention, or orientation of the heart (in Hebrew, *kavanah*). A person who has achieved a higher, more spiritual level is no less concerned with precise details of the performance of a *mitzvah* than with the preparation of his soul to a more intimate identification with it. It is not widely known that meditation as a religious praxis is not restricted to followers of Eastern faiths. In Judaism it is practiced before and during the performance of *mitzvot*. These contemplative procedures (*kavanot*), exist in a number of forms. For those who are so inclined, there is a detailed system of mystical exercises; for others, there are intellectual contemplative procedures; and everyone, irrespective of his spiritual state, is enjoined at the very least to recite a blessing before performing a *mitzvah*. In addition, there are many intermediate acts and spiritual preparations whose performance is not fixed in time and whose purpose is to bring the individual to a state of readiness for the momentous event—the *mitzvah*. The deed itself is, of course, indispensable, and physical performance always entails a certain spiritual experience. In every case, however, the preparation of the soul for the performance of the *mitzvah* is primary. This is achieved by discipline, and it involves the miracle of ordering all the elements of one's being toward the experience.

Certain contemporary trends of thought will doubtless denigrate this approach, seeing in it an unjustifiable relinquishing of experience, a loss of spiritual and emotional spontaneity. A whole romantic world subsists on the supposition that one should cultivate spontaneity of feeling and reject all rigid or clearly defined anticipation of spiritual or emotional experience. This attitude is not restricted to the religious life and is applied to other realms of feeling as well, such as romantic emotion and artistic creativity. It informs such concepts as "love at first sight" or "artistic inspiration." In fact, it is precisely in these other realms that one can see the illusory quality of this romantic approach. Inspiration as the primary source of artistic creativity is no more than an attractive fiction, for spontaneity plays as relatively minor a role in art as it does in philosophical and scientific thinking. Creative action generally results from a combination of many factors, including subjective preparation, professional training, and a considerable amount of hard work.

A more critical, penetrating observation reveals that existence as a human being depends largely on achieving distance from the pressures of physiological spontaneity and on focusing consciousness on activity. The lower a creature is on the ladder evolution, the more it is subject to the demands of its instincts, that is, to its natural spontaneity. Each higher level of development demands a further release from these pressures and their displacement by processes of learning and training. A child cannot learn to walk without a long period of preparation. Now this is a relatively simple motor function, and it is obvious that psychological activities, which are more complex and subtle, require even more training and conditioning. A total spontaneity of love, for instance, rarely occurs in man (in most animals it is a function of the sexual cycle), for the feelings involved are much too complex and are, to a large extent, learned.

Many Jewish sages have noted that the two Hebrew words *emunah* (faith) and *emun* (training) are derived from the same root, and they have interpreted this as showing that the soul must train itself in order to be capable of achieving meaningful religious experience. This need for training, however, does not mean that there is no place for spontaneous religious experience, but rather that such spontaneous experience by itself cannot serve as the basis of the religious life. Only by cultivating awareness and understanding, by conscious, ongoing preparation can a person draw from the inner resources in his soul the capacity for meaningful and profound experience.

Throughout his life the religious person is confronted by the task of consciously drawing upon his inner resources; he must constantly maintain and strengthen his inner discipline, the same discipline that enables the artist to create. And, of course, he must be able to receive from these inner resources the authentic experience he needs and desires. These religious experiences do not flow from the freedom of spontaneity, but they are nonetheless genuine, and, by virtue of being guided and prepared, are even more human.

Thus, on the date assigned by our calendar for rejoicing, the person who has prepared himself, the man whose life is more than a series of reflex responses to internal and external stimuli, can attain real happiness; he knows how to rejoice wholly.

13

Teshuvah

The word *teshuvah* is the Hebrew word for repentance. But it should be stressed that the meaning of *teshuvah* is not entirely conveyed by the word "repentance." *Teshuvah* is somewhat broader and deeper, and it is most important to notice that in a more general, accepted definition *teshuvah* means "return." Hence, the keystone of *teshuvah*: It essentially represents a lifelong journey back to unflagging soul-searching. For it is a spiritual disquiet, much more than a guilty feeling, that makes us feel the urge to take a look back. Indeed, we feel we are no longer the right person in the right place, we feel we are becoming outsiders in a world whose scheme of things escapes us.

This is why we decide to turn around and go back. Naturally, the itinerary of the way back will depend on the person, and the uniqueness of a personality logically ensures that each of us will follow his own personal route, and that there will be no fellow traveler to rely on. Fortunately, the Gates of Heaven are numerous. Each of us may lay claim to have his own, as long as our desire to go through is really overwhelming, in other words, as long as we really feel the need to repent. Witness the case of King Manasseh (whose name is high up among the worst kings of Judah) when, according to the Talmud, the angels closed the Gates of Repentance on him, God Himself created for him a new opening.

To feel the need to repent means to realize that a change is imperative. There is no moaning about our past wrongdoings: in contact with evil, you always get dirty, as surely as you get dirty in contact with dirt, even when you intend to remove it. What is less common, some of us, more or less prone to masochism, might well take pleasure in arousing old memories of this kind. When we say that we must avoid pondering over the past, we mean that we should not rethink and relive our past as it happened, with its faults and mistakes. What we should ponder is our past as it ought to have been. The main thrust of *teshuvah* is indeed to show the definite intention of changing the scheme of things. Someone who repents, someone who, as we would say, does *teshuvah*, is someone who feels the need not only to redeem but to rebuild his past, in the literal sense of the term.

Naturally, an epistemological obstacle looms up, which we will have to bypass if we are to follow that strange principle of thermodynamics known as entropy. It becomes clearly established that time is strictly unidirectional, that any reversion to a former situation is unthinkable, and that as a result, doing *teshuvah* sounds like a paradox. But what should be remembered is that we are not expected to do *teshuvah* in a conventional universe. We do *teshuvah* in a universe that is quite unaware of physical laws, a universe in which the present, the future, and and the past merge into a timeless duration, a universe in which a lethal arrow is liable to fly back and to be as free of all suspicion as if it had never left its quiver. In a word, through repentance we penetrate into a sort of physical weightlessness, where we can choose, for instance, to reverse our conventional value by replacing a plus sign with a minus sign, or vice versa.

There are things on this lowly earth of which we are particularly fond, but each of us has his own peculiarities in this regard. To give money, for instance, is for some of us a molehill, whereas to apologize for having offended someone is a mountain. Now beware! If you offer a sacrifice to God, make sure that you offer what really costs you dear, for God would not appreciate a fool's deal.

To achieve this result, we shall have to know ourselves thoroughly, we shall have to sound our souls. And if we decide not only to repent but also to execute our about-face, things will get still more complicated: we shall have to reach the inmost depths of our being, the nadir of the abyss, you might say. For in this abysmal zone we are entitled to believe our souls are not far from God, and unless we reach this zone we cannot be convinced that a radical change has taken place deep down in our hearts, a change liable to transcend all the data of the universe. It is obvious, therefore, that to repent is not merely to recognize a misdemeanor. To repent is to dig down to the very bottom of one's soul, and to realize that the feelings we experience there are quite beyond those we experienced when we committed the transgression, to such an extent that the former soon cancels out the latter.

This journey back is obviously a difficult achievement, the more so since it represents a continuous process. Indeed, for a few moments we may believe we have reached the required depth, when suddenly we become aware that our spiritual disquiet surfaces once more, thus obliging us to dive further down without delay. Notice that the inaugural disquiet, if we may call it that, does not compulsorily proceed from the memory of some fault; it may just as easily proceed from the memory of some laudable action which, in view of our personal evolution, no longer meets our intimate requirements.

Besides, if we are to raise ourselves up to more philosophical levels, we must confess that the Manichaean distinction between good and evil is too clear-cut, that even in westerns the good guys and the bad guys have something in common, and that, accordingly, we should not expect of repentance to grant exclusive rights either to good-doers or to evildoers as such. In fact, what repentance strives for is a far-reaching plan. Its ambition is indeed to supply a new scale of values to human existence, the notion of increased profoundness being accorded particular attention. And this is why it is no use ruminating over the faults committed in the past. Those faults ought to be regarded as the seeds of virtue, in that they represent the trigger mechanism of the journey back, which enables us to rebuild our personality and our past.

In the main book of the Kabbalah we read that those who are "the highest of all—those who can turn darkness into light and bitterness into sweetness—are those who enter by the higher gates." No wonder. Achievements of this magnitude bear witness of a high degree of repentance: the transformation of the past is complete, the sign of inversion perfect. Consequently, whenever you turn your attention to somebody's life, to the history of a people or a religion, do not content yourself with asking forgiveness for the evil you may have done. This is not repentance; this is not what is required of you. Instead, you should regard the faults as something constructive, like the beginning of a new and beautiful story. Put more succinctly, come to grips not with your failing but with your past that gave birth to it.

$=14=$

Repentance

Repentance is one of the ultimate spiritual realities at the core of Jewish faith. Its significance goes far beyond the narrow meaning of contrition or regret for sin, and it embraces a number of concepts considered to be fundamental to the very existence of the world.

Certain sages go so far as to include repentance among the entities created before the world itself. The implication of this remarkable statement is that repentance is a universal, primordial phenomenon; in such a context it has two meanings. One is that it is embedded in the root structure of the world; the other, that before man was created, he was given the possibility of changing the course of his life. In this latter sense repentance is the highest expression of man's capacity to choose freely—it is a manifestation of the divine in man. Man can extricate himself from the binding web of his life, from the chain of causality that otherwise compels him to follow a path of no return.

Repentance also comprises the notion that man has a measure of control over his existence in all dimensions, including time. Time flows in one direction; it is impossible to undo or even to alter an action after it has occurred and become an "event," an objective fact. However, even though the past is "fixed," repentance admits of an ascendancy over it, of the possibility of changing its significance in the context of the present and the future. This is why repentance has been presented as something created before the world itself. In a world of the inexorable flow of time, in which all objects and events are interconnected in a relationship of cause and effect, repentance is the exception: it is the potential for something else.

The Hebrew word for repentance, *teshuvah*, has three different though related meanings. First, it denotes "return," a going back to God, or to the Jewish faith. Second, it can mean "turning about," or "turning to," adopting another orientation or direction in life. Third, *teshuvah* signifies "response."

The root meaning is "return" to God, or to Judaism, in the inclusive sense of embracing it in faith, thought, and deed. On the simplest, most literal level, the possibility of return can only exist for someone who was once "there," such as an adult who retains childhood memories or other recollections of Jewish life. But is it not possible for someone to return who was never "there," who has no memories of a Jewish way of life, for whom Judaism is not a personal but a historical or biological heritage, or no more than an epithet that gives him a certain meaningless identity? The answer is unequivocally in the affirmative, for—on the more profound level—repentance as return reaches beyond such personal configurations. It is indeed a return to Judaism, but not to the external framework, not to the religious norms that man seeks to understand or to integrate into, with their clear-cut formulas, directives, actions, rituals: it is a return to one's own paradigm, to the prototype of the Jewish person. Intellectually, this paradigm may be perceived as a historical reality to which one is personally related, but beyond this is the memory of the essential archetype that is a part of the soul structure of the individual Jew. In spite of the vast range of ways in which a Jew can alienate himself from his past and express himself in foreign cultural forms, he nevertheless retains a metaphysically, almost genetically, imprinted image of his Jewishness. To use a metaphor from the world of botany: a change of climate, soil, or other physical conditions can induce marked alterations in the form and functioning of a plant, and even the adoption of characteristics of other species and genera, but the unique paradigm or prototype persists.

Reattachment to one's prototype may be expressed in many ways, not only in accepting a faith or a "credo" or in fulfilling certain traditional obligations. As he liberates himself from alien influences, the penitent can only gradually straighten himself out; he has to overcome the forms engraved by time and place before he can reach his own image. He must break free of the chains, the limitations, and the restrictions imposed by environment and education. If pursued aimlessly, with no clear goal, this primal search does not transcend the urge to be free; without a vector, it can be spiritually exhausting and may never lead to a genuine discovery of the true self. In this respect, not in vain has the Torah been perceived as a system of knowledge and insights that guide the individual Jew to reach his own pattern of selfhood. The mutual relationship between the individual Jew and Judaism, between the man and his God, depends on the fact that Judaism is not only the Law, the prescribed religious practice, but is a life framework that embraces his entire existence; furthermore, it is ultimately the only framework in which, in his aloneness and in his search, he will be able to find himself. Whereas potentially a man can adapt himself, there exists—whether he acknowledges it or not—a path that is his own, which relates to him, to his family, to his home.

Repentance is a complex process. Sometimes a man's entire life is no more than an ongoing act of repentance on several levels. It has been said that a man's path of spiritual development, whether he has sinned or not, is in a certain sense a path of repentance. It is an endeavor to break away from the past and reach a higher level. However, notwithstanding the complexity and the deeply felt difficulties involved, there is a clear simplicity in the elemental point, which is the point of the turning.

Remoteness from God is, of course, not a matter of physical distance but a spiritual problem of relationship. The person who is not going along the right path is not further away from God but is, rather, a man whose soul is oriented toward, and relating with, other objects. The starting point of repentance is precisely this fulcrum point upon which a person turns himself about, away from the pursuit of what he craves, and confronts his desire to approach God; this is the moment of conversion, the crucial moment of repentance.

It should be noted that generally this does not occur at a moment of great self-awareness. Although a person may be acutely conscious of the moment of repentance, the knowledge can come later. It is in fact rare for repentance to take the form of a sudden, dramatic conversion, and it generally takes the form of a series of small turnings.

Irrespective of the degree of awareness, several spiritual factors come together in the process of conversion. Severance is an essential factor. The repentant cuts himself off from his past, as though saying: "Everything in my life up to this point is now alien to me; chronologically or historically it may be part of me—but I no longer accept it as such." With a new goal in life, a person assumes a new identity. Aims and aspirations are such major expressions of the personality that renouncing them amounts to a severance of the old self. The moment of turning thus involves not only a change of attitude, but also a metamorphosis. When the process is fully realized, it includes a departure from, a rejection of, and a regret for, the past, and an acceptance, a promise of change in the future. The sharper the turning, the more deeply conscious it is, the more prominent will these aspects be: a shaking free of the past, a transfiguration of self, and an eager thrust forward into a new identity.

Repentance also includes the expectancy of a response, of a confirmation from God that this is indeed the way, that this is the direction. Nevertheless, the essence of repentance is bound up more with turning than with response. When response is direct and immediate, the process of repentance cannot continue, because it has in a way arrived at its goal, whereas one of its essential components is an increase of tension, the tension of the ongoing experience and of yearning. As long as the act of repentance lasts, the seeking for response continues, and the soul still strives to receive from elsewhere the answer, the pardon.

Response is not always given, and even when it is, it is not the same for every man. Repentance is a gradual process; final response is not awarded to specific, isolated acts, but to the whole. The various components—the desire to act, the performing of the deed based on anticipation, the yearning, disappointment, and hope—are rewarded, if at all, by partial answers. In other words, a response to turning is given to a man as "something on account," the rest to be paid out later. A person generally hears the longed-for answer not when he puts his question, not when he is struggling, but when he pauses on a summit and looks back on his life.

Jewish thought pays little attention to inner tranquillity and peace of mind. The feeling of "behold, I've arrived" could well undermine the capacity to continue, suggesting as it does that the Infinite can be reached in a finite number of steps. In fact, the very concept of the Divine as Infinite implies an activity that is endless, of which one must never grow weary. At every rung of his ascent, the penitent, like any person who follows the way of God, perceives mainly the remoteness. Only in looking back can one obtain some idea of the distance already covered, of the degree of progress. Repentance does not bring a sense of serenity or of completion, but stimulates a reaching out in further effort. Indeed, the power and potential of repentance lie in increased incentive and enhanced capacity to follow the path even further. The response is often no more than an assurance that one is in fact capable of repenting, and its efficacy lies in the growing awareness, with time, that one is indeed progressing on the right path. In this manner the conditions are created in which repentance is no longer an isolated act but has become a permanent possibility, a constant process of going toward. It is a going that is both the rejection of what was once axiomatic and an acceptance of new goals.

The paths of the penitent and of the man who has merely lost his direction differ only in terms of the aim, not in the going itself. The Jewish approach to life considers the man who has stopped going—he who has a feeling of completion, of peace, of a great light from above that has brought him to his rest—to be someone who has lost his way. Only he whom the light continues to beckon, for whom the light is as distant as ever, only he can be considered to have received some sort of response. The path a man has taken is revealed to him only in retrospect, in a contemplation of the past that grants confidence in what lies ahead. This awareness is in fact the reward, and it is conditional on the continuation of the return.

The essence of repentance has frequently been found in the poetic lines of the Song of Songs, "The King had brought me to his chambers." This verse has been interpreted as meaning that he whose search has reached a certain level feels that he is in the palace of the King. He goes from room to room, from hall to hall, seeking Him out. The King's palace, however, is an endless series of worlds, and as a man proceeds in his search from room to room, he holds only the end of the string.

It is, nevertheless, a continuous going, a going after God, a going to God, day after day, year after year.

Repentance is not just a psychological phenomenon, a storm within a human teacup, but is a process that can effect real change in the world, in all the worlds. Every human action elicits certain inevitable results that extend beyond their immediate context, passing from one level of existence to another, from one aspect of reality to another. The act of repentance is, in the first place, a severance of the chain of cause and effect in which one transgression follows inevitably upon another. Beyond this, it is an attempt to nullify and even to alter the past. This can only be achieved when man, subjectively, shatters the order of his own existence. The thrust of repentance is to break through the ordinary limits of the self. Obviously, this cannot take place within the routine of life, but it can be an ongoing activity throughout life. Repentance is thus something that persists; it is an ever-renewed extrication from causality and limitation.

When man senses the wrongness, evil and emptiness in his life, it is not enough that he yearn for God or try to change his way of life. Repentance is more than aspiration and yearning, for it also involves the sense of despair. And it is this very despair (and, paradoxically, the sin that precedes it) that gives man the possibility of overleaping his past. The desperation of the endeavor to separate himself from his past, to reach heights that the innocent and ordinary man is not even aware of, gives the penitent the power to break the inexorability of his fate, sometimes in a way that involves a total destruction of his past, his goals, and almost all of his personality.

Nevertheless, this level of repentance is only a beginning, for all of the penitent's past actions continue to operate: the sins he committed and the injuries he inflicted exist as such in time. Even though the present has been altered, earlier actions and their consequences continue to generate a chain of cause and effect. The significance of the past can be changed only at a higher level of repentance, called *tikun*, or correction.

The first stage in the process of *tikun* is of equilibration. For every wrong deed in his past, the penitent is required to perform certain acts that surpass what is demanded of an "ordinary" individual, to complement and balance the picture of his life. He must build and create anew, and change the order of good and evil in such a way that not only his current life activity acquires new form and direction, but the totality of his life receives a consistently positive value.

The highest level of repentance, however, lies beyond the correction of sinful deeds and the creation of independent, new patterns that counterweigh past sins and injuries; it is reached when the change and the correction penetrate the very essence of the sins once committed and, as the sages say, create the condition in which a man's transgressions become his merits. This level of *tikun* is reached when a person draws from his failings not only the ability to do good, but the power to fall again and again and, notwithstanding, to transform more extensive and important segments of life. It is using the knowledge of the sin of the past and transforming it into such an extraordinary thirst for good that it becomes a Divine force. The more a man was sunken in evil, the more eager he becomes for good. This level of being, in which failings no longer exert a negative influence on the penitent, in which they no longer reduce his stature or sap his strength but serve to raise him, to stimulate his progress—this is the condition of genuine *tikun*.

Thus the complete correction of past evil cannot be brought about merely by acknowledgment of wrong and contrition; indeed, this often leads, in practice, to a loss of incentive, a state of passivity, of depression. Furthermore, the very preoccupation with memories of an evil impulse may well revive its hold on a person. In genuine *tikun*, everything that was once invested in the forces of evil is elevated to receive another meaning within a new way of life; deeds once performed with a negative intention are transformed into a completely new category of activity. To be sure, forces of evil that had parasitically attached themselves to a person are not easily compelled to act in the direction of the good. Spiritual possibilities, of which a man who has not sinned can never even gain an awareness, have to emerge and become a driving force.

The penitent thus does more than return to his proper place. He performs an act of amendment of cosmic significance; he restores the sparks of holiness which had been captured by the powers of evil. The sparks that he had dragged down and attached to himself are now raised up with him, and a host of forces of evil return and are transformed to forces of good. This is the significance of the statement in the Talmud that in the place where a completely repentant person stands, even the most saintly cannot enter; because the penitent has at his disposal not only the forces of good in his soul and in the world, but also those of evil, which he transforms into essences of holiness.

15

Sin

The Hebrew language, in both biblical and postbiblical literature, has numerous names for the concept of sin, each with its own unique sense and shade of meaning. Moreover, from the books of the Bible—especially the Prophets—to the latter-day homiletic writings, Jewish literature is filled with reproachful discourses inveighing against all manner of sins.

Nevertheless, the concept of sin in and of itself is never fully developed or clarified in Judaism. Despite the existence of so many definitions of an endless variety of sin, and despite the stern reproof voiced against sin and sinners, concern with sin itself occupies an insignificant place in Jewish thought. The problem of sin (and even, to a large extent, the problem of evil) is, in effect, treated as a secondary issue. Sin is viewed as a correlate of *mitzvah*; it is treated not as a separate, independent entity but rather as a shadow-essence or even, at times, a reverse image of *mitzvah*. The concept of sin and the attitude taken toward it thus stem directly from how mitzvah is understood. For example, Judaism divides the world of religious activity into two groups of commandments: positive and negative. Since sin is defined, from both a halachic and a theological point of view, as the negation of *mitzvah*, where positive commandments are concerned it consists of abstention and where negative commandments are concerned it consists of action. In every case, that is to say, it is conceived as the negation of something else and not as an independent entity in its own right.

The several theological understandings of sin to be found in Judaism are not concepts in their own right, and several of them appear in the extensive religious literature only by way of allusion. We arrive at them by first understanding the definition of *mitzvah* and then drawing conclusions with regard to the meaning of sin. But the various concepts of the nature of the *mitzvot* are only rarely to be found in distinct and defined form, and far more frequently (even in the case of fairly systematic thinkers) several of them come into play at once. The concept of sin, too, thus often has several ideational components coexisting alongside one another.

One conception of *mitzvah* sees its principal significance in the Divine command. The performance of a *mitzvah* is essentially an act of obedience, through which man approaches God by accepting the yoke of heaven, the supernal discipline. Sin, from this point of view, is thus primarily an act (by deed or default) of rebellion. The sinner is one who will not obey, one who, on account of external or internal factors, refuses to accept the "sovereignty of heaven" and prefers a different kind of rule, whether it be that of other men, other gods, or his own appetites. This conception in a sense gives equal value to all of the *mitzvot*, in that all of them alike express man's acceptance of the sovereignty of God. All sins, similarly, can be reduced to a single one—that of disobedience.

Another understanding of *mitzvah* conceives of it as the right way, the straight and good path. The commandments, for example, as an expression that has its source in the Zohar would have it, are viewed as God's good counsel for man, his revelation of the true path that it is natural and right for man to follow as he makes his way through life. Sin, then, is conceived as a straying or deviation from this natural path. If it is committed unwittingly, it is the consequence of a mistake, of lack of knowledge or understanding. If, on the other hand, it is committed intentionally, it is essentially an act of perversity, an intentional distortion of nature. This conception, too, does not make a qualitative distinction between sins of different kinds. In a psychological sense, however, it does differentiate between obvious, easily recognizable distortions and those that can be known only to one who has already learned the true path.

Another conception views the *mitzvah* essentially as an act of rectification or completion. The world is not a fully perfect entity, and the task of the *mitzvah* is to bring about the perfection that is lacking. Sin, then, is essentially the want of something, a defect in reality; if a sin is one of default, it consists of a failure to rectify some aspect of the world or of man, whereas if it is one of deed, the sinner has added to the imperfection of reality. Man, possessing free will, is the active force in the world, and he is therefore its guardian and keeper. When he does not fulfill this function he blemishes reality or allows it to deteriorate. In this view man is not the exclusive subject of *mitzvah* or of transgression but rather an instrument, an implement in the service of reality as a whole, in which he exists both as an active agent of influence and change and as a passive part.

These conceptions appear in most ethical and theological discussions in various combinations. The same thinker will at times emphasize one aspect of the problem while in other contexts view *mitzvah* and sin from a different perspective. Nevertheless, a deeper look will show that all these approaches have a common denominator: They do not see evil as a concrete subject or entity existing in and of itself. Even in those descriptions that view the history of the world or the inner spiritual life of man as a battle between good and evil, evil is not grasped as an essence to be defined independently. It is but the "other side" (*sitra achra*, in the terminology of the Kabbalah) of reality, which is good, and it has no existence or essential definition of its own.

This view of evil as something purely negative is found in a great many Jewish sources, despite the differences among them. The evil deed is viewed as an empty activity, an exercise in futility, a meaningless labor that must come to nothing. Evil is merely "chaos" or "vanity," not an entity in its own right.

Another common aspect of the different attitudes toward *mitzvah* (and so also toward sin) is their view of individual actions within the framework of a comprehensive whole. Despite each man's individual responsibility and obligations, he functions as an integral part of the world as a whole. Moreover, this is not only a matter of the societal influences he exercises upon his surroundings. Even a sin committed privately and in secret is part of this comprehensive fabric, just as the *mitzvah* incumbent upon each individual is part of the comprehensive network of relations between the creator and the world. Sin, however it is conceived, not only blemishes the connection between a particular person and his creator but also corrupts the general quality of the relations between God and man. That is why there is a need for extensive individual involvement in the conduct of society, why each individual has an obligation to concern himself with the *mitzvot* and sins of his fellowman, and why society as a whole has an obligation and responsibility toward its individual members. The influence of the defect caused by a single sin, by its very commission, extends to the people as a whole and even to the world as a whole.

Nevertheless, sin and the sinner, as we have said, are but shadows of the network of Divine–human relations, and they are not a subject for study in and of themselves. Even scholars who have studied and held forth upon the good qualities for which man should strive have not concerned themselves with defining bad qualities in their own right. Bad qualities can be defined only within the context of the world of *mitzvot*, and not beyond it. We might say, in fact, that the qualities of the soul are objective entities that can be evaluated as good or bad only in terms of how they relate to the sacred domain. Certain of these qualities, to be sure, are generally considered worthy of reproach: jealousy, lust, striving for personal honor, pride, laziness. Even these reprehensible qualities, however, are not evaluated in terms of their intrinsic nature, but only in relation to their specific context or in light of the manner in which they are manifested. We see in the Bible that even qualities or deeds that would normally have a negative connotation can at times, in different contexts, express positive motivations (compare the varying expressions of "jealousy" in Numbers 5:14 and 25:11, 13).

Even traditional Jewish works on the problems of ethics concern themselves primarily with describing the right way and scarcely treat the problem of sin and the sinner. Rather, these works focus almost exclusively on exhorting their readers or explaining to them how they are to do good or attain to a higher level of righteousness or piety.

We likewise find very few inquiries into the psychology of the sinner or the question of what causes man to sin. To be sure, the disregard of this subject is to be explained in part by the pessimistic view generally taken of man's nature. The presumption that "the devisings of man's mind are evil from his youth" (Genesis 8:21) appears already in the Scriptures, and this evaluation has not changed much with the passage of time. Precisely because evil is not grasped as an independent entity, however, man's attraction to it is seen as stemming not from a specific pull toward perversity but rather from other factors that have primarily to do with his weaknesses and not with some particular wicked quality. The conflict between body and soul often cited as an explanation for man's inner struggle is not really a conflict between good and evil; it occurs, rather, because of man's preference for a partial, immediate view of things over a more comprehensive understanding, for the good of the moment over that which is everlasting, or, sometimes, because of an incongruence between the merely pleasant and the truly desirable. Sin is also at times defined as forgetfulness, as a situation in which man temporarily fails to recall his obligations and his true needs and concerns himself with other things instead. Following another classical explanation, according to which "man sins only when a spirit of foolishness has entered him" (Sotah 3a), sin may also be seen as an act of foolishness or self-delusion. Knowing transgression and even conscious rebellion stem only from error, whether it lies in a failure to see things in their proper proportion or in a generally misguided understanding.

The approaches we have outlined do not necessarily lead to sin and the sinner's being seen in a forgiving light, but they do make a difference as to how the significance of punishment is understood, both where the punishment is meted out by heaven and where it is meted out by society. Punishment from heaven is viewed not as revenge but rather as the natural consequence of distortion or error. Just as deviation from, or rebellion against, the laws of nature really harms only the person who is at fault, so too in the case of deviation from the *mitzvot*. The principal purpose of punishment by society is also seen as rectification, either of the world as a whole (which has been blemished and perverted by the sinner or by his action) or of the individual sinner. Improving one's ethical conduct, moreover, lies not in exercising greater strength in the act of choice but in activating or raising one's consciousness. The higher mankind's level of consciousness, the less possibility there is for sin. The bearer of reproach, from the very earliest image of the prophet, has always been described as the man of clear vision; his function is to awaken others, to teach them to see, and to guide them to a more perfect understanding.

16

The Test of Jewishness

Many thinkers have attempted to define the uniqueness of the Jewish people: What is the nature of our difference from other nations, and why indeed have we been singled out to be the *Am Segula*, the Chosen People? Virtually all great Jewish thinkers agree that beyond our having been chosen by the Almighty, the Jewish people possess characteristics that justify our selection. In support of their conclusion, many cite the brilliant personalities who have emerged in each generation as examples of the Jewish potential for greatness, while others point to the prophetic revelations as the clearest proof of the unique spiritual worth of the Jewish people.

Yet all of these answers may leave one difficulty unresolved: How is this uniqueness apparent in the life of individual Jews who have not achieved greatness? Others have indeed suggested that our status as the *Am Segula* is not manifest in every single Jew, but is rather that of a collective, an attribute of *Klal Yisrael*, the entire nation. The Jewish people, as this collective, carries the God-idea through the ages, and from this collective there emerge the chosen few—those chosen for greatness who reach, as it were, "the higher spheres where the Almighty dwells."

But this still leaves unanswered the question: What role does each individual Jew who lives an "ordinary" life play in the chosen collective that is *Klal Yisrael?* Just as all the *mitzvot* and all the spiritual and moral imperatives are imposed upon every individual Jew without exception, so too is the potential for greatness the heritage of every Jew. Not only is it an attribute of the Jewish collective, but it is engraved on the being, on the soul of every single Jew.

The deepest understanding of this characteristic of each Jewish *neshomah* is found in the *Torat HaKabbalah*, the mystical aspect of Torah instruction, as it is expounded upon and interpreted through the teachings of Rabbi Schneur Zalman, founder of Chabad, who is reverently known as the *Alter Rebbe*. In the Alter Rebbe's approach, the greatness of the Jewish people and their uniqueness begins with, and is composed of, the hidden strength in every Jew, no matter how low he has sunk, and no matter how sinful he be. It is this hidden strength that makes even such a Jew ready to give up his life: to die when forced to choose between renouncing his Jewishness or losing his life. This power to withstand the ultimate test of human endurance, to give one's life so as not to compromise the collective Jewish holiness, is the manifestation of the uniqueness of the nation as a collective, and the Jew as an individual. This capacity is not confined to the great and the wise among our people; it is shared by every Jew, great and small, learned or illiterate, even by a Jew who has throughout his lifetime turned his back on all of the Torah imperatives and led a life virtually devoid of *mitzvot*. A Jew, given the option of choosing *shmad*, publicly denying God and renouncing his Jewishness, or death, will choose to die rather than cut off his *neshomah* from *Klal Yisrael*.

It has often been demonstrated that people who have been cut off from every manifestation of their Jewishness, living virtually as gentiles in every respect, when faced with the ultimate test of their Jewishness have chosen to endure even the worst deprivations and tortures, and to die *Al Kiddush HaShem*, as a final expression in this life of the Holiness of the Almighty, and the oneness of His Torah and His people.

Among other peoples and other nations there have also been men and women who gave their lives willingly for their beliefs; but it has been as a rule those few who had a high degree of spirituality and devotion to their faith. Not so the Jews: even the most distant, bereft of spirituality, carries within himself this supranatural capacity to renounce life rather than to renounce God. Again, it is apparent that this force derives not from the life-long efforts of highly motivated Jewish believers, but from something built into the fiber of the Jewish soul. And it is in this light that the biblical passage, "*V'amaich koolom tzadikim*" (and Your people are all righteous) takes on a simple and literal meaning: They are all ready for the ultimate righteousness—terminating their lives for the sake of Heaven.

But the Alter Rebbe's definition of the *Yiddishe neshomah* raises yet another question. If indeed every Jew has this spiritual integrity to give his life when called upon for the sake of Heaven, why does it lie dormant? Why does it demand the most terrible circumstances to bring it to the fore? Why does it not operate in the normal course of events? Why must a Jew first turn his back on all the sanctities of Torah and Jewish life, and only under extreme duress display his true loyalty? The Alter Rebbe explains it roughly as follows:

Every Jew, no matter who he is, has a holy *neshomah* virtually a *Chailek Eloka MiMaal*, a sort of microcosm of the Almighty. This gives the Jew the power to overcome every temptation of worldly pleasures—even cutting short his life for the sake of Heaven—so as not to be separated from God. This "identification" of the *Yiddishe neshomah* with the Almighty is not simply one aspect of his life that derives from "religious" commitment; it is the essence of his existence, of his life-substance. His being bound to God is not only a part of his "I," which consists of his corporeal and earthly existence; it is the "I" that encompasses every aspect of his being on every level and in every sphere. All living creatures—even the simplest forms—have a desire to live, to survive, and they will muster forces that normally lie dormant, when their lives are at risk. In that same manner, the Jew confronted with the threat of spiritual death, the threat to his fundamental life desire, will muster every iota of energy to go on "living" by dying to this world.

It is said that "all that a person has he will surrender for his life." And as this is so in the physical sense, so too will the Jew give all that he possesses to maintain his bond with God—even his earthly life.

But having made this case, the question once again arises: "Why cannot these incredible spiritual resources be put into play to make this same Jew manifest his ties to the Almighty by living all his days as a Jew must live if he chooses to be close to God?

The Alter Rebbe answers this question by drawing on yet another insight from our sages. "*Ain odom choteh, ele im kain nichnas bo ruach shtus*" (No one sins against God unless a spirit of folly overcomes him). The sages are not reacting here to the question of how a person who believes in God and His Torah can knowingly commit a specific sin, but rather to the broader question of how anyone aware of God and aware of His will through Torah can ever transgress the Divine will. Why does not the force that can overcome his desire to go on living, and motivate him to choose death rather than cut himself off from God, stand by him in resisting the very desire to sin? The answer is that the *ruach shtus*, the folly that overpowers him, keeps him from considering what he is about to do. Better, he knows what he is about to do, but he does not believe this particular transgression will sever his ties with the Almighty. The spirit that takes hold of him consists of this—whether he verbalizes it or not, whether in his consciousness or in some sort of intuitive response—that *in spite of his sin, he is still a Jew!* This spirit expresses itself in making it possible to deceive himself that life—and especially in relationship to the Almighty—can be compartmentalized to the extent that one area does not intrude on another. On the one hand, he can commit the most horrible transgressions, and on the other, he remains a faithful and obedient servant of God.

Yet this folly has its limit in its capacity to deceive. When the Jew reaches the point of choosing between surviving as a renegade Jew or giving his life to sustain his ties with God, the *ruach shtus* loses its force, and without a moment's hesitation, the choice of eternal life becomes his only option; he is prepared to lay down his life to sanctify God's name.

Certainly the uniqueness of the Jewish people and the *Yiddishe neshomah* is not limited to a readiness to renounce worldly life, yet it demonstrates the tenacity with which the Jewish soul is bound to the Almighty.

=== 17 ===

Destruction and Redemption

The gloomiest day in the entire Jewish calendar is *Tishah b'Av*. A long series of national disasters, from the destruction of the First Temple to the Spanish expulsion, are historically identified with this date. Moreover, in every generation this day has been looked upon as the essence of all national mourning, and the lamentation prayers of *Tishah b'Av* recall not only the events that occurred on that day but also the story of the sufferings of our people throughout its exile. Nevertheless, the focus of mourning is the destruction of the Temple, and this represents both the beginning and the symbol of all that occurred thereafter. The destruction of the Temple is not an isolated event (important or even basic as it is) in the chronicles of our sufferings; it constitutes both a key to, and a definition of, all the troubles of Israel. It is this destruction that lifts isolated events, persecutions, exiles, and oppressions from the plane of mere historical episodes and gives them a transcendent significance.

For the Jewish people, the Temple was the only place for complete worship. It was the recognized center for all the Children of Israel, wherever scattered. Indeed, the Temple was the only holy place recognized by Judaism. The central importance of the Temple can only be fully appreciated by studying Maimonides's list of the *mitzvot*. Of the 613 listed, less than half have been applicable (and some of the others only partly so) since the Destruction. And the situation is similar in the Oral Law and in all the other areas that make up the life of the nation. It may be said that most of the structure of Judaism was suddenly cut out from under it with the Destruction, not only in activities directly connected with the Temple and the worship there, but also a large body of *mitzvot* and customs indirectly bound to it. This picture of the effect of Jewish law gives us some conception of what really occurred with the destruction of the Temple.

Aside from the direct and indirect functions that the Temple served, it was also the pinnacle of Jewish life, and its absence represents a basic flaw in the very fabric of the Jewish people. We must remember that, of all of the spiritual and governmental institutions that arose in Israel throughout the generations, none achieved a comparable position of centrality in the life of the entire people. The centers of learning that became more and more important to the Jewish people throughout the generations depended on a substantial connection with the Temple. Not only the Temple service and the force of the historic events, but the Torah itself made the sole repository of religious authority "the priests and judges who will serve in those days," located in this specifically designated place, "the place which God will choose"— the house of His choice, the Temple.

The destruction of the Temple, therefore, deprived the Jewish people of the central axis about which the life of the people revolved and toward which all other life expressions were directed. Since that time, the Jewish people lack that central axis needed to direct the religious life, the national life, and the very existence of the people as a national body. Thus the destruction of the Temple was not only metaphysically but also historically and actually "the removal of the *Shechinah*" (the Divine Presence) from Israel ("exile of the *Shechinah*"). As long as the Temple exists, there is direction and significance to the flow of life and the direction of life. Whatever the number of Jews in the diaspora, and whatever the political and material position of the Jews in Israel, as long as the Temple exists, the entire nation knows that "the Lord dwells in Zion," and for the life of the nation there is not only a center but also a direction: there is a beginning and an end in the structure of life.

The Exile really begins with the destruction of the Temple. We must remember that even with the destruction of the First Temple, and certainly with that of the Second, there was not a massive exile of our people from the land. However, if in a practical way the situation of the nation changed little with the Destruction, as long as the Temple stood, Jews outside of the land were only a "diaspora," a scattering of people who happened to live in another country. The loss of national independence made little change in the situation, as our people had had complete national independence in their own land for a relatively short period anyway. But upon the destruction of the Temple there came that feeling of orphancy that is implied in the concept of exile. The far-flung communities of Israel, which had possessed a center toward which all life was directed, were suddenly no longer in a state of mere temporary absence (which would eventually be terminated), but, in a deeper sense, in exile, under the yoke of foreign slavery in every land, including the land of Israel. Therefore, the sufferings of Israel are unlike those recorded in the history of any other nation. The destruction of the Temple was the "expulsion of the Divine Presence" from Israel, and all the subsequent sufferings of Israel are understood as merely a repetition of that same event, the continual loss by the people of the center of its being.

All these sufferings are qualitatively the same, turning as they do on the fact that the nation is not unified by a single center but is, rather, broken into separated parts, subject to continual injury. In the course of the generations, therefore, all the days of mourning commemorating particular inflictions and sufferings were canceled and the heightened mourning of *Tishah b'Av* made the center and symbol of Jewish sufferings throughout the generations. Undoubtedly, even the days that have been designated in our generation as commemorations of the Holocaust will quickly be forgotten, and the recollection of even this great tragedy joined to the accumulation of national mourning throughout the generations, which is the ninth of *Av*.

The legend that on the day of *Tishah b'Av*, at the very time of the Destruction, the Messiah was born, is a key to the understanding of one aspect of the problem of the destruction and the notion of redemption. For redemption to take place, the repair of the various individual destructions alone is insufficient. Even if all people of Israel were to return to their land, this would be insufficient for the redemption of the Destruction. Furthermore, even the building of the Temple in and of itself could not repair that which had been damaged in the course of the generations. Only the Messiah, who will bring redemption to the world on a higher plane and in a more complete fashion than ever before possible, can undo the Destruction. Redemption cannot simply be a return to the situation as it previously existed; it must be much more than that, a higher stage. The reestablishment of a Jewish state, in the sense that it is merely a restoration, is therefore only a small part of the scheme of redemption. It is only true redemption that can reconstruct the Jewish people, not only as it formerly existed but on an even higher plane. The redemption of the Jewish people cannot be complete until it is accomplished by a change in the entire world. Only a redemption that rises above the sufferings of two thousand years, which leads from them to a higher level of existence, can be considered full reparation for the Destruction.

PART IV

SOURCES

18

Abraham

Now Abraham was old and at peace.

The hard times had passed. The pain, the cruel pain his son Ishmael had caused him had gradually dissolved into old age, into tranquillity. Not long before, he had made a pact with the warlike king of the Philistines. The two men were both kings, both leaders: the king of the Philistines and Abraham, a proud tribal chieftain and a prince anointed by God, He too a king. All was stable and peaceful, and so it was to continue indefinitely. And between faith and hope, Isaac grew.

"And it came to pass, after these things, that God tested Abraham." Was he still Abraham? Did he still hold fast to the charge and the destiny and the unending path?

"And He said to him, "Abraham!" " A question, a call, an examination: Are you still Abraham?

"And he said, 'I am here!' " Here I am, a vessel, ready and waiting. In tranquillity and tribulation alike, here I am. I am always prepared.

And this test is to be the cruelest of all. It is the one that confronts everything—hope, love, even faith itself—with that which transcends everything, the Divine essence, that something that knows no law or path, arbitrary, ever-changing, infinite, holy. It is He who asks, stamping His divinity on every word. It is no human speech, but the voice with the power to create and bring into being. He builds anew, moulds, stirs: "Take your son . . ."—your son, with the whole weight of meaning, the whole fabric of associations the word bears. ". . . your only son . . ."—to emphasize that there is no other, that no one will every take his place. ". . . whom you love . . ."—how profound is the feeling aroused when the Lord speaks the word "love." The whole is greater than the sum of the parts: "namely Isaac." And when all this had been stirred up, when Abraham's loving heart is filled to overflowing, there comes the cruel ambiguous command: "Give him to Me!" A pointless gift, against all principle, a "caprice" of the Divine will.

"Go forth!" That is the way all great tests begin. Go, leave everything behind. Leave all that you know, all the sensations and feelings that are familiar to you, for . . . for something far away and unknown, something undefined, somewhere else. Such was the trek from Ur of the Chaldees. But harder, immeasurably deeper and more painful is the other kind of leaving, not the cutting of mere external ties but the abandonment of the most profound inner tie, the trek toward the great unknown. Where? "To one of the mountains of which I shall tell you." You will find out soon enough!

Abraham is the servant of the Lord; he can withstand the test. And though his heart be filled with despair, his entire world destroyed, he remains, he must remain, the Lord's servant. Neither questioning nor inquiring, he is forever obedient. That which has been entrusted to him he shall return to its giver. It is all to be carried out correctly: not in a fit of madness or a drunken stupor, but calmly, to outward appearances even coldly. He is still a father, a leader, a king. His heart might be on the verge of exploding with emotion, but the absolute imperative takes full control. He gets up in the morning; resolutely, coolly, dispassionately, he loads the donkey; he takes his two servant boys with him. This is the way a leader conducts himself. He leaves nothing behind, not the wood, nor the fire, nor the knife. And he heads for the place to which God—the God of judgment, of might, of fear—has directed him. He follows Him.

For three days, he makes his way along the mountain path. Outwardly, routine; inwardly, unimaginable anguish. He turns the Lord's words over and over in his mind, for the hundredth, the thousandth time. He tries to understand, to find consistency in them, to ponder his own future, to draw conclusions, to be reconciled, and to accept with love the will of the Creator, the Life-Giver, the Destroyer. On the third day, he looks up. He is at peace with himself. He sees the place off in the distance. It is a mountain like all other mountains, but his eyes—not his fleshly eyes—see that this is the one that was meant. The boys are to remain behind with the donkey. They may not see or feel what it is like for a prophet of God to sacrifice his future and his faith. His voice is still that of a leader, and coldly, without emotion, he orders them to wait until he returns. What fine, bitter irony there is, too, in his choice of words: "We shall go, we shall prostrate ourselves, and we shall return." We, the two of us.

He loads up Isaac with the wood, taking in his own hands the sacrificial implements: the consuming firebrand and the death-dealing knife. Now, for the first time in his life, he must serve as an agent of death and destruction, with no hope for life, for rescue. And he walks along, this old man, this leader of men, this dignified sheikh, with his young son, a lively, bubbling lad who looks at the flowers along the way, the passing birds, the clouds above, and smiles: full of life, full of flowering, full of worlds unborn. He walks beside his aged father like an embodiment of spring. But as for the old man, how is it that despair does not retard his steps, that dark ruminations do not slow him down? "They walked, the two of them together," step by step, Isaac skipping lightly despite his load and Abraham plodding heavily with the burden in his heart. They march together. So the Most High has decreed.

How can the boy help but be puzzled at the unaccustomed gloominess, the silence, the strange seriousness of his journey? Looking about him, he begins to feel lonely and afraid. Never has he seen his father, this kindly old man, this epitome of goodness, looking this way: proud, mournful, and tense. He notices that his father does not look at him, and that there is grim determination in his eyes. Something awesome and terrifying lurks behind that face, and suddenly his father seems to him alien and threatening. Hesitantly, as if trying to recover a sense of closeness, he turns to him and asks gropingly, in a voice not his own: "My father?" His father, the servant of the Lord, now belongs to a realm beyond fatherhood, beyond this world; he belongs to the cruel Absolute. He has not overcome fatherhood by extirpating it; rather, he has transcended it. With all his heart, with all his love, he still holds fast to his son, and he answers with the fullest readiness, the greatest tenderness: "I am here, my son." I am here, I stand ready to attend to your needs. And you, you are my son and always shall be.

Now the son can ask on, for no matter how terrible the secret, even if it turns out to be the horrible thing that has already crossed his mind, as long as his father remains his father he has no fear, even of death. And being a child, he asks the innocent question: All is ready, "but where is the lamb for the burnt offering?" And the father's answer is vague, and in its vagueness, menacing: "God will provide Himself with a lamb for the burnt offering." God, the God of judgment, will arrange for His own sacrifice! How indefinite, how very frightening these words are. Isaac knows about the human sacrifice practiced by his Canaanite neighbors. He knows about the clay urns in which the bodies of their first-born daughters are collected. How horrible! He does not yet grasp what his father has told him, but it is clear that it is something terrible, and it casts over him a pall of dark dread. Now he is almost certain that it is he himself who is to be sacrificed; but at the same time he knows that this must be the decree, the command from on high for the sake of which his kin, the family of Abraham, are prepared to give anything. Looking up at his father's face, at the proud character and abundant outward confidence displayed there, he resolves not to hold back, not to falter.

The old man has already decided. His steps are firmer now. For the young, inexperienced son this is a further crushing blow; but after all, he too is a servant of the Lord, he too has been consecrated from birth to carry on. "And the two of them walked on together"—the same footfall, the same double thud of steps, the old man and the boy.

The altar is built, the wood is arranged, and Isaac is bound as well. He has not resisted. He may have trembled a bit, but he knew in advance this would happen. Now Abraham raises the knife to slaughter the greatest sacrifice, the most precious lamb he can give. His mind is clear, his hand steady, his eyes dry. He is fulfilling the command. Brimful as he is—with the pain and with the imperative— he nonetheless remains Abraham, the servant of God.

And when the Lord's angel calls out to him—"Abraham, Abraham!"—his answer is once again that of Abraham, of one who loves the Lord beyond all else: "I am here!" Here I am, ready, prepared. Then the Divine utterance releases him from the terrible obligation; for, in fact, it has already been performed; the sacrifice has already been offered up in the depths of his soul.

Yet it is not joy that first floods his heart. Still filled with the command, he feels somehow that it has not been completely discharged, that its execution is not yet perfect. So he looks up, searching for the fulfillment, for Divine guidance at this critical moment. Only now is the ram revealed to him. It is standing there as if that had been its place since time immemorial, since Creation, and as if its presence there were an answer to Abraham's question: the ram shall be Isaac.

Quickly, he unties the boy—there is no time now to pay him much heed, for the act is not yet complete—and he sacrifices the ram in Isaac's place, as if offering up Isaac himself. He slaughters it, knowing that it is his son he is killing, and he feels in every jerk, in every spurt of blood, in every hiss of the rising flames, the complete and perfect exchange of identities between Isaac and the ram. The ram *is* Isaac. The sacrifice is done!

Now, with everything finished and his sacrifice consumed by the fire, he knows that his family is no longer merely a family of believers. He senses that it has been transformed, has undergone some mysterious transmutation that has brought it wholeness. And so, with a sense of completion, he is now able to conclude the sacrifice by saying, "The Lord sees."

And the voice of the Lord gives approval, a blessing without end, a last supernal oath: "Inasmuch as you have done this thing and not withheld your son, your only son"—the ram having been Isaac, the sacrifice having been fully given—you shall be blessed forever. Isaac shall come down off the altar as the Lord's gift, a pure burnt offering, a sacrificial lamb. This is what Abraham's seed has been, and this is what it shall be for all time.

Abraham returns to his servant boys. They have not seen or heard a thing. Little do they know that Isaac, walking now alongside his father, is henceforth to be the burnt offering of the Lord. Little do they know that Abraham has become the eternal father. They are walking, these two, in the manner of ordinary desert nomads. Yet walking along, side by side, father and son, the two are filled with a supreme excitement never felt by any man before, and they know that this excitement and this attainment must remain hidden in their hearts, never to be seen.

"And they rose and walked on together." And Abraham was old, and tranquil, and content.

The following citations are intended merely to suggest the many sources from which the ideas expressed here have been drawn.

"Not long before, he had made a pact with [Abimelech]."—*Midrash HaGadol*

"Was he still Abraham?"—*Sanhedrin 89b*

"And he said, "I am here!"—*Tanchuma Vayera 22*

". . . which confronts everything—hope, love, even faith itself."—*Midrash HaGadol*

". . . the voice with the power to create and bring into being."—*Rabbi Yitzchak Meir Alter of Gür*

". . . your son . . . your only son . . ." *Abarbanel, Commentary on the Torah*

"That is the way all great tests begin."—*Genesis Rabbah 55*

". . . of which I shall tell you . . ."—*Genesis Rabbah 55*

"This is the way a leader conducts himself."—*Genesis Rabbah 55*

"For three days, he makes his way."—*Tanchuma Vayera 22*

"He turns . . . in his heart . . ."—*Genesis Rabbah 55; Midrash HaGadol*

". . . not his fleshly eyes—see . . ."—*Genesis Rabbah 56*

"The boys are to remain behind with the donkey."—*Genesis Rabbah 56*

"We shall prostrate ourselves, and we shall return."—*Mo'ed Katan 18a*

"How is it that despair does not retard his steps?"—*Genesis Rabbah 56*

"He . . . asks gropingly: 'My father?'"—*Genesis Rabbah 56*

". . . a realm beyond fatherhood . . ."—*Zohar I, 20*

". . . the greatest tenderness . . ."—*Abarbanel, Commentary on the Torah*

"God, the God of judgment . . ."—*Zohar I, 20*

". . . will arrange for His own sacrifice."—*Targum Yonatan*

" 'I am here.' "—*Tanchuma Vayera*

". . . still filled with the command . . . "—*Genesis Rabbah 56; Numbers Rabbah 17*

". . . as if that had been its place . . ."—*Yonatan ben Uziel; Pirkei deRabbi Eliezer 31*

". . . as if offering up Isaac himself. . ."—*Genesis Rabbah 56; Midrash HaGadol*

"The ram *is* Isaac."—*Tanchuma Yashan, Shalah 27*

"You shall be blessed forever."—*Midrash Tadshe 14*

". . . old, and tranquil, and content . . ."—*Genesis Rabbah 56*

= 19 =

The Downfall
of Rabbi Eliezer

It is impossible ever to forget that day, the greatest day of Rabbi Eliezer's life and the most lamentable, the day he rose to the peak of his existence and then fell, so completely that we never set eyes on him again. To be sure, those of us who witnessed the events of that day have, like myself, often wondered whether they really happened—even though over the years they seem to become more clearly focused than ever. Even while it was all taking place, we experienced the same mixture of wonder and incredulity, as though we were in two worlds at once. To this very moment, I cannot tell where we were. Altogether, there is something awkward and painful about the whole thing and, being now an old man, I may even be mistaken about certain details. But since there are few of us left to tell of it and no one, so far, has ever divulged the scarcely-to-be-believed facts, let me try to render as complete an account as I can.

The whole thing started as something quite inconsequential; it was one of those minor debates in the *Bet Midrash*, most of them leaving nothing more behind than case material for the students to learn by rote. The subject was a contrivance of some sort, an invention by a potter, or rather a craftsman working with clay and bricks, who had a new idea about making a baking stove. Now this potter, whose name was Akhnai, or something like that, had conceived an ingenious way of getting around the strict regulations concerning the purity of an oven. He constructed it in sections, and between the sections he poured sand, which was then plastered over. The whole oven could be taken apart and put together again. It could thus be considered a broken vessel and, according to strictly legal tradition, broken pottery was in the nature of material returned to earth and was not subject to rules concerning purification. In that sense, it remained legally pure no matter how much uncleanness it gathered. Akhnai considered that making and selling them could turn into a profitable enterprise. Before proceeding further with the development of his invention, however, he thought it would be advisable to get the opinion of Rabbi Eliezer.

The industrial-minded potter was probably a decent enough fellow, with a smattering of learning and perhaps even with some pretensions at artistic as well as technical innovation—which doesn't explain why he chose to consult Rabbi Eliezer of all people, especially since Rabbi Eliezer was known to be contemptuous of new ideas and could, as likely as not, reject this oven out of hand. It may have been a provocation, of course, on the part of some of the more mischievous pupils, a deliberate misguidance. Or, the potter may have been led by circumstances we cannot now fathom. Whatever it was, the oven was brought to Rabbi Eliezer and, to everyone's surprise, Rabbi Eliezer's verdict—in no uncertain terms—was that it was pure and would always remain legally pure, because it was not in the category of implements. The inventive manufacturer was himself dumbfounded. On the one hand, he could now sell any number of such ovens to his fellow villagers, on the other, he was more perplexed and uncertain than ever about the legal purity of his oven. He therefore decided to bring his contrivance to the *Bet Midrash* to get it confirmed by the sages of that worthy assembly.

In those days, the problems dealt with by the *Bet Midrash* were numerous and varied, and we lived in the exhilarating conviction that it was all very important somehow, that whatever we decided was precedent and would become *halachah* for generations to come.

When this oven-maker appeared—a rather broad-chested, simple artisan with a Galilean accent—we were inclined to make light of the whole thing. We of the back rows, the scoffing novices, felt that this was an obvious trick, a device to get around the *halachah* regulations of purity. Those in the front rows with outstanding memories restated the words of earlier sages on the matter of an oven constructed in sections, and how it had been clearly condemned as something that accumulates uncleanness. It was all in good humor, and I recollect the phrase used by someone of the House of Betira, who still spoke a lot of Babylonian: "*Hukha Vetlula*," he said, and when one of us asked what it meant, he jokingly translated it as "stuff and nonsense." Anyhow, as this would indicate, there didn't seem to be much to concern or trouble us. We were even wondering whether a vote was needed when Rabban Gamaliel, who presided over the assembly, rose to sum the matter up.

He was tall and autocratic and a trifle impatient. "Is there anyone who disagrees that this oven is impure?" he asked. Whereupon, to our consternation, Rabbi Eliezer stood up. He wasn't called Eliezer the Great for nothing, for he was immensely tall but unlike his princely brother-in-law, Rabban Gamaliel, he was very heavy and ponderous. What is more, he was extremely grave and dignified; one hardly ever saw him smile, and when he spoke, his voice had an impressively sonorous tone.

"I have declared this oven pure," he said, "and I still maintain that it is pure." A few moments of shocked surprise followed. An Elder, who sat a couple of rows ahead of me and who was already a little hard of hearing, blinked his eyes and, turning from side to side, called aloud, "Eh, what? Pure?" The astonishment in his voice reflected the feelings of the rest of us, especially since we were well aware that Rabbi Eliezer never jested in the *Bet Midrash*, and if he said something, he really meant it.

The occupants of the front rows looked at one another to see who would speak up and, when no one did so, the same Babylonian of the House of Betira, who had previously called it all a "*Hukha Vetlula*," now rose and suggested that, with due respect to the previous speaker, the oven had to be considered unclean. He then proceeded to reiterate all the arguments that had already been given—about the need to preserve purity in respect to vessels of clay and the various precedents—and supported them by the weight of words spoken by the sages of the House of Betira and things learned from the great Rabban Yochanan ben Zakkai and other sayings ascribed to earlier sages such as the son of Hillel the Elder. All of which was presented out of respect to Rabbi Eliezer; a lesser dignitary would have been exposed to a snort of contempt from Ben Betira for daring to defy the assembly. Finally, he admitted he could not help wonder how anyone could conceivably declare this oven to be pure.

Rabbi Eliezer, who had been listening quietly, waited to make sure he was finished, and then uttered only one word. He spoke without bothering to get up, in his rich, clear voice, and this somehow goaded the others to answer vehemently.

Another worthy of the House of Betira, a cousin I believe of the first, quickly came to the defense of his relative. Not that any of us were ignorant of the past greatness of the Betiras nor did anyone cast any doubt on their piety and erudition. Anyhow, when he had had his say, another sage felt compelled to voice his opinion on the matter, and he was followed by a whole rush of arguments on the part of additional front row sages—some long-winded, a few brief and concise.

Rabban Gamaliel sat throughout all this with more than his usual tranquility, indicating with a word or a gesture who was to be the next speaker. Some of the rest of us, especially those in the back rows, I'm sorry to admit, were keen to hear how Rabbi Eliezer would react to the weight of the arguments against him. Too many of us had known the lash of Rabbi Eliezer's contempt for all innovation or novelty.

Of course, there were a few personal pupils of Rabbi Eliezer who tried half-heartedly to defend him. There was one, I remember, we used to call the little Eliezer, or Elai, a name that later became famous on account of his son, the great scholar, Yehuda ben Elai. Anyhow, this Elai now endeavored to lend some support to his teacher by insisting that the appliance being discussed was of a different nature than the usual oven, because of the sand between the sections and so on. All very commendable as an act of devotion to a teacher, but hardly convincing.

Rabbi Eliezer himself sat in his customary calm, listening with the attentiveness he gave to everything that had to do with Torah, but also showing that cold noncompliance we were used to seeing in him whenever he was opposed. As the arguments against him became a deluge, his face became stonier and more set.

Rabban Gamaliel remained serene and quiet, the tense glow of his intelligence evident in his eyes, which shifted up and back from interpreter to speaker, and alighted on someone in the second row, whose chief claim to recognition lay in his hoary age. It was from this moment that the whole matter began to assume a different aspect. This old man of the second row was originally from Alexandria and was said to have been a pupil of Yedidiah, or Philo, as he was called. Like most of that school, he was an extremely pious fellow, very scrupulous about observing the *mitzvot* but not too knowledgeable, so that even though he was well on in years he sat in the second row, and even that was more in deference to his being related by marriage to the family of Nakdimon ben Gurion than to his wisdom. It was no secret that Rabban Gamaliel preserved a certain respect for all the first families of old Jerusalem, the Jerusalem before the destruction, even those that had fallen from their greatness or their wealth. He would go out of his way to show his regard, such as in this instance of the elderly fellow now being allowed to speak, who was someone we knew as a bore and a sermonizer.

He used to deliver Sabbath afternoon sermons in the synagogue on Aggadah, somewhat in the style of the Philo school. Although he knew Hebrew very well, his accent remained Greek and it was re-marked, rather slyly, that the suspect Greek philosophy also spoke through him. At the same time, as mentioned, he was punctiliously observant about his religious duties and was a loyal follower of the school of Hillel. He would occasionally run diplomatic errands in which his fluency in Greek was useful. On the other hand, he didn't speak much in the *Bet Midrash*, and when he did he used to talk like one of the extremists of the Hillel School, arousing the secret scorn of many and not only the survivors of the School of Shammai. To be sure, no one said anything, perhaps because he was a relative by marriage of Hyrcanus the elder, father of Rabbi Eliezer, who, incidentally, because of his own age, he addressed by his first name, Eliezer.

This old man now began his speech by quoting *halachah* prec-edents, not omitting several that had been thoroughly expounded by previous speakers, and adding words of wisdom he had heard from Hillel the Elder. Some of the more roguish novices around me winked and smiled at each other whenever he repeated what the Elder Rabban Gamaliel had said (it was the one *halachah* he remembered of that sage and it later became fixed in his name in the Mishnah scripture). His tone, at any event, was that of a patronizing older person addressing a younger colleague, his being related by marriage to Rabbi Eliezer giving him a right to do so somehow.

It would all have passed without leaving much trace—everyone having become restless and eager to finish the whole affair without further ado—except that, for some reason or other, the old bore suddenly veered away from the routine *halachah* framework and began to talk about what he called the inner content of the discussion, "the idea," in Greek.

With this his speech assumed the enthusiastic tone of his sermons in the synagogue and he forgot that he was not talking to the simple folk of the congregation of Alexandria but to the sages of Israel. He got carried away and said that the things spoken by Rabbi Eliezer were an example of that mode of thought that we, the pupils of Hillel the Elder, had proven to be of no value whatever. Such notions were remnants of the repudiated approach of the School of Shammai and it was indeed to be wondered at, how someone like Rabbi Eliezer, a pupil of Rabban Yochanan ben Zakkai, could let himself fall into such a patently wrong reasoning, because it was so obvious to all that the oven was impure. Rabbi Eliezer was merely an example of that formalistic legalism that did not accord with the inner spirit of the Torah, which teaches us that we should not let ourselves be beguiled by trivialities or outer details but should go along the way of truth of the inner spirit of things, for we cannot follow after the play of logic or build the *halachah* on the basis of an idea or a formal arrangement that does not take into consideration the essential reality of things.

Truth to tell, we pupils did not pay much attention to all this; we felt we had already heard it before. We were only astounded at his daring to tell it to Rabbi Eliezer to his face. After all, we were not too concerned about the principles of the matter. But when I lifted my head, I saw that Rabbi Eliezer's face was more fiercely negative and noncompliant than ever. As we knew from experience, when Rabbi Eliezer became hurt and angry, it was not like anybody else suffering a personal affront; it was the wrath of the Torah, the response of sublime purity to offense or disrespect.

He had been known even to burst out at Rabbi Akiva in words afterwards recalled with dread and anguish, and now that he showed all the signs of such a fierce inner rage, we all trembled a little. The old man, as soon as he also became aware of it, dropped his voice and concluded his speech almost in the middle of a sentence. Whereupon, without even waiting for permission to do so, Rabbi Eliezer rose to his full height, more impressive and grave than ever, and in the taut silence that ensued his voice boomed forth.

"What is the meaning of this thing you call formalism?" Here it may be mentioned that Rabbi Eliezer had himself grown up in a Greek-speaking household and in his youth had studied with a master who was learned in Greek philosophy. He was, thus, far more sensitive to the nuances of the criticism leveled at him than were many of the ordinary members of the *Bet Midrash* who, although they were familiar with the Greek terms, did not grasp the full import of the concepts involved.

Now it was no longer a matter of a simple stove but a matter of the relation to Torah. "What is formalism?" he asked and answered his question by quoting something Rabban Yochanan ben Zakkai had said to the Sadduccees. We were all familiar with the whole story, of how the great teacher had said, "Can the Law of the Torah be compared to your rules of nature and your logic, your whole shaky philosophy, the philosophy with which you sow confusion among us?"

He continued, "Torah is an essence unto itself and everything in it is independent of the world. By what authority do you say that, according to the Torah, this oven is a deception, an attempt to get around the rules of purity? The Torah is altogether made up of pathways and signs, all its words are guidelines for the world, and it is far beyond the stupid laws of the earth. Whatever the Torah makes obligatory, whether it seem possible or impossible, is not to be questioned. Do not try to make the Torah an instrument for human needs, for it is not the Torah that serves the world but the world that serves the Torah. We cannot be responsible for the blunders of the ignorant, and we cannot adjust the Law of Torah to accommodate man or nation. What, then, is the meaning of formalism here? There is Torah, the unswerving obedience to Torah, and that's all. We sit here, and we study Torah only for this purpose and not to discuss or argue or consider public opinion. Whether a thing is right or wrong, correct or incorrect, will be decided by Torah; I will not accept any other authority!"

Thus it was that Rabbi Eliezer let himself go, and we who should have perhaps restrained him, heard him out with growing dismay. Indeed, he went too far in denying the connection between Torah and life, and in rejecting all the many laws and regulations passed by the *Bet Midrash* itself, which had the power of Scripture over the lives of the people. He had gone too far and had exceeded all bounds, not only of the subject under discussion but of good manners.

Even Rabban Gamaliel showed extreme displeasure at this subversive attack on himself as well as on the School of Hillel; and Rabbi Yehoshua, who almost never was upset by anyone or anything, was provoked to bursting point. Rabbi Tarfon, whom we would expect to ease the tension with a quip or a jest, seemed to have curled up in himself as though personally insulted. There was a strong feeling in the *Bet Midrash* that what had been uttered should not have been and could not have been said.

When the sages of the house finally rose up to speak, we heard much that was memorable and rare. Several of the speakers expounded not only on *halachah* matters but also on the way each one understood the *halachah*. Rabbi Tarfon, for instance, rose up finally and spoke eloquently. A stirring talk was delivered by the young Rabbi Elazar ben Azaria, whom we already recognized as one of the great minds of the generation, even though his beard was hardly grown.

Some of the addresses were drawn out, others were brief, but all of them without exception insisted that is was impossible, it was forbidden, to think of the Torah as not being alive and as not being connected with the ongoing existence of the world. Torah could not be considered by itself, separate from the world, as though what it had to say did not relate to, and guide, the course of events.

In a variety of ways it was mentioned that Rabbi Eliezer's approach could have been correct in a vastly different world. One of the speakers said that at the End of Days, long after the rebuilding of the Holy Temple, it might perhaps be possible to adopt such an approach.

I remember that Rabbi Akiva also spoke, and in his speech there was a vague hint of something we gathered was of an esoteric nature, so that not all of us knew what he meant. He, too, asserted that the Torah has to be bound up with the essence of things. His words had the ring of authenticity. I will admit I never did get to the bottom of Rabbi Akiva, even then when he was still at the beginning of his greatness.

At the conclusion of his talk, Rabbi Yehoshua got up, and as he began to speak, one was, as always, reminded that he was one of the poets of the *Bet Midrash*. His voice, too, was soft and pleasant, and the way he ordered his ideas was clear and convincing. At first sight, he may have seemed small, dark, and even ugly, but to us, who listened to him talk, he was enormously enchanting and delightful. Although he repeated some of the things that had already been stated, about the Torah and the way of Torah, he did not linger over them. He made a point of speaking *halachah*, as though there was nothing at stake but the matter of Akhnai's stove. Clearly he wished to restore the discussion to a definite subject and to the halachic framework of normal *Bet Midrash* activity. At the same time, he very decidedly indicated that it was out of the question to consider this stove as anything but a deception and consequently impure.

Even though the followers of the School of Shammai were few in number, they stubbornly clung to a certain conservative point of view. Now that the issue of a basic approach was let out of the bag, these followers of the School of Shammai did not wish to be cheated of a chance to express themselves. I recall especially Yochanan ben Hyrcanus, sturdy and youthfully alert in spite of his gray head of sixty years. His nickname, so apt it was known to us from his very first years at home, was "Devil boy." At any rate, he now spoke at length, bringing up various arguments, most of them out of place, and tried to get to the root of the matter, the root of *halachah* itself. I must admit I understood only a little of what he said; although his logic and wit made one feel it was all very clear, there was also the feeling that it wasn't quite the whole truth, that there was something twisted in what he said. It was almost as though he were trying to lead one astray.

Afterwards, several of Rabbi Yehoshua's disciples tried to go into more detail on the specific issue at hand, but neither Yochanan ben Hyrcanus nor any other followers of the School of Shammai responded in kind. They simply were pulled back to the old conflict and the spirit of dissension between the Schools of Hillel and of Shammai, which we had thought was long since over and done with.

The day waned and twilight set in. We had extended the discussion far beyond the usual time and Rabban Gamaliel decided to come to a conclusion. The interpreter, Hutzpit, called everyone to silence, and Rabban Gamaliel, in his customary tone of address, no different from that heard at the end of any ordinary controversy in the *Bet Midrash*, said, "Gentlemen, we will count the votes. All those who grant this stove ritual purity will say so, and those who disagree will declare that they do not grant it purity."

Rabban Gamaliel was very careful about his choice of words and never uttered any expression of blame if he could possibly help it, so that he never said "uncleanness" if he didn't have to; and now he launched the vote by saying, "Gentlemen, I myself do not grant purity." After him all those present rose up, one after another, and gave vent to their opinion, I among them. In fact, only Rabbi Eliezer and one other sage of the first row voted to grant purity. It was years since such a decisive majority had been expressed in a vote.

I don't know whether the matter would have ended there, peacefully enough, had it not been for an unexpected outpour on the part of one of the veteran disciples of Rabban Yochanan ben Zakkai. This elderly person, never conspicuous for his wisdom, now got up, and without being given permission, began to speak very agitatedly. "You see, dear sirs, at the conclusion of all the very sharp and deep words that have been uttered here, the overwhelming majority has been able to judge correctly and to find the truthful halachic solution."

He then continued to tell us how the words of sages were like firm stakes in the ground, like trees planted by the waters, and so on; how the truth must always win, as it did here in this discussion; and he finished with a saying that used to be quoted by certain scholars when they completed their addresses. "Behold, my friends, just as this great tree stands firmly rooted in its place and does not budge, so is this *halachah* fixed and immovable; just as the water flowing in this channel does not move backwards, so does truth never flow back."

This tree, which he now pointed to, was a giant carob tree, heavy

with age. It stood next to the *Bet Midrash*, and the pupils would frequently sit under its leafy branches, studying, their backs against the
broad trunk and their faces turned toward the shallow channel of water
that ran nearby and irrigated the tree, making it grow to such proportions. This tree was thus one of the landmarks of the *Bet Midrash*;
and even though it did not give much fruit, no one ever dared to think
of cutting it down. I must confess, too, that as we glanced out at the
tree in response to the last remarks made about it, and saw the light
of the setting sun leave its golden imprint on the upper branches, and
heard the soft rush of the water on the channel nearby, we were all
reassured somehow by its stability and serenity.

Rabbi Eliezer's voice suddenly broke the stillness—an altogether
different voice. There was something else present in his face, too,
something that made us suddenly afraid to look at it. He was no longer
with us in this place, discussing *halachah*; he was more like someone
who sees that which is taking place at a great distance, and we who
were near him were invisible. He seemed to be somewhere else, on
a different level. We were aware that Rabbi Eliezer was one of those
who had gone deeply into the occult mysteries of the Chariot, and
his whole appearance now betokened some such inner vision.

Suddenly, before he even began to speak, we were overcome by
a nameless fear—a fear of the hidden and the esoteric, of those
mysterious things known only to the initiated and as terrible in their
power as prophecy. Although in a certain respect he seemed to be
removed and distant, and extremely tall, indeed towering above us
in every way, he remained bound somehow to that which had been
happening here before. And in a voice that was not his—after all, his
characteristic voice was familiar enough—in a voice that was resonant
with other forces, alien powers and unknown worlds, he turned to
the ancient carob tree: "This carob shall testify that the *halachah* is
with me!"

Whereupon something happened, and although I saw it with my
own eyes, I am not sure whether it was a seeing such as men usually
see. We had not stirred from our seats, but before us something happened that shook the very foundations of our certainty in all that existed. Nothing was clear or definite any more, because this enormous
tree moved suddenly from its fixed spot, and we all saw it move, trunk

and branches together, sliding along the earth away from the wall of the *Bet Midrash* to a point about a hundred cubits away, where it came to a halt and stood still. It must be admitted that not only I, but all those present—even though we never spoke of it, except perhaps for the glance of astonishment we exchanged with our eyes—felt that never again could we rely on the law and order of nature. Rabbi Eliezer had called upon the powers above this world to help him prove his point. And whether we agreed with him or not, we could not but be shaken to the core by the feeling that we no longer knew what the truth was.

It was the sound of Rabban Gamaliel's voice that now woke us out of this strange, uncanny state. With the same cool tone of the most ordinary daily affairs, he said, "Despite which, no proof can be drawn from the carob tree."

Although Rabbi Eliezer did not seem to be listening, he stirred, and in that vibrating, prophetic voice he called out, "The channel of water shall testify that the *halachah* is with me!" And now the open conduit that had become completely exposed with the shifting of the carob tree, this same rushing channel of water now became still and then, before our incredulous eyes, the water began to flow in the opposite direction, up the slope of the rise, light, easy waves running up the conduit of water.

Once more the cool tone of Rabban Gamaliel's voice broke the silence: "There is no proof in the channel of water!" This time Rabbi Eliezer turned his face away from the window, through which, as I mentioned, he was looking without seeing. Scanning the entire assembly with those frightening, unseeing eyes, he called out: "The walls of the *Bet Midrash* shall testify that the *halachah* is with me!" Whereupon we heard the walls of the *Bet Midrash* begin to stir. The structure was not exceptionally massive, but it was a building that had been made to last, and we now witnessed the thick walls shifting and cracking and leaning from the horizontal outward and then more and more inward. Were we terrified? I can't be as certain of our physical fear as of our terror of the nature of the event. The power of Rabbi Eliezer's words frightened us beyond the sudden dread of being crushed by a falling building. After the shifting of the tree from its place, nothing was self-evident and certain anymore, and I personally was no longer able to be astonished by anything; all was possible and at the same time, it seemed as though I, and only I, survived within a dream, and as in a dream, I could not budge, could not remove myself from the scene. Those who sat next to the walls were likewise frozen into immobility, although they felt the walls bending over them more tangibly than the rest of us.

But the whole thing did not last more than a moment. In the instant of our panic, we heard the voice of Rabbi Yehoshua speaking to the walls. Strange that a man should address walls, and even more strange that he should do so in the same way that one rebukes young pupils or children who take advantage of a master's kindliness. However that may be, this chiding tone, even though the subject of it was so utterly unbelievable, was in itself extraordinary in its very ordinariness. We dearly loved Rabbi Yehoshua, knowing that he never really got angry and that he only pretended to be vexed, like a good-hearted father who could not hide the affection from his soft and pleasant voice even when he was reprimanding us.

But now, as he admonished the walls, his voice carried an additional quality, of mystery and power, a resonance beyond this world, on planes and levels of being beyond the known and ordinary. "If scholars contend with one another about the *halachah*, what is that to you?" he asked. And just as children will fall back, discomfited at being scolded, so did these walls now recede shamefacedly, to their erect position. What we think is an unbridgeable difference between man and things was suddenly obliterated, and the walls were very definitely hesitating, wobbling aslant for an interval in time before deciding to remain firmly erect.

The only one who had remained unmoved throughout all this, standing as though to gather all his forces, was Rabbi Eliezer. He now lifted his gaze upward and called out, in a mighty voice: "The Heavens shall testify that the *halachah* is with me!"

Whereupon we heard the Voice. This was the first time in my life I had ever heard a *Bat Kol*, a voice from Heaven. When others used to tell me about it, I understood only the words, because there is no way of describing what a heavenly voice is. It is not like the sound of speech, and yet it is a voice. If there is anything to which it can be compared, it would be more like the reverberating echo of a cry in the mountains. And even though the sound of it is clear enough, one cannot locate it; it doesn't come from any definite place, or from any creaturely throat, and the effect of it is indeed indescribable. At any event, that which was uttered by the Voice cannot be forgotten: "What have you against Eliezer, my son, with whom the *halachah* is always in accord?"

It was more than a reverberation of sound from all sides; this that was beyond anything that can be called a voice made us feel with an absolute certainty that whatever it said was true and could not possibly be otherwise.

We remained stunned and petrified into silence. The *Bat Kol* had uttered its injunction from Heaven, shattering all our convictions and prejudices. Thereupon, once again, the voice of Rabbi Yehoshua was heard, and this time in the accents of prayer: "Lord of the Universe, You revealed Yourself in all Your glory on Mount Sinai. There You gave us the Torah, the one and only Law, and in it You spoke the Truth and the Judgment and the Right, and in Your Torah You wrote saying that in council one should follow the decision of the majority. But what if the majority do not agree with Rabbi Eliezer? Are we not to abide by that which is right?"

What happened after this was so very simple, it is difficult to put it on the same level as the Heavenly voice. Even though there was absolutely no sound, no voice or great crackling thunder, we all experienced the vivid sensation of the passing of the *Bat Kol* from the *Bet Midrash*, as though it had been renounced by some greater power above—as though, if I may dare to say so, the Holy One, Blessed be He, Himself had agreed with Rabbi Yehoshua. Because after all these dramatic events, the world was restored to us, a different world, but still the world of Torah, and we understood the holiness of this Torah in our possession, a holiness derived not from heaven but from that which was here and now, from this *Bet Midrash*. When the sages, whether great and wise or whether simple and ordinary, studied the Torah, the Torah they pored over was Truth, the words of the living God.

At this moment, then, we were restored to the *Bet Midrash*, to the walls that no longer seemed to slant, to the channel of water that again flowed as usual, to the sun that was setting as usual—and everything was as it had always been. We were relieved to know that

the Heavens did not coerce us, did not compel us to make one decision rather than another, that the obscurity of doubt was suddenly
cleared away and it was we, in our freedom of the majority vote, who
decided the substance of truth. It was a feeling of immense relief shared
by all of us, even Rabbi Eliezer I think, because he did not turn and
take his seat with dignity but sank down into it, sweating profusely,
stricken with sorrow and fatigue.

When Rabban Gamaliel spoke, we were back in the customary
Bet Midrash atmosphere as I said, even though it could never again
be the same. Nevertheless, the usual tone of Rabban Gamaliel helped
us to feel right, as he said, "Members of the Assembly, since we have
decided that this oven is impure, its bread is hereby declared unclean,
for it was not prepared in accordance with the laws of purity, and so
the attendants will gather all the loaves and burn them in the compound next to the *Bet Midrash*."

The attendants gathered up the loaves of bread and took them
outside. The Galilean inventor of the oven disappeared, but no one
saw him take his departure. A few of the younger pupils went out to
gather wood to burn the loaves of bread. We had witnessed enough
such halachic proscriptions—on cakes of meal and offerings, and the
subsequent burning in the compound—so that there was no reason
this should be as different and strange as it seemed to us. Perhaps the
whole ordinariness of the world had changed: the attendant carrying
the loaves, the pupils preparing the fire, and the fire itself. Smoke began
to rise. It was already dark when we heard Rabbi Eliezer give vent to
his anger. His anger was full of a terrible bitterness, an abysmal
humiliation.

"How dare you alter the decision of Heaven!"

Wrapped in this fierce mortification, he rose and left the *Bet
Midrash*. But it seems that he was not the only one to feel anger. Rabban Gamaliel, always so wonderfully self-controlled, now raised his
voice an octave, so that it was just a trifle more decisive, and yet profoundly sad.

"Men of the Assembly," he said, "we cannot tolerate such a refusal
to accept the decision of the Sanhedrin of Israel. If the Sanhedrin
decides, then no one, not even if it be Rabbi Eliezer ben Hyrcanus . . ."
Here he hesitated, almost as if he were about to add "my brother-in-

law," and he continued, "can say such things as were heard just now."

Then, almost as an afterthought, he added, "There is the precedent of Akabia ben Mahalalel." We all knew about this Akabia, a great mind, one of the outstanding men of his generation, who had defied the decision of the majority, with the result that he was excommunicated. Indeed, many years had passed since any of the great sages had been excommunicated; there were other ways of keeping them in line. But now, precisely because of the prestigiousness of Rabbi Eliezer, the hint was clear.

No one offered to say anything. Everyone waited for one of the sages to express it more explicitly. The old men, who had spoken so glibly a while ago, were now silent, and even those in the first row waited for someone else to speak up. All eyes were gradually focused on Rabbi Yehoshua—Rabbi Yehoshua of the kindly disposition, the one who was the close friend of Rabbi Eliezer from their difficult years at school together. There was a long pause. At last he stood up and said it:

"It seems we have no choice. We cannot divide the one Torah into two Torahs." A long, hushed interval, and he continued, "I am of the opinion that we have to consider whether to excommunicate him."

Once the word was uttered, it was clear that it would be so. There was no more desire to discuss the matter. And Rabban Gamaliel, unable now to hide the extremity of his emotion, was obviously torn; he had to force himself to remain calm. It was, however, in a clear and firm voice, hiding all his personal feelings (as befits a leader of Israel), that he called out, "Stand and be counted!"

Now, too, there was a majority, and the majority decided to excommunicate Rabbi Eliezer.

═ 20 ═

Rachel and Rabbi Akiva

No one in later times has ever seen Jerusalem in all her beauty. The city of consummate splendor. What remains today of that city are only a few houses, ruins, memories.

But I shall not speak of that Jerusalem—the Holy Temple and the holiness of the city—or of the great learning of Jerusalem, in the larger body of the Sanhedrin and in the smaller Sanhedrin. Who, indeed, can describe all the holiness, the divine worship, the priests, the sages of Israel in their hundreds and their thousands with their numerous pupils.

Yes, Jerusalem was a city of consummate beauty, full of remarkable people and a certain magnificence of its own. And it was also a city of great wealth. The profusion of gifts that poured in from kings and merchants and pious Jews from all corners of the world added to the splendor of the city, as well as to the majesty of the Temple and the royal palaces.

To be sure, there were very many different kinds of people in Jerusalem, poor as well as rich. But the rich had a certain opulence about them. Money seemed to have no meaning for them. Some were more than generous in their charities, others were far from the ways of the Torah and went the way of the gentiles. Most of these wealthy families lived in the upper city, in grand palaces, the like of which could be seen only in the urban centers of the Empire, like Antioch or Rome. And among these houses of legendary wealth, there were three great families whose richness of style and power exceeded all others: the house of Nakdimon ben Gurion, that of Ben Tzitzit Hakesset, and the house of Ben Calba Savua.

These three families were superior to all the others, also by reason of the fact that the individual members of the families were close to the world of wisdom, close to the Holy Temple, and were involved in the glory of Jerusalem. They were the ones who, when the great rebellion came, gave huge sums of money to sustain the people in their struggle. Some of them were entirely wiped out, all their wealth lost. Others remained, even if greatly reduced in wealth and power.

One of these was the family of Calba Savua. They were not quite like all the other great houses of Jerusalem, even though they dwelt in palatial enough residences in the city. They were actually of the old aristocracy of the tribe of Judah, and most of their houses, lands, and property were situated in the hill country to the south, in the region of Hebron. The members of Calba Savua traced their ancestry back to the biblical family of Caleb ben Yefuneh, and they possessed vast stretches of land in southern Judea: vineyards, olive groves, flocks of sheep and goats, broad fields of grain. Conscious of their noble lineage, they never tried to intermarry with the respectable houses of Jerusalem, though their wealth and power were enough to warrant entry into any of the venerable families of the priests and illustrious sages. They preferred to adhere to the ancient customs of Judah, which drew upon the traditions of the land that nourished them.

Altogether, they were conservative in their ways, clinging to the old customs of the fathers. Their hospitality was famed far and wide. And always there were guests in their houses—guests of all sorts, not only those who were formally invited to the splendid feasts, but also simple folk who were hungry and came to eat. The family of Calba Savua prided itself on its hospitality according to the example set by the patriarch Abraham.

As I have said, they were essentially a landed aristocracy, the Calba Savuas, so that even though their wealth was less conspicuous perhaps than some of the great houses of Jerusalem, it was more stable and permanent, and was able to endure the wreckage of the destruction. In the security of their lands and power and noble ancestry, they did not bother to enter into politics; they were not among the ministers and the administrators even in the days of the Hasmonians, and certainly not in the time of the Herods. Similarly, they made no effort to marry into the families of the high priests. Their princely nobility was sufficient unto itself. And so they carried on, an aristocracy occupied with their responsibilities to the land, their houses open and their interests broad enough to include all aspects of Torah. Though they were not considered among the sages, they were proud of their learning and boasted some genuine scholars. As a matter of course, all their sons and daughters received the very best education that Jerusalem could offer. And this included the wisdom of the gentiles as well as of the Jews.

One of the chief characteristics common to members of the house of Calba Savua was a certain proud stubbornness. They were quick to make decisions, easy to anger. And when once a decision was made, an anger or an ardor ignited, they could not be deterred. No matter what suffering it brought them or others, it was extremely difficult for them to digress from a chosen path of action or feeling. It used to be known that those whom the clan of Calba Savua favored would be supported in any situation, under any circumstance. And the opposite also was true, whether justly or unjustly: when once they had reason to dislike or hate someone, nothing could make them alter their opinion.

At the time of which we speak, Rachel was the only daughter of this family. There were a number of brothers, and as was to be expected, Rachel was spared no love or affection, nor did she ever lack whatever could be obtained with money or influence.

I, myself, never knew her in her early years; I first saw her when she was already a mature woman and I was still quite a young man. But certain members of my own family—which was not as rich as the Savuas, but occupied an honorable place in Israel—did have occasion to be on good terms with that illustrious house and knew her as a young woman. So that I am able to speak of her on the basis of more than just hearsay.

She may not have been considered a beautiful woman, but no one could fail to be impressed with her appearance, even then: a slender maid with a great abundance of long black hair, blazing eyes, and a personality that suited her famous pedigree; generous, quick-thinking, resolute, and proud; equally amiable to everyone, big and small; naturally sure of herself in everything. It was hard to deny her; and she did not refrain from taking part in practical matters of the family fortunes— land and money and decision-making of all kinds. Unlike the other daughters of the palaces of Jerusalem, Rachel had spent much of her time on the family estates in the country, where she knew all the folk and they knew her. She was not obligated to do so, of course; it was a matter of personal preference on her part to become involved in the life and problems of the countryside, to haggle with the merchants over the sale of produce, to discuss worldly matters with the many visitors to the house, and to converse with the simple workers of the land. Sometimes the brothers would try to restrain her a little, feeling that a daughter of the aristocracy and a possible wife of the greatest in the country should not be friendly to such diverse sorts of people. But, as I said, even then, as a young woman, no one could control or deny her anything; neither her brothers nor her father, the head of the family, could do anything.

She was already of marriageable age, and there was certainly no lack of the most dazzling offers, especially since it was common knowledge that, as the only daughter of the Calba Savuas, she would be given a considerable part of their inestimable wealth. She herself, however, was not in any hurry to decide, and since no one would dare decide for her, she continued her life of culture and study in Jerusalem, and her active life among the people of the land in the countryside of Judea.

No one knows when and how she first saw Akiva ben Yoseph. He was then one of the shepherds of the many flocks belonging to the estates of Calba Savua and, in the nature of things, hardly in a position to meet the daughter of the one who was lord and master of the vast holdings. Moreover, his family had a relatively low status. His father, Yoseph, had become a proselyte, and was said to have originated from one of the native Galilean families in the north. Later, stories circulated to the effect that his family had not been ordinary folk, but belonged to a certain noble line of princes of the gentiles. But this was all story.

The fact was that this Yoseph was not only a convert, he was also poor and had no clearly defined occupation, as far as anyone could tell. He had married a simple woman of Judea and lived in such poverty that his son, Akiva, could not even be sent to school. Even in those days, such a thing was rare—a Jewish child who did not have the minimum of education: reading, writing, Torah. Only the poorest of the poor were unable to pay for a village teacher of children. Subsequently, too, there was not much chance for the young Akiva to learn any estimable trade, and he became a shepherd, which was perhaps the lowest of occupations.

The flocks did not graze in the fields, except in the season of the year after the harvest. Generally, they were led down to the edge of the desert of Judea, and there the shepherds would remain with the sheep and the goats for months at a time. Akiva was thus alone for a large part of the year. A very tall man, dark and already close to the age of forty, he was becoming bald. Later in life he would be completely bald and would be known as a taciturn, silent man who had learned to keep his thoughts to himself in the great stillness of the desert. Only occasionally did he express himself, and then with astonishing clarity and sharpness; the other herdsmen used to remark how for months on end he would say nothing at all except what was essential to communicate. No one had the slightest clue as to what he was contemplating, or the nature of his thoughts. At this time, too, he had an additional reason to be reserved. He had married a woman, no longer young, and they had had several children. It was one of those poor households where one was grateful for whatever one was given. But then his wife died suddenly, and he was left with the small children, more solitary and pensive than ever.

As I have mentioned, the house of Calba Savua was of a generous temper and close in relation to their lands and their people. When they learned of Akiva's misfortune they gave him work near the village so that he could take better care of his children. Some women of the village took it upon themselves to feed the children during the day, and at night upon returning from the fields, he would assume all the duties of the household.

It seems that once, toward evening, when Akiva was hurrying home, tall and taciturn, looking at the sky as though to hold back the quickly descending darkness, Rachel noticed him and asked about him. When she heard the details, she made up her mind to be of help, and the next day when she saw him striding toward his house, she accosted him. Naturally, he knew who she was. But it was she who spoke first—even though it was not quite right for a woman, and a young one at that, to address a strange man. However, she was the mistress, in a sense, and could allow herself liberties.

She spoke in the proper manner, rendering condolence for the loss of his wife. "Be consoled from Heaven."

In the accepted manner of the one in mourning, he merely nodded with his head.

"Are you in need of anything?" she inquired.

He answered, "Your family are very kind and they have allowed me to herd the flocks near the village so that I can be close to my children. But there is no one really to take care of them during the day. My old father is in the house, but he can really do little."

"And do you require anything more? Do you not need help of some other kind?" she asked.

"No," he said "there is no need for charity."

"But how can you make your Sabbath if no one assists you?"

For the first time, he lifted his eyes which had been riveted to the ground and looked at her. "My lady," he said, "better that my Sabbaths be weekdays, and I be not needful of anyone." And he continued on his way.

Walking home slowly, she reflected on the strange quality she felt in this unusual man. He had spoken with the respect and gentleness to be expected of a shepherd addressing a mistress—but there was something else that baffled her. It was not that he was one of those poor folk who were so proud that it was frustratingly impossible to help them. He had made no effort to hide his distress. On the other hand, he had made no gesture to receive assistance from her; he seemed simply to be a person in his own right, a rather wonderful person in an odd and compelling way. In spite of his poverty, he seemed more composed and complete in himself than anyone else she knew. The few words he had uttered seemed to come like parables from the lips of the wise. Every word he said seemed to be pregnant with meaning. She would have to learn more about him; was he not, perhaps, one of those rare sages whose wisdom comes not from books, but from life itself?

On the following Saturday, she joined all the people of the village in the synagogue, sitting among the women who received her with inquisitive courtesy. Unseen, she was able to watch him. He stood among the group of herdsmen and peasants who were illiterate and like them he repeated word for word the utterances of the reader. It was for their sake that the prayers had been arranged in such a way that they could repeat it after the one who read them, with the proper additional responses. Akiva stood apart, dressed in a very old robe, which had clearly been patched more than once. At his side stood his two sons. He was very straight and firm, and yet loosely quiet, joining the others in intoning repetitions of the reader's words.

She could not hear his voice and could not keep staring at him too long. But from that first glance she was aware of an extraordinary expression on his face, which held her spellbound throughout the duration of the prayer. She was not certain whether he even understood all that was being said—after all, he was unlearned. Nevertheless, there was something about him that made her feel that he did not need the words. For the first time in her life, she saw a person who seemed to be in a state of beatific union with God, a state of radiant contact with the object of his prayers. And it was not supplication; he was not appealing for help or forgiveness from his God, as one was able to see men doing in the Temple in the days of spiritual awakening. He was simply in a state of soul communion with the Creator of the Universe.

He was not a particularly good-looking person, yet she seemed to be aware of some glow or radiance, an inexpressible beauty on his sun-scorched and toil-lined face. Without being aware of it, a thought rose in her subconscious, that here stood one of the prophets. It was such a ridiculous thought she almost laughed aloud. An ordinary shepherd, an illiterate man of the soil—this Akiva, a prophet! She had seen many of the great men of Israel in her father's house; Rabban Gamaliel, son of the President of the Sanhedrin, who was then still quite young, but looked like a king; Rabbi Eliezer, the stern-faced aristocrat in every fiber of his being; Rabbi Yehoshua, the relatively small and ugly one, but brilliant and charming; and the other young leaders of Israel, brimming with wisdom and Torah. How their words came forth, like jewels fallen from the Holy Tablets of the Covenant. All those sages of Israel had a certain dignity and learning, with generations of Torah tradition behind them. At the same time, she remembered somehow that the prophet Amos, whose birthplace at Tekoa she knew quite well, had also been a simple shepherd. Could that Amos of ancient times have looked like this Akiva here?

At the end of the service, he seemed to be jolted back into the world. Again he was one of the common shepherds, humble and useful, but bereft of anything unique or outstanding. On the contrary, he was heavier of speech, more taciturn, almost as though lacking even the impoverished fund of expression of these men of the earth.

During the following days, she found herself wondering what it would be like if this man were one of the aristocracy. What would happen if a person of his caliber were to study? The idea was strange to contemplate. A shepherd was always a shepherd, and as such was at the very bottom of the scale of society, hardly worthy of being considered a witness in a legal action.

Before returning to Jerusalem, she saw Akiva once again. It was before evening, among a large group of field workers returning to the village from the harvest. They were a lively group, with a relatively large number of girls and women, as is usual among harvesters and gleaners. The yield was good this year, so that they were a good-humored, if tired, bunch of laborers, with some independent farmers thrown in—men and women talking together and joking with the well-known wit of Judea. Akiva stood out among them by his height and aloofness. He did not chat with the women or jest with them; his eyes were cast down like a scholar, although he did respond cheerfully enough whenever anyone greeted him.

The straggling group caught up with a few slower-moving old men and women who were gleaning in the fields already harvested. No one paid any attention to them, even though some of them were cripples who could barely keep up with the others. Only Akiva turned to one of the old women who was tottering under the weight of a large bundle of sheaves. "Mother," he said, as one addresses old women, "may

I carry your bundle?" The old women very happily turned over the load to Akiva and he put it on his back. It did not look so large and heavy on his back, and he walked alongside her deliberately and quietly, like a nobleman who knew how to be kind without any display. And again, Rachel found herself wondering how much he looked and acted like a true scholar of Torah, even though he was an empty vessel, an unlettered herdsman.

Jerusalem at festival time was an entirely different city. It was full of the preparations for the *Shavuot* festival, with many farmers on donkeys or in wagons streaming in, bringing their produce to feed the expected pilgrims, and shepherds with their flocks to provide the animals for the sacrifices at the Temple. Among these were the choice sheep and goats of the herds of Calba Savua—not only for the Temple sacrifices but also, as was natural at such huge gatherings of people, for sale and exchange. So that the city was filled with noise and bustle, and at the family mansion there were many distinguished guests. The father of the family sat at the head of the table, joyfully welcoming each new arrival and guest, no matter whether rich or poor. And he would even joke with some of the guests, to the point where it was almost embarrassing for the rest of the family.

"Do you know why they call us the sons of Calba Savua?" he would ask teasingly. And answer, "Because even a dog (*calba*) who comes to us, leaves satisfied (*savea*)."

Since the joke was in a way on himself, no one took offense, not even the poor, who jostled each other to get to the table; and there were, of course, plenty of rich men, too, some only too eager to be in high society, and others anxious to lay eyes on Rachel, the daughter of the house. The women were not in the same room, but the men knew they were nearby and probably watching them through the lattice work, so that the young men were careful to look well and be on their best behavior.

At the termination of one such evening's festivities, the father asked Rachel, "Did you notice the young man with curls sitting at my side? He is well spoken of. Comes of a famous family, the Pi Avi. His cousin was the high priest, Ishmael ben Pi Avi, and he himself is very rich, besides being quite learned and clever."

Of course Rachel had seen him, and she understood why he had been given the place of honor at the feast and where all this was leading to. But although he was no doubt a pleasant and intelligent young man, well-dressed in proper Jewish robes, and at the same time evidently familiar with the Hellenistic style of the day, she could not bring herself to say what was expected of her. Instead, she broke out in not atypical family manner: "True, he seems rich and well-bred and may even be a scholar, but what is he in himself? What kind of man is he? To me he's just a well-dressed dummy. Why, even a shepherd, like our Akiva, seems to have more to him. More . . . something."

Her father and some of her brothers who had in the meantime entered, all burst out laughing. That was a real Calba Savua answer. There were, of course, few matches more prestigious than the house of Pi Avi, with their high priests and their wealth, but, after all, the Calba Savuas were just as illustrious a family, if not more so, even if they never were connected by marriage with those noble houses of Jerusalem, and it tickled their vanity to think that one of their own shepherds was, in the daughter's eyes, preferred over the highly esteemed scion of the Pi Avi.

The feast of *Shavuot* that year was like all the great festivals of those days before the terrible disaster—with much rejoicing and amicability, in spite of the crowds of visitors and pilgrims. But right after the festival, life returned to its routine flow and Rachel, too, was glad to get back to the village.

When once again she saw Akiva, it seemed to her more important than ever to get to know him—perhaps because of the very different kinds of people she had met in Jerusalem. She found herself strolling toward the direction of the sheep pens, either by herself or in the company of an occasional companion or a servant maid. And since contact with the common people was not unusual for the members of the Calba Savua family, she was able to move freely and to converse with Akiva at leisure. She confirmed that in spite of his lack of learning, he had a profound wisdom of the heart. He would say things that, on her return home, made her wonder whether he had indeed intended to say so much in so few words. He was, on the whole, more tranquil and reconciled after the festival, and sometimes would even smile in the middle of speech. And, as with some rare people who do not have particularly handsome features, his smile brought

a new quality to his face; the whole personality was suddenly lit up
with an internal light, and he became heart-renderingly beautiful for
a moment.

In this way, a sort of contact was established between her and
this man who was probably twice her age and so vastly distant from
her world. She continued to call him by his first name, Akiva (as lords
and masters have the right to do) and he spoke to her respectfully as
"the lady," with his eyes modestly cast down. And when she realized
that this modesty was his general attitude to women, not only to her,
she also noticed that oddly enough, women were attracted to him.
But altogether, he seemed to be under some profound constraint in
everything he did, like someone who really knew the meaning of awe
and fear of Heaven. It showed itself in the way he performed the
mitzvot—even though his lack of education should have proven a
hindrance.

This brought home a contradiction she had preferred not to
notice. The sages and scholars of the day were not at all admired by
the poor and unlearned. What was worse, the feeling was mutual; the
sages and scholars had nothing but contempt for the uneducated
masses. True, the ignorant ones could not help feeling respect for the
Torah scholars, but it was tinged with a certain disappointment, even
hatred.

Once, when there had to be an inspection of the firstborn in the
sheep pen by the scholarly experts to see if they were unblemished,
she noticed that Akiva, like the other shepherds, tried to keep apart
from these scholars, and he wore a certain cold expression every time
he had to answer their questions. She could not restrain herself afterwards from asking him, "Akiva, what do you think of those scholars?"
And he answered, distinctly and more sharply than was his wont, "Give
me a scholar and I'll tame him like a donkey."

This odd combination of images made her laugh aloud, and she
asked him, "Why a donkey and not at least a dog?"

He replied without even a smile, "Because a dog bites but doesn't
break anything, while a donkey both bites and breaks."

The feeling of intense dislike behind the words made her shud-
der a little inwardly. Nevertheless, she continued questioning him.
"Why this hatred, Akiva?"

To this there was no sharp reply. He seemed to hesitate, search for words, and finally said, "If there really were any Torah in them, they should be like angels, while they . . ." and here he paused and then awkwardly continued, "they're not even decent human beings."

When she left him, she was rather shaken. Of course, respect for sages and scholars was so ingrained in her that she was shocked to the core by any assault on them. On the other hand, she knew that far too many scholars were not like the angels; they were hypocritical and bigoted and greedy. And again she let the thought rise to her mind, "What if this Akiva had learned Torah properly; what kind of a scholar would he be?" But this thought was instantly followed by the knowledge that the poor remained ignorant, and only the wealthy could afford to give their sons an education.

That very evening, at the feast, with the candles burning low and the diners lounging comfortably, all attention was focused around the learned conversation of the scholars, who, uninhibited by their usual hair-splitting dissection of the law and relaxed by the abundance of good food and the convivial atmosphere, could allow themselves to talk freely. One of the older of these pundits, whose rotund torso more than hinted at a certain leisurely indulgence in the pleasures of this world—all very clearly within the circumscribed rules of piety and good conduct, of course—told anecdotes about some of the outstanding sages of the generation. He spoke of Rabbi Eliezer, friend of the great saint, Rabban Yochanan ben Zakkai, and a man of great mystical power in his own right. It was said of him that he never lost a drop of all the wisdom that he imbibed.

"And do you know," the old pundit exclaimed, "that this selfsame Chiger ben Hyrcannus never studied at all in his youth? True, he came of a wealthy family, but he was raised to be a man of affairs, to be able to manage the family estate and finances. It was only after he came of age, when he was twenty-two, that he entered the *Bet Midrash* of Yochanan ben Zakkai. There his hunger for knowledge was so great he was able to be oblivious to the privation and hunger of the body for years on end, until he became one of the giants of the generation."

The loquacious old-timer continued to tell anecdotes of those former days, especially of fervor and zeal of study. Others there added details and additional facts and stories to those already known.

Amongst the latter, someone told about Hillel the Elder, how he learned Torah in the midst of great poverty—even when his own family was in dire distress. And one of the listeners remarked, "One cannot draw conclusions from the life of Hillel. He was already a scholar at a very early age, when he first came from Babylon."

Someone else interjected, "And what about the sages Shemaiah and Avtalyon? They started as unlearned sons of converts and still they rose to be leaders of the Sanhedrin! Who guided the people with knowledge and wisdom in the time of Herod, if not they? More than the priests or the scholars of the age."

Rachel listened to these latter comments with the utmost interest. Were they not somehow directed to her most secret thoughts, as though in answer to her reflections on the man Akiva? If he had been born of a noble family and could study, would he not be called Rabbi Akiva? It sounded ridiculous—Rabbi Akiva. And yet, she could not rid herself of an image of him, dressed differently, speaking differently, standing in front of an audience, teaching, lecturing. It seemed right for him to be wrapped in a prayer shawl like the scholars of the Torah, his eyes agleam, his whole bearing full of great dignity and power. If such were the man Akiva, he would be the man to whom she would like to be wed. The very thought made her tremble. It was madness! What outrageous thoughts rise to one's mind!

During the following days, these reflections, outrageous as they obviously were, did not leave her. She was drawn, as by a magnet, to the sheep pen where Akiva was to be found. She found herself watching him, unable to throw off the superimposed image of the scholar. And he, taller and stronger than the others, and far more youthful and agile than most of those younger than he, seemed to be oblivious of her. In fact, he paid scant attention to anyone, men or women, though many of the latter—shepherdesses and wives of herdsmen— were clearly attracted to him. To be sure, it was not only a physical force that emanated from him, it was a kind of light, something to which everyone joyfully surrendered. She wondered whether anyone else was aware of it as she was.

Was she in the grip of a fascination, or a love, that was out of bounds? Or was her feeling of strong certainty something beyond what could be interpreted as womanly passion? It was not a desire to possess or to be possessed. It was rather a need to do something for him, an irrepressible urge to save him from the oblivion to which he was doomed by the circumstances of his life.

She was delighted to observe that when she approached him, his face brightened and he listened to her without his usual reserve. On one occasion, after a few polite exchanges, she blurted out: "Akiva, why don't you go and study Torah?"

He lowered his eyes and answered, "But what have I to do with Torah? I am a simple person, a shepherd."

"But don't you want to know the Law of God? All its greatness and wisdom?"

He looked at her with a certain confusion. "My Lady knows that I am no longer young. And I can't even read."

"Don't you want to?" she persisted.

"People like me can't want anything that is beyond them," he said quietly and turned away to his work.

The next day, she continued to feel frustrated in a way she could not explain, though she could not help smiling to herself when she learned he had asked to be transferred back to the routine of the field shepherds, away from the precincts of the village. At this time of the year, however, they did not take the flocks to the desert; they brought them to the grain fields, which were rich with the leavings of the harvest. All the shepherds had to do was see to it that the sheep did not get near the orchards and vineyards on either side. Otherwise, they came home in the evenings, and so she was able to accost him again in a few days with the same question. "Why won't you try to study?"

This time he spoke more freely. "A few days of the field have given me a chance to think about this more seriously. Even if the heart is a stone in its hard resistance to wisdom, will not the soft drops of water of Torah, dripping on the rock, serve to crack it?"

She suddenly felt a sense of release, as though a great barrier had been removed. The pride of the House of Calba Savua and the modesty of her womanhood vanished in the rush of this happy release.

"Akiva," she exclaimed, "if you promise me that you will study Torah, I would like to be joined with you in the sacrament of marriage."

He could not conceal his astonishment. "But, my lady!" he stuttered, "much as I wish it . . ."

"Do not call me anything but Rachel," she pleaded.

"But that is impossible! I am a poor and miserable creature!" he said.

"You are nothing of the sort," was her prompt reply. "You shall be a light unto Israel, a man great among men, and I shall be your wife!"

And then, without waiting for his reaction, she added: "Wait for me tomorrow at sunset near the old olive tree by the well, and bring some money with you." Upon which she left him, with a look of gladness that made him realize that she had already triumphed somehow over all that was impossible for other men and women.

The next day, Rachel chose two of the older servants of the House of Calba Savua, faithful retainers who had known her from her childhood and were ready to do her bidding on all things, and asked them to accompany her. They found Akiva already waiting at the appointed spot, and she said to him: "I have brought witnesses."

The old servants had no idea what was meant, and she was not even certain whether Akiva was fully prepared. But she quickly ascertained that there was no need to underestimate his resolution. Once a decision was made, he would carry it out—simply and firmly, without arrogance or pride. He shook out the paltry contents from the purse he had brought, picked the silver coin, and handed it to her. Then he recited the accepted formula of marriage: "With this coin I sanctify thee ..."

The two servants stood there, dumbfounded. Unable to speak, they looked on unbelieving, while Rachel and Akiva completed the ritual and turned to one another with calm and glowing faces. As soon as they could, the servants took to their heels, as though frightened of what they had just witnessed.

There was no point in trying to keep the matter a secret. At first, the head of the family of Calba Savua was too astonished to be angry. When he asked whether it was true, he hardly expected her to respond simply, "Yes, I am married to Akiva, the shepherd."

His reaction was even more violent than she had anticipated. He shouted and cursed and filled himself with such passion, the words came out choked, scarcely articulated. She stood there quietly with downcast eyes, listening. "You, who could have married into any of the leading houses of Israel, dare to tell me that you chose some creature in the dirt, a shepherd!"

"He's not a creature in the dirt, even if he is a shepherd," she said calmly. "He is a man of noble mind and I know what I am doing."

Finally, realizing that she was as proud and adamant as any of them, the father disinherited her. "You are no longer my daughter; this is no longer your house. Go with him to your death!"

And so the two were banished to years of poverty and destitution in another village far away. But Rachel made Akiva abide by his promise. He studied. It is said that he learned to read with his sons. It is said that he made such phenomenal progress in all written and unwritten knowledge that few living men could be compared to him. Most wondrous of all, he became a great leader of Israel—the undisputed head of the Sanhedrin, where the law of the Jews and the vast body of postbiblical literature called the Talmud were formulated.

And of all the great teachers of the centuries of the Talmud period, scholars and sages of profound wisdom and purity of life, the greatest of them all was Rabbi Akiva. But that is another, a much longer story.

Much of what happened to Rachel remains in obscurity, as she herself preferred. Her joy was in his triumph, which, in barely twenty years, exceeded all that she could ever have imagined. Moreover, since Rabbi Akiva lived to a very ripe old age, he managed to impress on the law and the wisdom of Israel the power of a unique and rich personality, more so perhaps than any other single individual since Moses, the lawgiver himself.

It is recorded, too, that only after many years did the House of Calba Savua relent, long after he became the most illustrious and eminent of scholars and leaders of his generation.

PART V

THREADS

═ 21 ═

The Ari

The book that first made known the personality and life of Ha-Ari (The Lion) was written only a short time after his death. Called *Shivchei Ha-Ari* (*Praises of the Ari*), it attempted to relate whatever was known of the life of the Ari—as Isaac Luria was called—and to enhance the memory of him with stories of divination and miracles. Much was afterwards told and retold of his visions and revelations and of his ability to see the depths of the souls of his disciples—of Elijah the Prophet, who used to appear before him—of his power to cast out *dybuks* (demons), and other works of wonder that he performed. But the greatest wonder and the supreme miracle of the Ari is not in any of the marvels with which he may have impressed certain of his disciples—it is the historical fact of his achievement.

In the year 1570, a virtually unknown man came from Egypt to the city of Safed in upper Galilee. He lived in Safed only two years; he hardly wrote anything at all and merely taught a small group of disciples. At the end of these two years he died, being no more than thirty-eight years of age. But through the teachings of these two short years, the Ari, or Isaac ben Shlomo Luria, created an entirely new world. Our Divine Rabbi Yitzchak, as he has been called ever since, created a new system that in many ways changed Judaism, theoretically and historically. He is numbered among those few singular personalities who, by themselves, created an epoch, and without whose achievement it is impossible to understand the history of the years after them. What is incredible is the extremely short period of time in which this work was accomplished.

When the Ari came to Safed, he found an enchanting little city, a city almost as fascinating as himself. For some quite inexplicable reason, this obscure place in upper Galilee, which was even then older than recorded memory, had become in the sixteenth century the spiritual capital of the whole Jewish people. Some of the greatest Jewish minds of the age had begun to gather there, drawn from among those who had been forced out of Spain and other European countries as well as from the East. For several decades during the middle of the sixteenth century, so many learned scholars lived in Safed that the last bold attempt was made at that time to renew the institution of the Sanhedrin and establish a high court and governing body for the Jews of the world.

Among the outstanding figures gathered there were great codifiers of the Law, like Joseph Karo, author of the famous *Shulchan Aruch*; the last of the great poets of Spanish culture, like Shlomo Alkevitz, composer of the Sabbath hymn, "*Lechah Dodi*"; and Israel Najara, the poet. Also living in Safed were some of the writers of the profoundly moving books on moral action, works that had such a lasting influence on the people. Finally, there were the great kabbalists of the time, chief among them, Moses Cordovero.

The city was remarkable, however, not only because of the great men who lived in it, but also for the general atmosphere, which included all the inhabitants. It was a sort of dream city-state, a realization of certain spiritual ideals, almost Messianic, to which the people of Israel had always aspired. What characterized it was the extreme spiritual tension in which the whole city was absorbed. Artisans and merchants, scholars and converts just returning to Judaism, and people of all ages and backgrounds were devoted to studying the Torah and practicing the Torah. The city was full of synagogues, schools, and houses of study, all of them permeated with the belief that it was possible to bring all Jews to this level of responsiveness, and that the final redemption was imminent.

Just when this city was at the height of its spiritual flowering, Isaac Luria came and conquered it with his personality and gave it his teaching, which spread with amazing rapidity from this city—then the very center of Jewry—to all the scattered Jewish communities of the world, so that in a few years, there was hardly a single community, from Yemen to Russia, from Iraq to Germany, that had not been dazzled by the revelations of the Ari and did not accept them as the fulfillment of Jewish thought.

The Spanish expulsion had been a historic turning point not only politically and practically but also intellectually and spiritually. Besides being uprooted from a land where Jews had lived for a thousand years, countless Jews had failed to stand the test and had converted. These converts were merely a handful of renegades; they included people from the finest and most aristocratic families, those imbued with Jewish culture as well as a broad general culture. The disappointment of the Jewish community in the converts caused the Spanish émigrés to reexamine their relation to culture, in particular to religious philosophy. It appeared that the magnificent intellectual structure of their Judaized Aristotelian philosophy could not support them in times of trial. Thus, the old controversy about a satisfactory system of thought that would also provide an inner incentive for the life of Jewish piety and *mitzvot* was finally decided: the true values and ideas of the Jewish people should not be sought in systems foreign to it, but in its own esoteric teachings—the Kabbalah. In fact, within a generation or two after the expulsion from Spain, it was acceded that the Kabbalah was the closest thing to a theology that Judaism had.

The teachings of the Kabbalah go back to antiquity. It is said that even the "sons of the prophets" of the period of the First Temple developed certain mystical concepts that became the beginning of the Kabbalah. In any case, by the time of the Second Temple, we find many indications of systems of esoteric lore, such as *Ma'aseh Breshit* (*Concerning Genesis*) and *Ma'aseh Merkavah* (*Concerning the Chariot*), which were passed on orally, from one generation of wise men to the next. In time, Kabbalah (that which is received) gradually revealed more of itself; basic books were written and circulated, and outstanding figures at various times in history hinted at their relation to the Kabbalah and at the way in which they drew from it.

In the fourteenth century, the Zohar was discovered in Spain, and this book became the basic kabbalistic text. Although not at all organized in any systematic way, the Zohar still has a fairly clear system of its own, and much of the work of later generations has been nothing more than clarification, expansion, and development of the system. Altogether, the literature of the Kabbalah is vast, including thousands of books, but the fundamentals, to a degree, can be summarized briefly.

According to the Kabbalah, God acts on the world and reveals himself through ten aspects, or emanations, called the *Ten Sefirot.* These *sefirot* are the instruments through which the Divine fullness is revealed, God Himself being infinite and devoid of all limits and attributes in the world. The mutual relationship between these *sefirot* and their various combinations determine the essential manner and working of the world, and especially of men. More particularly, the people of Israel react to the union or separation or constellation of the various *sefirot*, with all their power for good and for ill. The evil in the world is derived from a distortion of certain forces, and they can, in turn, have a bad effect on the rest of creation. The Torah, or Jewish scriptures, is, on the whole, a revelation of the right way to behave so that the Divine plenty will flow into the reality of the world. The carrying out of the commandments (*mitzvot*) of the Torah acts in a concrete way to make the *sefirot* combine properly to cause this plenty to flow, while the transgression of the commandments is an act of absolute evil that adds strength to the forces of wickedness and pollution in the world. The esoteric teaching, the Kabbalah, is the inner part of the Torah that explains the metaphysical significance of every single movement and thought, and ultimately of the whole essence of the world. The man who attains genuine knowledge of the wisdom of the Kabbalah can, in certain respects, use the keys provided by this wisdom to reach a deeper and more complete closeness to God, and is able to change and "repair" the world in which he lives.

When the Ari came to Safed, he found the greatest systematizer of the Kabbalah, Moses Cordovero, still living there. Although the work of Kabbalah scholarship was at its height, the Ari had no new way of arranging the material, nor was there a new philosophic system to explain the Kabbalah. Modestly, he explained to his pupils that what he had acquired was the result of a long and wearying inner struggle and told of the joy of "doing" the *mitzvot*. Indeed, that which made him stand out was a new illumination, an independent and mystical revelation, and a new understanding of the Torah and the Kabbalah.

The system of thought propounded by the Ari did not merely add something to existing knowledge; it was an approach that, in its own way, encompassed and included previous forms of studying Torah and Kabbalah and provided a new interpretation. Thus, whole new fields of inquiry were opened up by the Kabbalah of the Ari. Its influence was so pervasive, it can be compared to the influence of the theory of relativity on modern physics.

The most thorough review of the Ari's revelation was set down in writing by his disciple, Chaim Vital. His book *Etz Chaim* (*Tree of Life*) contains thousands of the Ari's discoveries and interpretations, all written in the extremely concise and concentrated form of symbols traditional to kabbalistic rendering and with the addition of new symbolic methods. One of the most daring of his concepts was a new understanding of Creation, according to which the world was created by an act of Divine contraction. The infinite Divine light hid itself (contracted), and in the place that was formed by the absence of the light, there came into existence the place for the finite world. The world is therefore a reality drawing sustenance from the absence of a real being, and this nonbeing is derived from the infinite Divine power. The world is therefore encompassed and surrounded by the infinite essence of Divinity, while it, itself, consists of another kind of emanation of Divinity, in which the hidden and the revealed are intermingled. The Ari's system was in a sense a new theological approach in Judaism, emphasizing the somewhat pantheistic views of the Kabbalah, by which the world is seen to be included in the Divine but is not identical to Divinity. This system also provided a new interpretation to the meaning of evil, for at a certain stage in its coming into being, the world had to pass through a cataclysmic experience, "the breaking of the vessels." In other words, the *sefirot*, at an early phase of manifestation, did not fit together and were consequently shattered, and in their breaking up (the world of chaos), our world was created.

The world as we know it is a new combination and structure, made up of the contradictions and incompleteness resulting from the breaking of the vessels. The fragments of the higher world that was shattered, the "sparks" from the Divine light, are scattered throughout existence, some of them becoming part of the chain of Divine sovereignty in the world, or "chariot," and others falling out and becoming distorted, changing their form, and becoming the material world and even the forces of evil. Thus, it is the task of man to redeem these shattered fragments, or sparks, to find in them their higher significance, and to restore them to their Divine origin.

In fact, the entire course of life on earth toward its final redemption is the constant struggle to redeem the light that is hidden in the darkness, and when this process is completed, there will be revealed the true, whole structure. This is the meaning of the coming of the Messiah. Thus, according to this approach, the redemption of the sparks is the work of every Jew, and this work—which is done by keeping the Torah and doing the *mitzvot*, by ascetic self-discipline and moral restitution, by right intention in all one's deeds and mystical unity—this work is the decisive factor in redemption. Waiting for salvation is, therefore, not a passive state of being; it is rather the active doing of every person whose every thought and deed can contribute to the redemption of the universe. This is at least part of the reason for the enormous influence of the Ari's teachings on the daily life of Jews in subsequent generations. The entire people became active participants in the struggle for the "end of days."

It did not take long for the Ari's Kabbalah to become *the* Kabbalah, and everything that developed after that, like the Chasidic movement, grew out of it. His teachings were adopted by the common people—not only by the great minds who made a study of Kabbalah; it became the basis for a whole mystic literature and a broad moralist movement, and hundreds of new customs and prayers were inspired by it. Inevitably, it caused a change in perspective in the relations of man, and the world, the Torah, and the Kabbalah.

What of the Ari himself? He left us in writing no more than a few mystical poems, which are sung to this day with a certain awe on the Sabbath, and several Talmudic exegeses. Still, one can catch more than a glimpse of the man between the lines of what he wrote and in the disjointed descriptions of him by his disciples. A clear-eyed, saintly figure, whose look penetrated the unknown and who was at the same time extremely simple and straightforward in the small actions of daily life, seeing in them a great light. Together with this immense authority that he exercised was his profound humility, so natural to one for whom everything was open and manifest, so that he never seemed to have occasion to think about himself or his task in the same way that he used to tell about his visions and thoughts. Like a Moses, he stands at a crossroads in the history of the people, holding in his hand the key to the way through which the generations pass.

22

Religion and Mystical Powers

Our generation has been inclined to approach religion through psychology, to see religion as a problem of the human soul, essentially unrelated to the concrete world of reality. In this general modern approach, two different attitudes are apparent. One of them thinks of religion as an insubstantial dream, something the intellect and the emotions consider otherworldly. People who have such an attitude may even admire religion (or adhere to it) as one admires a work of art, and this is the way they would like to understand it or feel about it. Also, the use of religion for subsidiary purposes, or the lukewarm tolerance shown to it, all come from a view of religion as something pallid and indistinctly imaginative, a feeling that believers are dreamers of odd, romantic fantasies.

On the other hand, there are people who seek a certain reality in religion and in doing so reach different sorts of supernatural experiences—inner experiences that give one a feeling of reality, accompanied by perceived unnatural phenomena, which science cannot (or does not wish to) explain. In short, a kind of metapsychology, which has become a modern psychological substitute for metaphysics. The mystical experience and the supersensual experience have become matters of keen interest among broad circles of intellectuals who hope to find in such revelations of the soul something new and firm to cling to. They look for something beyond the known and the commonplace, which will provide man with the chance to contact God; they want to experience religiosity directly, without religion.

In any case, this contact with the subconscious (or if one prefers, with the superconscious) makes modern man feel that he is in touch with the untouchable beyond, with God. Then the religious reality seems clear and apparent, almost substantial enough for scientific experimental confirmation. And God himself is made more real, so to speak, with the assistance of the most scientific investigation and statistical analysis.

With all of this, there is room for another reflection. These depths and heights of mystical experience open up vast realms of being, raise man to a level beyond and higher than himself toward...what? And indeed, does this inspired sensation, which overwhelms all the other sensations of the being and which seems to be altogether too overwhelming, does it truly lead to something? Does it lead to God?

In other words, the question being raised is: What is the relation between religion (as the expression of the bond to God) and the various mystical experiences? Are they identical, do they supplement each other, or do they belong to entirely different levels of being? More specifically, these questions lead us to inquire into the place of mysticism in the Jewish tradition.

In Judaism there is nothing extraordinary or unacceptable about extrasensory experience. It is quite natural for people to have the capacity to rise above the usual human level of functioning and to reach a higher spiritual consciousness. Judaism even recognizes different forms and levels of this capacity, such as prophecy, magic, and mystical power.

The attitude toward each of these various forms, however, is very different. Prophecy in Judaism is a basic source of religious knowledge, and the prophet is a person on the highest level of being. On the other hand, magic is strictly forbidden, on pain of death. What interests us here is the attitude Judaism takes toward the superhuman capacity for the mystical experience—that which is still very individual and fairly common and which does not properly belong to either prophecy or magic.

A story in the Talmud aptly illustrates this. Once, Rabbi Chanina ben Dosa went to study Torah with Rabbi Yochanan ben Zakkai. Rabbi Yochanan's son fell ill and Rabbi Chanina asked for mercy for him, and he lived. Rabbi Yochanan said, "If Yochanan had beaten his head and held his legs all day long, he would not have been noticed." His wife then asked him, "And is Chanina greater than you?" To this he replied, "No, except that he is like a slave before the King and I am like a prince before the King" (Berachot 34b). From this it can be seen that in the encounter between the two types—Rabbi Yochanan ben Zakkai, the great sage, the superior personality, and Rabbi Chanina ben Dosa, gifted with the supernatural faculty for healing and for other extraordinary things—Rabbi Yochanan is by no means able to do what Rabbi Chanina does so easily. This does not mean that Rabbi Chanina is greater than Rabbi Yochanan; he is merely gifted with a certain talent or capacity to make contact with God, which makes it possible for him to perform these miracles. It does not make him "a prince before the King"; he remains "a slave before the King" (which may even be the nature of his extraordinary power). In other words, there is an evaluation here of the essence of the mysterious power to exceed the limits of nature. Admitting that it is truly a marvelous power, it is not considered one that necessarily makes the bearer of it superior to ordinary mortals.

As is apparent, the relationship of Jewish tradition to mystical powers (if we can call this assortment of supernatural forces that) is varied. It is respectful, but so reserved in its admiration as to hint at a certain scorn. This is quite in contrast to the relation to prophecy. Indeed, a sharp and fundamental difference is evident between the honor and esteem shown the prophet, and the reserved and distant respect for the person of mystical powers. For a proper understanding, therefore, it is important to note the main differences between these two phenomena, which seem, nonetheless, to be so similar. Outwardly, in fact, and even in terms of the visible effect, there may be little to distinguish the prophet from the magician or the possessor of supernatural powers. Both of them do things extraordinary, that exceed the limits of the natural. The difference becomes apparent only when one penetrates to the source: Where does the marvelous power come from? This is the profoundly basic difference.

Prophecy is an abundance that comes to man from without, from a higher source. This supernatural power is not necessarily a quality of his own being (although it may be), but he is essentially dependent on something external and objective, which is the source of the power. On the other hand, the possessor of supernatural powers who is not a prophet, is himself the source of this power, which is subjective and given to his free will. From this point of view, and from every other point of view, this capacity or talent may be likened to any other human talent—like painting or composing. The capacity to rise above the limitation of nature is given to people with a special gift for it; this gift, however, can be found in almost every type of person, irrespective of any other quality or trait. In other words, prophecy is an expression of supernatural influence coming from some source above and greater than the world, while other kinds of supernatural phenomena are expressions of human capacities for this sort of power, used within a personal framework of source and action.

In the literature of the Kabbalah and Chasidism, it is assumed that every human being has some capacity for making contact with a world above the concrete world, and that the way to the supernatural is available to everyone at a particular level. At the same time, there are exceptional individuals and exceptional revelatory situations in which this contact is much more intimate and meaningful. The supernatural capacity itself is a part of the whole concept of *madregot* (steps or grades). The term *madregot* comprises the various forms of supernatural revelation, vision, clairvoyance, telepathy, miracle, healing, release from the physical, and the like. The relation to all these *madregot* (though they may also be the basis for "miracles") is like that of the Talmud: an attitude of respect and deference, together with a certain suspicion and disdain. Thus, although *madregot* were considered valuable means, they were never felt to be the end in themselves. A person could be a miracle-worker and still not be great as a person; the *madregah* and the person are not always on the same plane. Much has been written about situations in which a person receives *madregot* without an accompanying elevation of personality or being, so that the *madregot* may later destroy the soul of the person who receives them. And clearly, these distinctions have to be made. The *madregot* are as marvelous as any other spiritual gifts, capable of bringing much benefit and grace. But if they are not used correctly, they can become the very opposite.

Many stories have been told about this, among them the tale of the rabbi who was discovered to be able to "see" at a distance when he was only a child. When he reached the age of six, his uncle, a *tzadik*, said to him, "I shall bless you to rid you of this holy spirit, because it will impair your Jewishness. Then, when you are thirty years of age and want the *madregah* back, I shall return it to you, with added powers" (*Megillat Sefarim*, Introduction to *Zohar Hai*). This shows the double attitude toward the supernatural—respect and suspicion—for if it is not clearly and directly Divine, it is very liable to be abused. There are many stories of people who were granted *madregot* in order to "confuse" them, for to those who do not know how to use them, the *madregot* become a very disturbing factor in real life. Thus there is the story of one who, on returning from his teacher, felt that he was being visited by marvelous higher powers. (This is not so extraordinary when one is immersed in scriptural study and concentration.) The sudden appearance of the gift shook him completely, for he felt it was not of his own choosing nor under his control and could therefore mislead him into an undesirable course; so he stood under a tree in the forest and prayed to God to take it from him.

If we thus distinguish prophecy from supernatural power by declaring the former to be Divine and the latter human, it is also correct to add that there is another, inward aspect to the difference. If *madregot* are human powers or gifts, then, as with all the faculties of man, they are ambivalent—good or bad as circumstances make them. Therefore, the greater the power or talent, the more dangerous, too, with as great a potential for destructive as for constructive action. Such an evaluation of human qualities and spiritual gifts means that there is no way of judging them in terms of good and evil (or anything else for that matter) and that to be kind or cruel, clever or proud, is merely a reaction to a particular context and has no intrinsic value. Thus, for example, kindheartedness, in certain instances, may be a bad quality; cleverness, a sin; pride, a pure and noble impulse; and so on. Everything that is human is, in itself, incapable of having only one meaning, or perhaps any "meaning" at all. The human is that which can take on meaning—it has meaning only in potential, in itself, intrinsically— but which is transparent and without content or meaning.

In contrast to the lack of intrinsic content on the part of the human, the Divine revelation is qualified by a very definite and fundamental content. This content may be hidden or open, pleasant or hateful to us, as the case may be, but it always has the Divine mark of truth and inner necessity. And the prophet is essentially, by the nature of his being, a messenger of God, who has to speak, and his speech, therefore, has content, which is Divine. The prophet is compelled to speak out; the one who possesses supernatural powers does not have to say anything. Prophecy is an expression of a Divine idea and the Divine will; a vision that is not prophecy is an expression of a hidden human force that has no idea or will of its own.

What is the relationship of these mystical powers to religion? One might think the answer is fairly straightforward: Mysticism of this sort has no essential connection with religion, since religion has a Divine content based largely on prophetic revelation, whereas mystical powers are human in origin and have no content of their own. Even though mystical revelations do present manifest matters hidden to the ordinary man, they cannot reveal more than what is already known or create a new content. Remaining as they are, human, they cannot even give meaning to other (higher) contents and are certainly unable to reach the Divine. In this respect, it has been said that the vision of a pillar of fire or a burning bush by Moses may be considered a wondrous experience—but a human experience in the sense of being a trial of God.

This is not to say that there is no use for these powers, or that mystical manifestations have no value. They are only worthless in themselves, when they are isolated from all else; but when they are properly understood, they can guide the soul better than any other forces in life. Here, too, as with all else, it is the use and direction of a faculty that determines its value: It may be turned one way to fantasy and empty vision or another way toward God. The decisive value lies with consciousness, the capacity of a person to make the right choice, because anyone who is gifted with the ability to see more and to act on a wider scale than ordinary people must discriminate continually and must decide where he wants to go. The mystical power is a higher power and is needed by a person on a higher level, who knows how to use it to the best advantage.

$=23=$

Chasidism and Psychoanalysis

At first glance it seems strange to join these two terms, Chasidism and psychoanalysis. In a sense, it is the union of two opposites: Chasidism, every aspect of which is religious—its inner drives as well as its outer forms, all are religious manifestations—and psychoanalysis, whose totally secular purpose, according to all its schools (save, perhaps, that of Jung), is clearly and most definitely nonreligious, if not antireligious.

It is not only the conflict of purposes, however, that creates the impression of dissonance, for no less striking is the difference in essence and direction. Chasidism is not, in any sense, a system of analysis of the psyche, nor is it an exact and defined discipline in the Western European sense. Its freshness and uniqueness are not to be viewed as elements in an ordered discipline, but rather as products of the exuberance and improvisation of the soul, itself, in its struggle with the problems presented to it by life. Psychoanalysis, despite elements of the purely hypothetical and the overemphasis of the uninhibited imagination, must be considered a scientific discipline. It is to be so considered since, at its very best, it strives to be scientific by formulating its postulates about many subjects clearly and comprehensively. An image of man, or at least an artificial construction that should approximate it, must be reached through psychoanalytic research. Chasidism, with its contempt for forms and formalities that lack content, never attempted to summarize its approach to the human soul by any definition or extensive analysis that would present, so to speak, man in his totality. Chasidism offers only random striking remarks on the theme, but these often penetrate to the depths of specific problems with all the vigor and insight of revelation; and yet, these are struck off only *en passant*, and never aim to derive patterns or rules from these specifics nor to draw them to any conclusion. Even the *Tanya*, the best organized of all the Chasidic books that treat matters of the psyche, which might seemingly give the impression of a truly systematized work, is found to be, after careful consideration and study, nothing more than a collection (edited in an amazingly well-ordered pattern) of minor, random inquiries into specific personal problems (as is, indeed, noted in the introduction).

This essential disparity renders ludicrous any attempted comparison of Chasidism and psychoanalysis—in short, at first glance there seems to be no point of contact between the two by which to compare or contrast them. To compare these two subjects would be similar to comparing darkness and sweetness, namely, the comparison of two totally dissimilar elements.

If, indeed, there is to be a correlation between these two systems, it cannot come by the usual comparison and contrast of two equal components. The only possible correlation is that comparison that renders one element central and the other peripheral to it, the peripheral being auxiliary to the center. This relationship would disclose many complementary and instructive features inherent in both disciplines.

Obviously, it is possible to set up the pattern of correlation between Chasidism and psychoanalysis in one of two divergent ways. One may treat psychoanalysis as the focal point and thereby render Chasidism a source from which to gain illuminating insights and further psychoanalytical observations. This would lead to an analytic study (Freudian or otherwise) of Chasidism. It is, however, also possible to arrange the correlation in an opposite manner, that is, making Chasidism the center and have it draw its points of reference, explanations, and systematic clarifications from specific problems in psycho-analysis.

The discovery of the unconscious is, undoubtedly, the basic element in all schools of psychoanalysis. The assumption that there exists in the psyche of man certain factors that operate without his being consciously aware of them but that, nevertheless, influence his conscious life, is fundamental to all analysis of man's psyche, which undertakes to reach to the roots of problems and not merely to their outward manifestation.

Freud understood that even before his time, there existed at least a basic awareness (though blurred and unconscious) of the existence of the unconscious. Certain oft-repeated expressions in the literature testify to the fact that in Chasidism there existed an awareness of this aspect of the soul. These expressions of the unconscious are noted in the characteristic manner of the Chasidic approach to the human psyche—profundity, lucidity of thought, and an overpowering reluctance to draw conclusions from random statements, or to generalize them into a systematic pattern. One example must suffice: There is a long-standing awareness of the exegetical difficulties that surround the verses describing the announcement of the birth of a son to Abraham and Sarah (Genesis 18:12–16): "And Sarah laughed within herself," immediately followed by, "Then Sarah denied, saying: 'I laughed not.'" The author of the Chasidic book titled *Sefat Emet* comments: "Sarah laughed inwardly—in her soul—she herself being unaware (unconscious) of her laughter and, therefore, when the Lord admonished her she denied it, since she was totally unconscious of her laughter."

The awareness of the unconscious is not limited in Chasidism (nor in Judaism in general) to a few chance or random remarks. However, the context in which these comments about the unconscious are made would not by themselves be very instructive, and were it not that psychoanalysis had defined and elucidated these terms, we might never have been able to ascertain them from our sources alone. The importance of this type of comparison for Chasidism lies in our confronting it with a scientific discipline with established terminology, by which it explains and defines the general concepts that have yet remained undiagnosed.

Jewish law differentiates between these different levels of responsibility as regards transgression: a conscious sin is an act committed with full consciousness and sane mind; an inadvertent act and sin is one performed despite one's will (either being forced by another party or lacking means of opposition).

Generally speaking, the law permits man (courts) to punish the offender only in acts committed with full awareness, and excludes from any type of punishment an act committed under duress (accident). Inadvertent acts from an intermediate category. Although man, generally, is not punished by human courts for a transgression committed unwittingly, nevertheless, he must offer a sacrifice to repent for his sin and, thus, the claim of inadvertence, according to Jewish law, does not automatically entitle one to forgiveness. This approach, however, is fully explained after clarification of the terms with the aid of psychoanalysis.

Although man may have committed an inadvertent sin without his full awareness he is, nevertheless, to some degree responsible. That is to say, that portion of man's psyche that operates in cases of forgetfulness and inadvertence (what psychoanalysis calls the unconscious), is not an entity separate from man but is rather an integral part of him. Although it is not possible to bring man to court for deeds of which he himself is unaware, he must, nevertheless, confess them before the Lord—for this inadvertent act discloses a segment of his will. (Similarly, the Midrash on this subject: A man who transgressed inadvertently must be concerned not with that one transgression but with the many that will follow in its wake. That is, the one transgression, though inadvertently committed, is one demonstration of the general inclination of that man.)

In Chasidic literature there is manifest a full description of the image of man that in many aspects parallels that of Freud (i.e., man's unending inner tension between the conscious and the unconscious). The *Tanya* places man within a complicated pattern of multiple personalities and makes a clear demarcation between the *I* (ego) of man and his conscience. According to the *Tanya* the essence of life is the struggle between the *I*, which is fundamentally unconscious, and the normal conscious self. In the opinion of the *Tanya*, however, the unconscious is not one-dimensional as it is with Freud and Adler but complex and involved, for man's unconscious self is composed of base animalistic elements as well as sublime and divine aspects. Man is actually the composite of these two aspects of the psyche (or as the *Tanya* expresses it, these two souls), and the conscious element is nothing more than the battleground on which the infinite conflicts of man are revealed.

The consciousness of man is a small fortress beleaguered by the subconscious and the superego, both of which are desirous of conquering and subduing it. The literature of Chasidism brilliantly formulates the idea that the conscious external phenomenon of man's life is not at all to be identified with his true being. The new psychological image described in the *Tanya* is that of the average man, who reckons not with his consciousness alone, which may be absolutely good in thought and action, but with his real image. His essential ego consists of those aspects of his psyche that do not act overtly on his consciousness. (Clearly, this unconscious element is not totally hidden from the average man himself.) Only in the imperfect saint is there to be found a part of the soul that is absolutely unconscious, for his consciousness and the more profound areas of his psyche are all directed toward the good. Nevertheless, there yet remains a concealed part of the psyche affixed to the sensual.

In order to prove that a person who has not attained total perfection is not totally free of evil, the author of the *Tanya* adduces several proofs, dreams comprising one source of his proof. That dreams—at least some of them—are an expression of man's desires, was understood by the ancients, who recognized not only that man sees (in his dreams) his own general reflections, but also that he specifically sees those thoughts that are most deeply embedded within him. One formulation of this is to be found in the Bible: "And it shall be as when a hungry man dreameth, and, behold, he eateth, But he awaketh, and his soul is empty; Or as when a thirsty man dreameth, and behold, he drinketh, But he awaketh, and behold, he is faint, and his soul hath appetite" (Isaiah 29:18).

In Chasidism these factors are more closely analyzed. As already mentioned, use is made of the phenomena of dreams as proof for the existence of suppressed desires in man. For example: "Even while asleep, man should be aware before Whom he sleeps . . . this is an even greater feat (than he who only recognizes Him while awake). And as I learned about the verse 'and as Jacob dreamed' the superiority of man can be detected in his dreams; while he slumbers and is inert, he reflects only on 'God who stands over him.' Indeed, few saints can boast of this." (*Tidkat Hatzadik*, Chapter 3).

According to Freudian theory, the unconscious is identical with the subconscious; that is, the unconscious aspect of the soul is seed-bed for everything base and evil in man (if we may use popular terminology). Chasidism, which also posits an unconscious element in man, sees it as composed of an additional element—the supreme element (or as we may call it, the superconsciousness)—made up of the sublime inner personality of man, which exists (consciously or not) in every individual. Much of the optimism and drive observable in man, according to the *Tanya*, is based on the awareness of the existence of a collective unconsciousness of the Jewish people, which may elude a person during his entire lifetime but which, at moments of crisis, is aroused and may overwhelm him, evoking a total revolution in his character and conduct. Aside from his superconscious element of the soul, Chasidism is fully cognizant of the subconscious in man, and it seeks above all to understand and to define the prime operative force in his soul.

Chasidism is unique, especially in all matters pertaining to its psychology, in its obvious lack of design and formulation; and its imprecision here, as in other fields, is quite manifest. Therefore, it was inconceivable for Chasidism to develop a theory that would base all of man's inner drives on one key motivation, and that would attempt to derive from it other psychological tendencies. Nevertheless, it does select a very small number of forces from which all the others derive; as a matter of fact, there are two prime drives: the sex drive and the expansion and dominance of the ego.

Rabbinic literature already classified the sex drive as a fundamental drive of prime import, when it states "there is no guardian in matters of sex"—thereby considering no one above suspicion (regardless of status and character) in matters of sex. (There is, by the way, no other sin for which every individual is classified as suspect.) Moreover, in rabbinic literature, "sin" *per se* refers to sexual waywardness. This approach, so evident in rabbinic literature, is further elucidated in the literature of Chasidism. Not only does it clarify the roots of this drive and the psychological phenomena accompanying it, but it reserves a central place only to those urges derived from it. Rabbi Nahman of Bratzlav and his followers speak of this drive as the "all embracing urge," for in their opinion this drive includes all the others. There is much made about the prime position of this drive in the structure of human drives. It is a drive that creates and is created by all others. "This is the drive that contains everything human, for it creates the human."

Although the comparison is only approximate, Chasidism also points to pleasure as the prime force in all creation. The primary urge in everything in the world of the sensual and the rational, as well as the most supreme will, is pleasure, the source of all, the unequivocal motive. However, pleasure in Chasidism is not a specific psychological entity, but rather includes the fundamental quality of the entire universe, since it actually makes up the deepest internal basic level in man's psychological structure—in essence, the soul itself. Alongside the inner recesses of the unconscious (or partially conscious) present in every individual as the expression of self-awareness, Chasidism also points to the drive of dominance—the drive to power and rule, which is often identical with pride and individuality.

Chasidism demonstrates that the drive for power is similar to the urge for pleasure (which is, in fact, the root of the sex drive) since it, too, is an all-embracing universal drive, operating on the highest levels of existence and reaching to the lowest. The drive for power is identical, according to Chasidism, with the essential expression of the inner will of the soul (or that of the world)—an intrinsic force that cannot be eradicated. This drive produces distortions and exaggerations of itself, resulting from a perversion of inner existence. Pride is this very basic awareness greatly exaggerated or is, perhaps, a more subtle expression of this feeling of self-awareness (which acts on man with greater intensity because it is concealed from him). It is an exaggerated feeling of personal existence, leading to hate, envy, and rivalry—all of which develop because the ego is unable to circumscribe itself and overreaches it essential limits, thereby affecting others.

Chasidism is not merely a theoretical doctrine, for in every field of its endeavor it prefers to ameliorate a condition, and therefore, when it deals with psychological problems, it does so not as a theoretical speculation but out of desire to mend psychological deficiencies and further existing positive features of the psyche.

A unique method was developed, in the past, to rid oneself of the evil in the soul—the method of suppressing to the utmost all negative drives by fighting them with every possible means and hoping thereby to destroy every lust and vice. Physical self-castigation, such as fasts and flagellations, was not meant simply as self-punishment (for the purpose of penance or for other reasons) but also as a way of suppressing the sensual and, thereby, removing every evil urge and desire.

As one of its first principles, Chasidism emphasized its strenuous opposition to both the theory and practice of asceticism and denounced this experience of self-renunciation and the "contempt" for the sensual, which the earlier ascetics developed. It strove to exalt and not destroy all things, including the material world, asserting that the reason for asceticism's failure to attain its goal was that the attempt to suppress drives does not result in their cessation, but leads to their taking root in deeper levels of the soul.

Chasidism followed a different course—the path of sublimation—by assuming (and this is a cardinal principle in its ethics) that the difference between good and evil is not a qualitative one, but a difference of object. The basic inclinations of man—good and evil—are identical. But man can change the direction, of his inclinations, and by reorientating them toward the good, attain to saintliness. Since the difference between good and evil lies in direction it is quite obvious that Chasidism should conclude that the more profoundly an individual experiences his various desires, the greater his opportunity (after redirecting these drives) of becoming a saintly individual.

Various solutions to many involved problems in the process of sublimation were elaborated and suggested, but once again, as in other areas, Chasidism never presented a comprehensive system, only basic principles and incomplete outlines, which it never fully explained. Nevertheless, one of the ways of "mending the soul" (*tikun hanefesh*), often quoted in Chasidic literature, is the oral confession before a teacher; that is, the *Chasid* goes to his rabbi and lays before him all of his problems and cares. This oral confession is considered one of the highest rungs in the healing and amelioration of an ailing soul (with no reference to the advice or instruction received from the rab-

bi, this being an entirely separate matter). The similarity to the practice of psychoanalysis is striking. It is essential to note that this oral
confession is in no way considered a religious rite, and is basically not
a confession of sins. This is a down-to-earth, very practical outpour-
ing of the soul, a self-analysis of various problems of the soul, in the
presence of the rabbi, who guides and directs the self-analysis.

This comparison, for all its brevity and tentative character, allows
certain conclusions. The relationship between Chasidism and psychoanalysis is bizarre since, despite their similarity, the conclusions each
one draws are mutually contradictory. If we examine this question more
closely, we discern that the reason for the difference lies essentially
in the difference between their respective fundamental attitudes and
points of departure.

The approach of psychoanalysis is, to all intents and purposes,
secular and materialistic and, therefore, it views the sensual drives of
the psyche as primary. This being its starting point, it undertakes to
build a structure of values on the basis of primary drives. Its approach
is to satisfy the subconscious to the fullest extent possible without
reference to sublimation.

Chasidism, on the other hand, views reality from the opposite
side, even though it is fully aware of the existence of the unconscious
and knows its content. (Indeed, the view that "man's heart is evil from
his youth" is already the Torah's view, and certainly the Torah expressed the need to triumph over the evil urge and redirect it to good.)
But despite its awareness of the existence of the evil urge, Chasidism
does not view man in his essence as an evil being, but attempts to
make of man a higher entity, one who will lift up his noble possibilities
to a loftier level by sublimation. One might say the goal of Chasidism
is to unite the superconsciousness and the unconscious within man.

The comparison itself suffices to demonstrate the essential truth
of the Chasidic doctrine concerning the difference between good and
evil, that difference lying not in essence but in orientation, in the interpretation man gives to his basic drives. It is evidently possible, according to Chasidism, to continually attempt to convert evil to good by
a change of direction; it is certainly possible for it to make use of
psychoanalytical procedures and methods. While Chasidism's orientation may contradict that of psychoanalysis, it could greatly benefit

from the vast materials the latter has assembled. For this psychological discipline, stripped of its philosophical garb, remains a practical system whose various techniques and discoveries may be employed by a system that aims to elevate the brutish in man.

= 24 =

Death Shall Be Defeated

It is one of the many paradoxes of Jewish history that whereas the Jewish people have known premature and unnatural death as a constant companion, probably more than any other nation, culturally and spiritually the Jews are remarkably unpreoccupied by death and the hereafter.

In the Exodus from Egypt, the Jews left a vast civilization that was obsessed with death and that devoted much spiritual energy and material resources to preparations for the hereafter. This cult of death was one of the evils from which Moses led the Children of Israel, guiding them toward a more wholesome outlook that put the stress on life.

The Jews never equated death with holiness. Cadavers, far from being treated as objects of sanctity and adoration, are regarded as impurities from which one must keep a distance. Of all the many forms of ritual defilement listed in Jewish law, the gravest is that caused by a corpse. And when a Jew, like a *kohen* in the synagogue or a priest in the Temple, is called upon to serve in holy functions, he has to take special precautions to avoid contact with death in any and every form. The same is true of the *nazir*, who voluntarily undertakes to follow an especially holy way of life. In Judaism, holiness is first and

192

foremost the sanctity of life. Where life abounds, holiness is at hand. "Life" is a synonym for all that is most exalted in Creation. One of the names of God is "the God of life." The Torah is described as "the Torah of life." The Torah itself speaks of "life and goodness" as of one and the same thing. "Living waters" are seen as a source of purity. It is thus not surprising that the Jews rejected all forms of the myth of the Dead God. Death is the negation of the Divine reality in all its manifestations.

The Jewish belief that "this world is the antechamber to the next" may well have inspired massive Gentile speculation on heaven and hell and purgatory, but, by contrast, Jewish literature and tradition engage in scant exploration of paradise. Judaism makes no attempt either to forget death or to smother it in false jubilation. "The dead praise not the Lord, nor do they who go down into the silence of the grave. But we will bless the Lord from this time forth and for ever more, Hallelujah!" proclaims the Psalmist; characteristically, he disdains death, but he does not, he cannot, ignore it. The natural reluctance to accept death is expressed in the conviction that the truly righteous do not actually die but "depart" or "ascend" to a different realm. Thus, Maimonides writes of Moses: "There occurred in him what in other people is called death." It is said that "the righteous live on even in death, while the wicked are already dead when alive." Here again we have the parallelism—goodness is life and life is goodness, whereas evil is death and death is evil.

The Jewish approach to death is that it is a problem to be solved by and for the living. Death, preparation for death, and mourning are all worked into the fabric of day-to-day life. The essence of mourning is not sorrow for the deceased, but rather compassion for the surviving relatives in their loneliness. "Weep not for the dead man who has found rest," said an ancient eulogist, "but weep for us who have found tears." Jewish law prescribes that all eulogies made at funerals are to life and to the surviving members of the family. Grief is defined within, as it were, concentric ripples of diminishing intensity. The ripple on the first day of death is the strongest and most critical. Also powerful, but somewhat less so, is the first week of mourning. The succeeding periods are the first thirty days and the first twelve months, getting less and less grievous. At all times, precautions are taken against unseemly outbursts of violent keening. There is an express injunction against self-mutilation as a token of sympathy for the dead, let alone suicide in order to accompany the dead.

The personal confrontation with death, perhaps the harshest test of a personality and of a culture, is of course frequently encountered in Jewish lore. The many variations on this theme all have one feature in common—the encounter with death is looked upon as a major moment of life, which must be met worthily. Unlike many other cultures, Judaism does not accept that any particular kind of death is glorious *per se*—with one exception, to which we shall return.

Even in biblical times, a hero's death was not regarded as a glorious achievement; the ideal was for a man to "sleep with his fathers" and to pass on the wealth of his life and strength to those who come after him. A special tome called *The Book of Departure*, which describes the deaths of the fathers of the nation, harps constantly on the need to maintain a calm, confident stance in the face of the enemy death, to stand up to the Angel of Death and to be prepared in all tranquillity to return "the bond of life to the Lord your God."

Nevertheless, there is one exceptional kind of death, Jews do consider glorious, and which we term "sanctification of God's Name." Martyrdom endured for the sake of sanctifying God's Name is a public act performed in the midst of the holy community, whereby the sacrifice imparts an added sense of sanctity to the living. When he is martyred in this way, the Jew embraces death for the sake of the survivors, so that their dedication to the Jewish way of life may be strengthened.

In this context, we can understand the extraordinary character of the *Kaddish*. Initially this ancient payer had no connection with death or the dead, and was an ordinary part of the liturgy. Only at a relatively late period—in the early Middle Ages when mounting persecution brought frequent martyrdom—did the *Kaddish* become a death prayer. However, it is devoid of even the slightest insinuation of reproach to God, who is throughout praised and glorified and sanctified.

The basic attitude of Judaism to death, which, it is said, was ushered in with Adam's expulsion from the Garden of Eden, is that it is not a natural, inevitable phenomenon. Death is life diseased, distorted, perverted, diverted from the flow of holiness, which is identified with life. So side by side with a stoic submission to death, there is a stubborn battle against it on the physical and cosmic level. The world's worst defect is seen to be death, whose representative is Satan. The remedy is faith in the resurrection. Ultimately, "death and evil"— and the one is tantamount to the other—are dismissed as ephemeral. They are not part of the true essence of the world, and, as the late Rabbi Kook emphasized in his writings, man should not accept the premise that death will always emerge the victor.

In the combat of life against death, of being against nonbeing, Judaism manifests disbelief in the persistence of death, and maintains that it is a temporary obstacle that can and will be overcome. Our sages, prophesying a world in which there will be no more death, wrote: "We are getting closer and closer to a world in which we shall be able to vanquish death, in which we shall be above and beyond death."

25

Religion
in the State of Israel

One of the interesting features about religion in Israel and, in a way, about the State of Israel itself, is the extreme variety of views on the subject held by people who look on from the outside. There are those who claim that Israel is basically a theocracy, only slightly camouflaged as a modern democratic state and that the real power is in the hands of a clerical caste who are assisted by, or who have under their dominion, the political leaders of the country. At the opposite extreme are those who feel that Israel is not only "un-Jewish," lacking in Jewish content and values, but that it is an atheistic country, a political entity in which religion has inferior status and less influence than it does in almost any other country in the world.

Oddly enough, both of those points of view are, to a degree, correct. To be sure, they are also based on shallow observations of the conditions in the country, making no effort to penetrate to the deeper Jewish aspects of the situation as a whole. On one hand, the first category of onlookers sees that the State is based on its Jews, and, to survive, has to maintain a dominance of the Jewish religion and of the Jewish people over and above other religions and peoples. Thus, they see that the State regards Saturday as the official day of rest, and

196

the Jewish holidays are the official holidays of the State. The sacred tongue of the Bible has become the language of the land (not without extraordinary social and educational effort), and the Bible is a major part of every school curriculum. In addition, the laws of marriage and personal status are entirely bound to the traditional, religious code of laws.

On the other hand, the others justifiably claim that all of these features of the Jewish State should be understood very differently. Instead of religious significance, almost all of the Jewish characteristics of Israel have secular and national meaning. Outside of the country, anyone (especially a Jew) who receives some religious instruction, will identify the Sabbath, the holidays, and the language of the Bible with religion, and only with religion. But in Israel, the Sabbath is kept pretty much as Sunday is kept in other countries. Hebrew has become a secular language and is increasingly under the influence of Western languages, mainly English, in respect to composition, new words, and lines of thought. The Bible is simply the basis of Hebrew culture, and the passages that are learned in schools are usually of general humanist content, or they form part of the national self-justification for contemporary political developments. Altogether, Israel is one of the states in the world in which religion has relatively little influence in culture or politics. The rabbis, as clergymen, do not constitute a factor in the lives of the great majority of Israelis. Even the word "religious" has become a blameworthy epithet among large segments of the population, and many, if not most, of the leaders of the nation consider themselves atheists, at least insofar as they are not active members of any religious community. It is a state in which an attempt by the late Kadish Luz, then the Speaker of the Knesset, to open a session with the blessing, *Shehecheyanu*, was met with fierce opposition from all sides (including his own party); and where most of the citizens of the country show little interest in anything related to religion.

We see, then, that both of these views of Israel are, to a certain extent, true. But the enigma of the apparent contradiction remains. In order to better comprehend the problem as a whole and to see clearly the attitudes presently involved, it would be helpful to note the approach held by the "founding fathers" of the State of Israel. The real founding fathers are doubtless the generation of the Second Aliyah, who established their influence within the half century before the State was born in 1948. To be sure, there was an even older *yishuv* of religious settlers in Jerusalem, Hebron, Safed, and Tiberias, and there was a First Aliyah of the Bilu movement and of the early pioneers. But it was the people of the Second Aliyah who shaped the country's image for generations. They, and the Third Aliyah, who hardly differed from them in most respects, supplied the majority of the country's leaders; they developed the language and customs, the political and cultural forms. In short, it is essential to understand the minds and personalities of the Second Aliyah in order to grasp what is happening in Israel today.

Spiritually and religiously, almost all of the people of the Second Aliyah derived their variety of political ideologies and moral ideas from the different socialist parties of the Russia of that time, which included Poland and Lithuania. In line with the general policy of the social-democratic movement (which only later changed its policy) and most of the other liberal and revolutionary movements, they were consciously atheistic and considered religion and everything connected with it as part of the old, corrupt world that had to be replaced by a new and "free" one. Furthermore, the Jewish religion was, for most of the Second Aliyah immigrants to Palestine, an intrinsic part of the Diaspora, which they vehemently rejected, in principle as well as in practice. The conservative Orthodox circles of Eastern Europe were not only opposed to "progress," in so far as this was bound up with atheistic social ideology, they were also opposed, to a lesser degree (although for similar reasons), to Zionism. Rejection of the Jewish life in the ghettoes implied, for them, a rejection of the religious ideas and traditions that constituted its framework. At the same time, these young people, who were so intellectually tied in with all the social idealism of the period preceding the Russian revolution, were also different from the young revolutionaries in at least one main issue—their relation to *Eretz Yisrael*.

Other young Jews, who were fascinated by the vision of freedom implicit in the progressive spirit of the times, tried to merge completely with the gentiles among whom they lived. They became a significant part of the vanguard of various communist, socialist, and revolutionary parties, while those who felt their allegiance to be primarily with their own people became the nucleus of a Jewish national-socialist movement called the *Bund*, which saw the future of the people within

Russia. It was only a small proportion who turned away from Russia to the Land of Israel. They did so not because of any political far-sightedness (although they may have ascribed it to themselves in later years); they were simply romantic souls who permitted their feelings about their historical tradition, the Jewish people and the legend of the Return to Zion, to prevail over their agnostic, socially "progressive" ideas. They were simply true to an undeniably deep, emotional relationship to their homes and to their upbringing in the Jewish traditional manner. For them, the transition to Socialist Zionism was not a complete break with their personal religious past, it was a kind of continuation, a raising of all that was good and beautiful in Judaism to a wider, freer, more universally human framework.

In any case, it was an attempt to sustain Jewish life. For this life seemed to them to have become distorted and spoiled, and they felt that it could be renewed and perpetuated only by drawing inspiration from its more distant past, such as biblical times, the era of the Maccabees, Bar Kochba, or the Golden Age of Spanish Jewry. Many of those who, for ideological reasons, had ceased to pray, could not repress their emotional attachment to the prayers themselves. Jewish institutions, such as the rabbinate, the *Shulchan Aruch* or *mitzvot* had become, in their eyes, negative and expendable—notwithstanding which they did not deny their own feelings of respect (and even love) for the figure of the rabbi, for the synagogue, and for the special warmth of traditional Jewish life. The majority of those who came from Chasidic homes remained great admirers of Chasidism and expressed it not only in their songs and dances and festivals but also in the way they gathered and organized themselves around the figure of a secular *rebbe*. Even though they fought against many Jewish religious images and institutions, they persisted in identifying Judaism with the Eastern European variety, to the extent that any other version was, in their opinion (even if not consciously so), a misrepresentation or a poor copy. This intricate composition of the Second Aliyah pioneers—their ambivalence toward traditional Judaism, and their deep emotional attachment to Jewishness, their romantic attitudes, so full of different types of faith, and their strong intellectual convictions—were among the chief factors that structured life in the State of Israel.

Education was one of the most vital fields in which this was evident, even long before the establishment of the State. Naturally, teachers aspired to reproduce the image of the older generation and to make it, if anything, a more healthy and free one. It was hoped that the succeeding generation would have the same synthesis of "instinctive" Jewishness and the best of human and national values, except the education could not help but be rather one-sided, because a vital part of their aspirations were of an emotional and scarcely conscious nature. There was, indeed, a large increment of nationalism in their education, but it was confined mostly to the question of the relation to the land and the people of the Bible. In general, the Bible became the corner-stone of Jewish education, with emphasis on national history, language, and folklore, and a deliberate minimalization of the religious aspects, especially those that touched upon keeping the *mitzvot*. (An extreme instance occurred in the early 1950s when an unsuccessful attempt was made among a certain minority to eliminate the Holy Name from current editions of the Bible.) Postbiblical literature, especially the oral tradition (Talmud and the like) and anything else that rested on religious faith, like the esoteric tradition (Kabbalah), was almost unknown to the pupils. The Hebrew literature taught was primarily that of the *Haskalah*, much of which had an antireligious and anti-Jewish ghetto bias. True, a certain place was granted to Aggadah literature and there was a positive relation to the Chasidic movement, but all this in rather romanticized fashion, disconnected from anything in contemporary life.

The product, therefore, of this Israeli education was a person who, despite a measured knowledge of Bible and Zionism, was often totally ignorant of postbiblical Judaism or of the religious contents of Jewish tradition. To the extent that a relation to the Diaspora existed, it was usually antagonistic, or even contemptuous (the adjective, *galuti*, still connotes shame and disgrace). Thus, when the news of the Holocaust first came to this country, it had a different effect on the youth than on the old-timers, and it took some time before the sense of identification could be felt. Many parents showed concern at this lack of strong connection with Jewish values and Jewish history in the Diaspora and, as a result, after considerable discussion both private and public, several national conventions, and many official pronouncements, the Ministry of Education decided some years ago to promote "Jewish" consciousness.

Special study programs were set up as part of the curriculum in every school, but it was too late and too little to make any noticeable difference in the prevailing attitudes. Jews and Judaism outside of ancient times were remote, uninteresting, and even something to be ashamed of, something that, at the end of a long and wretched history, had come to its humiliating last chapter in the Holocaust.

Religion was considered part of the shameful past and, at one time, in the early 1950s, this approach was given extreme expression by a small, though gifted, group of Israeli-born youth who called themselves "Canaanites" and who talked of the desirability of a complete severance with the Diaspora, both past and present, and of a return to the "common Canaanite past" of the "Semitic" entity. To be sure, this group did not last long, and its extremist views were not accepted by any significant part of the public, but some of its members continued to function in various public capacities and within responsible political frameworks. In a variety of guises, such as the League against Religious Coercion, the group managed to sway a section of public opinion, officially against religious coercion, but under the surface are deep-rooted seeds of the antireligious and anti-Jewish ideology of the Canaanites. There is considerable evidence indicating that the various mass media of the country have within them a numerous and influential group of people whose views are close to, or in sympathy with, the Canaanite approach, at least in several aspects.

Of course, a complete picture of the situation must include some description of the religious section of the country. The Orthodox communities of the Old Yishuv that existed before modern Zionism, could not cope politically with the Second or the Third Aliyah. As a result of organizational weakness and, to a degree, also because of an inner need, or even deliberate ideological decision, there was an increasing tendency toward withdrawal into their own specific, tradition-bound world. The few religious *chalutzim* who came to the country were unable to alter anything in the prevailing atmosphere and were looked upon unsympathetically, if not, at times, even antagonistically. This was especially true of those who did not belong to the Socialist camp, like the Kfar Chasidim immigrants. Also, the Fourth Aliyah immigrants, who came mainly from Poland in the 1930s (and many of whom were religious) could not, by themselves, contribute anything substantial

by way of change. Moreover, the general spirit of the land was na-
tionalist and secular, and many of the young people left the religious
homes in which they had been brought up to join either one of the
labor movement's settlements or one of the underground movements.
(The underground of *Etzel* and *Lechi*, which were more nationalistic
and less socialist, were more attractive to the religious youth, although
when it came to their religious identity, there was, in the long run,
little recognizable distinction between the different ways.) The
Holocaust, which also destroyed the great reservoir of Orthodox Jewry
in the Diaspora, seemed, for many, to be the end of a chapter—and
the end of Jewish religion as a whole.

    It should be noted that many of the concessions that were given
to the religious sector, on the establishment of the State (especially
the law of religious marriage and the exemption of *yeshivah* students
from military service), were not based as much on pressure or political
coercion on the part of the religious sector as they were on the supposition (frequently expressed in those days) that the problem would,
to all intents and purposes, solve itself in a matter of a decade or two,
as the religious sector would diminish and lose its importance. From
the very beginning, the Chief Rabbinate was not accepted by a considerable portion of the religious sector (the Old Yishuv, the Aggudat
Yisrael, and the like), and even the ostensible leadership of these groups
was ineffectual, so that there was practically no religious influence in
the prevailing atmosphere of the country, nothing that had a moral
weight. Even when, at the head of the religious sector, there was a
person of stature, with a positive relation to the Zionist upbuilding,
such as Rabbi Kook, no more influence was felt than in later periods.
For the most part, the religious leadership in the country was on a
rather low level.

    The situation changed significantly after the establishment of the
State. First there was a spiritual uplift: as the pre-State Zionist enthusiasm waned and the general, secular system of values lost its glamor
(the Second World War made many people aware of the crisis of
Western culture), the constant drain of religious youth to the outside
ceased. From that time on, it may be said that the religious sector re-
tained its numerical proportion in the country; if anything, it may
have grown somewhat, due to its high rate of natural increase. The

exemption of *yeshivah* youth from military service and the growing support they received from abroad increased their numbers and was instrumental in forming a new stratum of people who had received a more extensive Jewish education—at a higher level and for a longer period—and contributed to the near-cessation of the student drain to the outside.

Another factor was the religious background of the new immigration. Those who came, in part from Europe, especially Hungary and the surrounding area, and in vast numbers from Islamic countries of the Middle East, were mainly tradition-minded Jews who kept the *mitzvot* and abided by the Torah. Thus, in the context of the political setup of those years, with the various parties juggling for political status, many things were done that can only be termed *organized destruction*. Local government and authority were parceled out to the parties on a proportional basis, with the "religious" receiving 25 percent of the new immigrants into their educational, cultural, political, and administrative frameworks. Pressure was used to cut off the new immigrants, especially the children, from the religious tradition. These efforts succeeded to such an extent that many, if not most, of the immigrants from the North African and Middle Eastern countries abandoned either all or part of their own religious way of life. (This may well have prepared the ground for a serious social problem some twenty years later, which emerged when the succeeding generation became aware of the cultural, economic, and social gap among the communities.) Nevertheless, the new immigration reinforced the religious sector in a very emphatic way. As a result, the concept of a clear-cut religious sector was fixed in the political and cultural awareness of the population. Although politically that sector elected only about 12 percent of the Knesset members, it has the general sympathies (if one can judge by the numbers of children in religious schools) of about three times that number.

Within this religious sector, there are two distinct and opposite trends, the existence of which serve to explain many of the features characteristic of Jewish religious life in Israel. On one hand, with the growth of the more conservative elements (the Old Yishuv, Aggudat Yisrael, the *yeshivah* students) there has been a tendency to sever contact—in terms of ideas and in practice—with the State. This element consciously prefers to build religious "ghettos," scattered throughout the country, and to strengthen the religious core, even if this means the loss of many on the fringes. The other element (Hapoel HaMizrachi, made up of university graduates) is more open to the outer world and visualizes itself and the whole religious sector as an integral part of the life of the country, and even ascribes to this national life a certain religious value, which it also strives to make palpable.

The relation between the trends—toward inner withdrawal and outer involvement in the State—and between the bodies representing them, are not permanent and steady, and depend on a variety of external and internal factors. Thus, the increase in numbers of *yeshivah* students (including, to the surprise of the National Religious Party, also those *yeshivah* colleges supported by the Hapoel HaMizrachi wing) is among the factors leading toward inner withdrawal. On the other hand, long-standing political alliance with Mapai, the influence of the communications media, the time spent in military service—all these shift the balance in favor of involvement in the outer world. One of the decisive external factors is the attitude to religious questions on the part of the nonreligious sector. Every time there is public tension around an issue that has some religious overtones, the tendency of the religious sector to withdraw and retreat into isolation grows perceptibly. Whenever the relations between the two sectors are more relaxed and tranquil, the religious sector tends to become more open and accessible.

With the crystallization of a broad religious front in the 1950s, the political and spiritual issues in connection with religion in Israel were brought into relief. First, religious problems ceased to be general spiritual problems. Second, the State, as such, ceased to be interested in religion, except when, and to the extent that, it was directly concerned, as in questions of legislation and *halachah*. Finally, the problems of Judaism became controversial political issues, and their outcome depended on the alignment of the political forces involved. It seems, therefore, as though the problems are moving in the direction of a sociological confrontation between religious and secular sectors, but a religious problem no longer exists to any other degree or significance.

Various factors have led to this situation, in which Judaism and the religious sector of Israel have ceased to be the vital core of the nation. Most important, no doubt, is the education given to the children and the prevailing atmosphere of secularism. Concerning the latter, as described previously, the State got its spiritual orientation from people who considered themselves atheists. Therefore, there has been a general feeling in the country that matters of religious faith belong to the past and that enlightened and progressive people cannot be expected to put their belief in such "medieval superstitions," while those who do cling to the ancestral faith are considered backward and anachronistic, if not actually queer and strange. The problem, as such, is nonexistent, in principle—and there is no point in discussing it or contemplating it seriously.

On the other hand, the education itself, with its very small doses of Jewish tradition, acted as another, perhaps more formidable barrier to genuine faith than the scornful total disregard for religion, for it made Jewishness something odd and different. As a result, religious feeling was not necessarily bound up with specifically Jewish forms or expressions, and it did not even bring one closer to the ranks of the religious sector. Judaism was no longer the accepted way for any young Jewish person with religious inclinations; in fact, all the ways could be considered equally attractive. These facts, as they resulted from the prevailing atmosphere and education, were again extended to the mass communications media, which, in turn, reinforced the estrangement from Judaism. In addition, since problems have not been taken seriously, any public airing falls back to the political, legislative, or party administrative level, and Judaism is made to appear a matter of personality clashes, political intrigue, and election struggles. Consequently, the average man in the street has practically no idea whatsoever of a religious figure, whether in terms of creative activity, thought, or literature, who does not belong to the political arena.

All of this only reinforces the estrangement of religious personalities and religious ideas from the average Israeli. Gradually, chances for intimate communion with Jewishness in words, concepts, images, is diminishing. Therefore, the phenomenon of repentance—the one who returns to the fold is a *baal teshuvah*—is not common, and involves all the problems of someone converting to a new faith.

The formation of blocs has, of course, also had an immediate effect on the religious adherents, either making them withdraw into social and spiritual works that have little or nothing to do with secular life and people, or making them direct their energies into political activities, the aim of which is merely to strengthen their defensive position against attack from outside. A serious analysis of the political action of all the religious parties would indicate that, in spite of their being accused of exerting religious coercion (which, in fact, hardly exists), they are not concerned with matters that are valid for the State as a whole but with defending their own existence against the prevailing tendency to ignore their problems altogether. The laws of Sabbath and of marriage, or the regulations exempting *yeshivah* students from military service provide the religious sector with their only chance to retain some sort of contact with the rest of the population. But this very struggle restricts any deeper and broader possibilities of influence on the part of spiritual leaders, such as rabbis or heads of *yeshivot*. What is more, no attempt is made to exert any genuine spiritual influence on the State as a whole. There is not a single religious personality who carries any weight beyond the limited confines of his own very clearly defined public.

Similar obstacles face the efforts of religious groups like the Reform or Conservative congregations, brought primarily from the United States. Even though these groups, especially the Reform synagogues, have tried to make contact with a broader Israeli public, their influence is not marked. Mistakenly estimating that the negative attitude to religion could be attributed to certain harsh features of the *halachah* or to the pressure of religious coercion, they thought that by coming out against these aspects of religion they could overcome the obstacles raised by the Orthodox religious bloc. But, of course, as mentioned, these aspects were only political expressions of the absence of any ideological relation or real religious tension, and changing them would be of little avail. What is more, according to the approach of the founding fathers, a genuine emotional relation to Jewishness could be realized only through those forms familiar to them from Eastern Europe, and anything else seemed counterfeit.

On the whole, then, the gap between the average Israeli and Judaism is the result of a certain outlook that continues to operate even though it no longer presumes to be a clearcut ideology, and of an educational system that has had a very definite effect on the country even though it had no such clear-cut intention. The accumulation of forces is continuing to widen the gap between the Israeli and his religion and is creating an Israeli nation, whose inherent ties with Judaism, past and present, will probably continue to decline and diminish. As against these forces, however, there are others. First, the state of constant warfare with neighboring countries has not only isolated Israel from the world, it has also necessarily brought about a national unity that becomes stronger with every threat and danger and because of which the obstacles and antagonisms of conflicting blocs are overcome. Moreover, the influence of the founding fathers' orientation to Jewishness, in spite of its antireligious bias, also contains a kind of idealization of certain aspects of Judaism and a real, heartfelt connection with them. Thus, one should distinguish between the worship of the dead rabbi, with its deference to the sages of the past, irrespective of who they were, when they lived, or what they stood for, and an equal incapacity to relate devotionally to a living sage. Part of the great respect now shown to the late Rabbi Kook may be ascribed to this attitude, which largely ignores the disputes and the enmity that so harried him in his lifetime.

Another feature is the profound unwillingness of almost every sector of the population of Israel to cut its ties with Judaism. It is characteristic that even the sharpest criticism of religion or the *halachah* (*Shabbat*, conversion, or personal status) throws the guilt on the institution of the rabbinate and not on the principles of Judaism itself. Even when the persons leading such an antireligious struggle are well aware that the issue is not a matter of the stand taken by certain rabbis or by the rabbinate itself, they do not dare to come out in open war against Judaism. At the same time, factors of this kind, which are bound up with certain emotional ties with Jewishness, become weaker with the growth of a new generation, further removed from national-traditional or folklore sources.

In a variety of ways, the Six Day War brought a certain change in this whole situation. The trauma of the weeks preceding it initiated a crisis in the Israeli's sense of isolation. Whereas before he had tended to feel "more Israeli than Jewish" and closer to other normal nations than to the Diaspora, he suddenly discovered that all the political friendships and alliances were quite worthless and that the only reliable partnership was with the Jews of the world. Even though this period was very short, it caused a change of attitude and identification, so that the relation to the Jewish People was no longer a matter of Zionism, which was an unconvincing subject learned in school, but a very real and vital experience. Another postwar development was the growth of the movement for a greater Land of Israel (*Eretz Yisrael Hashlemah*). This was the first movement that broke through not only the party barriers but also the religious-secular barriers. Despite its strictly political-secular side, it also drew much from the historical Jewish past and, this time, not from the archeological aspect but from the ideas and concepts of ancient times. The notion that the people of Israel have an essential right to the land is derived from the Bible view of the Covenant, with all that this implies. A number of writers and public figures from different backgrounds have begun to discover a Judaism that has meaning not only for an irrelevant distant past but for contemporary life.

Still another influence on religious life may be expected to come from outside the country, especially from recent intellectual trends in the Western world. Such trends are usually absorbed by Judaism rather tardily, as one Israeli cynic put it—an academic quarter century late. Nevertheless, the general weakening of atheism as a solution to the problems of life, and the increasing interest in different religions for the sake of their spiritual message, are trends that have also reached Israel. Their effect on the intellectual life of the country seems to be a certain change in the attitude of rejection toward religion. And when the subject of theology, in its widest sense, becomes a legitimate problem in Israel (until now it has been out of bounds), then there is a good chance that the values of Judaism will also find their proper place.

The future of Israel, however, is still inscrutable. There are certain forces, both among the religious sector and among the secular bloc, that seek to sever all contact between the two. Such a severance can quickly become an unbridgeable gap. In addition, it should be kept in mind that the cultural essence of Judaism is such that it is extremely difficult to keep in touch with it superficially, by way of purely emotional "conversion," so that the very inability to reach the shut gates of Jewish culture can become a very important factor in blocking the way for later generations who would want such a more complete involvement. With all this, there still exists in Israel a silent majority that sincerely wants a national unity to evolve and that aspires to a cultural renaissance that will also be a total or partial return to the religious contents of Judaism. Because of the enormous importance nowadays given to political activity, and because of the way Israeli politics is structured with its opportunist platforms devoid of broader vision, it is possible that certain political maneuvers will weigh the balance one way or another without anyone consciously intending it to happen. Various intellectual trends from abroad, immigration, or the appearance of spiritual leaders of stature, whether from among the religious sector or from other sectors, may also bring about a certain solution to the riddle of the spiritual identity of the State of Israel.

26

The Rabbinate in Israel

Any broad discussion of the rabbinate in Israel inevitably turns into a discussion of the crisis of the rabbinate in the country. It should be realized, however, that the crisis of the rabbinate is not typically Israeli; it is a general Jewish crisis, connected with the social and spiritual development in Jewry in the last hundred years or so. A fundamental treatment of this problem is, of course, a whole subject in itself, but one should at least be acquainted with its basic points in order to understand the special nature of the problem in the State of Israel today.

The role of the rabbi is rather special because, on the one hand, the rabbi is indeed chosen by the community in which he serves, while on the other, his authority is derived from another source—the Torah—and he is its interpreter and representative. The rabbi, therefore, cannot really represent or speak for the people of his community beyond a certain very narrow scope, unless they, too, like him, accept the authority of the Torah over the whole spectrum of life. Another difficulty is that his role is not essentially a sacramental, purely religious one. Unlike the Catholic priest, who serves by virtue of holy orders (and actually holds in his hand the sole authority to perform the sacraments), the Jewish rabbi has no essential function that cannot be performed by someone else. In theory at least, a Jewish community could carry on its whole spiritual and religious life without the services of a rabbi, who, being learned in the Torah and Jewish law, has merely to help the members of the community when a religious problem arises.

But the importance of the task is, again, dependent on the degree to which the members of the community are genuinely in need of these services. To illustrate this problem, a joke is told about a rabbi in a city in Israel: "In the ten years of my official functioning as rabbi, there are only two questions that have been put to me—and both of them can really be reduced to one question, namely, 'what time is it, sir?' " which is not to say the Jewish community, like every religious community in the world, does not require the services of a religious leader. It is simply that these services do not stem from the traditional function of a rabbi as such. If, as in the Jewish communities of Europe or America, the rabbi delivers a sermon every Saturday or directs the community religious affairs and social services or gets people together for various religious functions—all these are, in fact, new functions. Even when they did exist in the past they were of a peripheral, secondary nature, and it is still not clear whether the rabbi is the personage most suited to perform them.

Another special Israeli aspect of this general question of the role of the rabbi is that the Israeli rabbi is compensated for his services by being an employee of the state. This bestows on him a certain happy independence from the community and its financial leaders, but it may thereby result in a lack of interest on the part of the rabbi to take an active part in the community or to introduce a personal note into his relations with the people. Additionally, there is the matter of the religious council, which exists in every community. The religious council is a body composed, according to law, of representatives of the public concerned; and the ones chosen to serve on it are largely selected by the political parties. The religious council is allocated its budget from the Ministry of Religions and from the local authorities, and its task is to supply the inhabitants of a given place with all the religious services required. The rabbi is not a member of the religious council but is employed by it, and together with the other religious

or semireligious functionaries, he has to provide all the religious services he can. The rabbi, therefore, represents the local religious-political
institution but does not stand at the head of it, and he cannot, by
virtue of his legal position, direct the activities of the council or influence it.

In addition to these factors, the problem is made more acute by
the existence of the *yeshivot* and the strong influence of the heads of
yeshivot and even of the *yeshivah* graduates in the community. The head
of a *yeshivah* is, actually, more than the spiritual leader of the school;
his influence often extends beyond the school and scholarly matters,
to the field of ideas and ideologies. *Yeshivah* students usually choose
to study at a particular school out of deference to the authority and
leadership of the head of the *yeshivah*. Usually this emotional and
spiritual bond is maintained in all its force even after a student leaves
the *yeshivah*, often throughout one's life. Clearly then, the influence
of the *yeshivah* heads is liable to be much greater than that of the
rabbis of the community, who are themselves former *yeshivah* students
with their own proclivities to such an influence. Furthermore, the existence of so many *yeshivot* creates a whole class of laymen who are
often authorized as rabbis and who have an education equal to that
of a rabbi. Such a congregation would require relatively little of the
routine halachic-legal services of the local rabbi, and, in fact, he is frequently in the position of an ideological or political opposition. What
is more, a *yeshivah* scholar who wishes to devote his life to religious
action will generally prefer to take up a career as a *rosh yeshivah* or
as a teacher, or else as an official *dayan* (rabbinical judge). Far too often,
therefore, those who become community rabbis are frustrated individuals for whom it is second or third choice of career and who,
even in the carrying out of their task, will dream of establishing a
yeshivah as a fuller expression of their personalities.

Besides the large number of *yeshivah* graduates, another con-
tributing factor to reducing the dependence on the traditional services
of the rabbi is the production of halachic handbooks and guides and
other works dealing with the solutions to problems of Jewish law. People
often prefer to read and learn for themselves rather than rely on the
opinion of the local rabbi.

The scope of the traditional task of the rabbi is narrowing down in Israel, whereas his education continues along the same traditional lines. The material he studies and on which he is examined has become less and less useful in terms of his real work, while the fields of operation that do engage him are quite outside the *yeshivah* curriculum of studies. Furthermore, the whole field of relations with the large nonreligious public is a serious problem in itself. The rabbi usually comes from a religious background, which is a different social and cultural milieu than that of most of his secular-minded community, and the gap between their respective views and values is often much greater than he can bridge. Even the formal respect shown to clerics in other countries is relatively absent in Israel. It is no wonder, therefore, that the rabbi in Israel is inhibited in his work, and his traditional title of *mara d'atra* (master of the place) has become an ironic reminder of his condition.

A possible solution might be the emergence of the rabbi from the confines of religious party politics and the narrow scope of his ritualistic duties (as one rabbi put it, from the butcher shop to the *mikve*), and his active participation in public life, on the basis of a definite moral and Jewish point of view. This may well make him a controversial figure, but it will at least reinforce his role as a representative of a living Jewishness in all realms of life. Another possible solution to the problem is a return to the traditional task of teacher of Torah to the people. In other words, the rabbi should see himself as obligated to instruct anyone who asks for it—young or old, religious or nonreligious, those close to his own mode of living and those far from it. This obligation to teach, if properly carried out, could make the rabbi in Israel a genuinely influential factor in the future of Jewishness and the Torah.

— 27 —

Remembering Jerusalem

On the ninth day of Av, the anniversary of the destruction of the Temple, when the Jews mourn the long years of their exile, the congregants sit upon the floors of their synagogues to chant the traditional Lamentations, and the one who leads the prayers declares, "So-and-so many years have passed since the destruction of the Temple." For the grief of banishment and dispersion is identical with, and emerges from, the grief at the destruction of the Holy City and the Temple.

At the same time, the mourning for the ruin of Jerusalem is far deeper and more personal than would appear from its public nature. It betokens more than the loss of the most sacred of the holy places or of the national capital. It is a blow to the very existence of the people. Indeed, the whole world feels the hurt, and according to tradition, it will not return to primal perfection until the city is rebuilt. For Jerusalem is indispensable to the well-being of the world.

We find reference to this thought in an early talmudic saying: "This world is like an eye: the white of the eye is the ocean that surrounds the world, the pigment is the world itself, the pupil is Jerusalem, and the face reflected in the pupil is the Temple" (*Derech Eretz Zuta*).

Thus, in mystical evocation, harm done to Jerusalem strikes at the light of the world. The sages of the Talmud said: "From the day on which the Temple was destroyed no day goes by without a curse, and the curse of each day is greater than of the one before it" (*Sota, 49a*). They imagined a cloud of mourning that veiled the face of the world: "And from the day of the Temple's destruction the sky has never been seen in all its purity" (*Berachot, 59a*). Again, the emphasis is on the injury done to all creation, whether it be conscious of it or not. Poignant anguish over the fallen city is, therefore, shared by all. Even the Holy One, Blessed be He, is said to sense its pangs. And the truly devout pilgrim who visits the vestiges of Jerusalem hears "a voice murmuring like a dove, 'Woe to my children for whose sins I destroyed My house, burnt My palaces, and dispersed them among the peoples of the earth. Woe to the father who exiled his son! Woe to the children banished from their father's table!' " (*Berachot 3a*). For this reason it is said: "From the day that the Temple was destroyed, there has been no laughter before God" (*Avodah Zarah 3b*).

Consequently, the lament for the destroyed city is not limited to a single day, and much of Jewish life is marked by a continual mourning. The dramatic verses of the psalmist: "If I forget thee, O Jerusalem, may my right hand forget its cunning; if I do not remember thee, let my tongue cleave to the roof of my mouth" (Psalms 137) are no empty phrases for the Jewish people, but a living reality, an actual part of their daily awareness. "A man is forbidden to indulge in laughter in this world, until the time of redemption." All the occasions of life, even those of rejoicing, are marked by the pain of the loss of Jerusalem. No joy is ever total, no building ever finished. If a repast is spread for guests, the observant Jew will leave something incomplete, in memory of the destruction of the Temple. Every newly constructed house remains unfinished, even if it is only by a fragment of wall left without plaster or paint. At a wedding ceremony, ashes are scattered over the head of the bridegroom instead of a garland, because Jerusalem must be put above all other joys. And the wedding ends with the groom breaking a glass vessel underfoot, to remind the participants that no bliss can be perfect so long as the City lies waste. Jerusalem has been closer to the Jews than any other place for nearly two thousand years, an inseparable part of every rejoicing, at the core of every sorrow.

What is more, during the centuries of exile, the recollection of

Jerusalem expanded and deepened. The Holy City became a concept transcending the specific spot. Jerusalem began to signify the Land of Israel as a whole, and a Jew coming from the Land was for generations called *Yerushalmi*, a Jerusalemite. The Talmud, compiled over long years in the Land of Israel and assembled in Tiberias and Caesarea and other cities of the Land, is entitled "The Jerusalem Talmud," for Jerusalem was seen to contain within itself the quintessence of the Land as a whole. Ultimately, Jerusalem and Zion—another name for the city—came to represent more than any kind of geographic location or spiritual center. In Jewish mysticism, it became a symbol of the eternal "Rose," sign of the *Shechinah*—Divine presence—identified with the mystic term *malchut*, kingdom. In mystic thought it was the point of contact between the infinite and the finite. It was where time and place met, and all that was beyond time and place. It was the point where "the silver cord" of Divine influence touched everyday creation. The poem "Come My Beloved" by Rav Shlomo Alkavets, which, almost as soon as it was composed, was adopted as a central song in the Sabbath liturgy, is in fact a mystic song of yearning for Jerusalem: it blends the redemptive longings of the people of Israel and of the world, and focuses those longings on the Holy City. When the Jews used to say "the city," they meant Jerusalem. For this earthly city of God reflects the essence of the people as a whole. It stands for the *Shechinah* in exile, and stands no less for the world in its agony and suffering. Thus, the ravaged and abandoned city awaits redemption and fulfillment. Its rebuilding signifies alike the renaissance of the Jewish people and the revival of Jerusalem's ancient covenant with that people and with the whole world.

Mystic Jerusalem did not blur the conception of Jerusalem as a real earthly center of habitation. Even in the darkest days of tyranny and persecution, when no Jew might dwell there, Jerusalem was held to be the capital of the children of Israel. As long as outer circumstances do not permit the life of the nation to be centered in Jerusalem, the institutions of Jewish religious law (*halachah*) cannot have their full effect. Meanwhile, all over the world, Jews turn toward the city when they pray, and synagogues are so built that the Holy Ark faces Jerusalem.

It is also the ardent desire of the individual Jew to be in Jerusalem and to live there. Even the dry legal code affirms that the will to live in Jerusalem overrides all other reasons given for a course of action. Over the centuries, this was very seldom a practical possibility, but the hope never faltered. So that, at the end of the Passover feast, with its celebration of release from bondage, the last words declaimed are: "Next year in Jerusalem." For many generations, it was customary to write in every marriage contract: "The wedding will take place on such-and-such a date in Jerusalem. However, if by then redemption has still not come, it will take place in ... (another specified place)"—which is to say that the only suitable place for the couple to live was Jerusalem.

The psalmist says: "Jerusalem is built as a city that is compact together" (Psalms 122), and this is traditionally interpreted as referring to its double nature. On the one hand, there is the earthly Jerusalem below, on the other, the higher Jerusalem, wherein is to be found all the majesty of the celestial world. This higher Jerusalem is conceived as hovering over its counterpart. Yet, it is dependent on the terrestrial city and springs out of it. "Said the Holy One, Blessed be He, I will not come into the heavenly Jerusalem until I come into earthly Jerusalem" (*Taanit 5a*). The two cities, the one arrayed against the other, cannot find perfection until the people of Israel are once again in their own unique capital: "Jerusalem is built as a city that is compact together, whither the tribes go up ... to give thanks unto the name of the Lord."

PART VI

CONVERSATIONS
WITH
RABBI ADIN STEINSALTZ

═ 28 ═

The Private Gate

Q. Rabbi Steinsaltz, in your dialogue with Peter Berger at the Jewish Museum you referred to man's inner meeting with himself as his most pressing challenge. Do you regard this as a search for man's identity in which he expands, or one in which he comes in contact with an unknown area in himself?

Steinsaltz. You see, I am in a certain way not so very much interested in man's search for himself. It is done by psychologists better or worse. What I was speaking about, then, was a Jew and his connection with his own traditions. Whether he has some knowledge or he doesn't have some knowledge of them, there comes a time when he has to re-meet and re-understand his tradition in a way that will be applicable to him and say something to him as he is. You see, every person has to at some time re-create Sinai for himself. He himself has to accept the Law. There is a very famous saying, and a very old one, that the Law was given so many years ago, but it was not *accepted* at that time. At least not by everyone. So I am speaking about the experience of completing

---

Conversation with Irving Friedman, *Parabola* 3(2):22–31.

what was given at Sinai by receiving, and receiving is always a very personal thing. For some people it may be a mystical and perhaps a shattering and destructive experience; others may do it in a very easy way without any pain. But for everyone it is a new feeling of meeting—of meeting again or for the first time.

There is a verse from the Psalms, "I know that God is great." And the emphasis is on *I know* —what *I* know, and the special form and way in which I know. I can sometimes talk about it, but I cannot transfer it and I can't learn it. This feeling that *I know now* is just what I was referring to. In our time I don't think that the tradition by itself is sufficient—everyone has to have a personal meeting. Even though I may be inclined to mystical thinking, I don't think that is the only way. People can do it in many ways, but they must be personal ways.

Q.   You have said that "the crucial moment of repentance generally does not occur at a moment of great self-awareness," and that "irrespective of the degree of awareness, several spiritual factors come together in the process of conversion." Do you believe that the metamorphosis of man can take place in the dark, without the active participation of his awareness? Do you draw a distinction between his consciousness at the moment and his later awareness?

Steinsaltz.   My experience is really with Jews. And at first my experience with Jews regarding conversion was very puzzling. It seemed to be entirely different, say, from William James's description of conversion. Speaking about those things I know from observing quite a number of people, I would say that, at least among our people, violent, one-minute conversions are extremely rare. Perhaps we are too obstinate. I pride myself in being a descendant of generations of very obstinate people. In our obstinacy we stand very fast, even to our errors. So that any change seems to be not very easy, and not instantaneous. Now, that means that if there is a change, the change comes not by leaps and bounds, not in an immediately illuminating moment when everything is changed, but very gradually. If our people do have such moments, they seem to have them much later on in the way of their development—not at the beginning, but as one stage in the long work of a lifetime. That is why I say that sometimes the change cannot be perceived when it is happening.

Looking backward one may say that the change was at a certain moment—the one where I made the real choice—but it may take years and years to discover what that point was. Sometimes without really being conscious that there are changes in oneself, a process may be going on. One can see that most processes of growth in nature, whether in animals or in plants, are done in darkness. They seem to do the initial, most important growing in darkness. The experience of birth, or the first time that something peeps out from the earth, is really a special experience. But the point is that this is the culmination of a process, not the beginning of it. The process *began* in the dark, quite a time before. When it appears later, it seems inevitable that it would appear, but the powers were at work for a long time before. It may take many years, or it can come very easily.

Q. In regard to man knowing himself, I'd like to ask about *Daat* [Knowledge]. Although it occupies a central place in Judaism, it does not appear as a basic force on the diagram of the *sefirot*.

Steinsaltz. You know, I usually do not talk about technical things. It is often not too useful. But in this case it is of interest that the *sefirah* of *Daat* appears as an exchange. It is important to remember that it does not mean knowledge in the usual sense; it is the power and the ability to make decisions that result from abstract thinking. It is an exchange with the other *sefirah* of *Keter* [Head, or Crown]. One of them is an outward look and one of them is an inward look. The kind of knowledge a person has when he says, "I know, I accept this" is not the result of his inner contemplation but the result of some higher force working within him. But a person cannot experience it this way and experiences it as an inner perception. So from the individual's point of view, the formation becomes *Chochmah* [Wisdom], *Binah* [Understanding], and *Daat*. But from what I would call an objective perspective, the formation changes.

Objectively, I would say, the decisions and results we experience as our own do not really come from us. In a certain way a person makes a decision and finds out later the reasons why he made it. That is what I would call an objective view of the process; subjectively, it is not experienced that way. So I would say the exchange of these two points of view creates a kind of rhombus formation, a perspective of symmetry. There are two fixed points and a third point is sometimes above (*Keter*) and sometimes lower down (*Daat*).

Q.   Isn't *Daat* sometimes identified with *Tiferet* [Beauty], the seat of the heart, and therefore referred to the feelings rather than thought? Also is it not sometimes regarded as an axis running the length of the body, thereby identifying it with a corporeal type of knowledge as well?

Steinsaltz.   To translate the idea of *Daat* as Knowledge is not quite accurate, because knowledge is usually associated with a process of the brain. Now, *Daat* has in it much more, and very strongly, the idea of identification. To know something is to be connected with it completely. The first time the word is used in the Bible is when Adam knew Eve, which does not have a theoretical, cerebral meaning. In many cases it has at least the additional connotation of not just knowing but of being attached and moved in many ways. This brings us to one of the points about the Tree of Knowledge. You see, when I understand good and evil it is very nice, but when I *know* good and evil it means that I am involved. I cannot know evil without being involved with evil. The whole concept of knowledge is always connected with the emotions and with the idea of attachment. In the Kabbalah, *Daat* goes along the middle line of *Tiferet* and *Yesod* [Foundation]. That means it is the connecting line, connecting things with one another. It is called the line of truth, the line that extends from one end of existence to the other, the line that goes from the highest point to the very lowest.

Q.   You just spoke a moment ago about evil, and of course Judaism makes a strong distinction between the good and evil impulses and bids us to "choose life." It also teaches that evil is natural to man's lack of balance and that it can be made sacred. Kabbalism as I understand it teaches that God is a source of evil as well as good.

Steinsaltz.   That is a biblical verse. The verse in Isaiah says, "I am the creator of light and of darkness. I make peace and I create evil." It is now in the prayerbook as "He makes peace and creates everything," which is a kind of euphemism.

Q.   The question comes up then as to how man must face evil. I understand that some kabbalists taught that evil had to be exhausted rather than opposed, and you speak of the transformation of evil by spiritual possibilities. Is this the way in which you would reconcile the natural view of evil with the strong moral viewpoint in Judaism?

Steinsaltz.   Well, first of all, Judaism knows that there is evil. Second of all, Judaism asserts that evil exists in everyone, not to exclude the smallest child. So evil is a part of our being. But we must keep in mind that creation is not something complete. If something is complete it has no way to go on. Creation is something that goes from a certain point on. So while evil is a part of our existence it doesn't mean that it *should* be like this. There is a very, very old story about circumcision that deals with this same problem. The Roman governor of Judea asked Rabbi Akiva, "If God wanted a person to be circumcised, why didn't he create him that way?" And he answered, "If the Lord wanted, let us say, cakes, why did he not create them?" He creates certain incomplete things and allows men to perfect them.

   Evil exists, but existence doesn't mean justification. Sometimes I have to accept things, many times I have to change them. Now this change can occur—and I find it fascinating in Judaism, which is supposed to be a very monolithic and rigid way of thought—in many different ways. We believe that the Law has at least 600,000 different paths within it for individuals to enter. There is what is called the "private gate" for each of us. And we each have to find our own gate. The search for my own particular gate can be a very arduous one. A man may search for years and find only doorways that are not his; he may go on through all his life without really finding it. That is the basis of the transmigration of the soul, which is, contrary to what so many nice people wrote, a part of Judaism. It is a part that is not publicized very much—intentionally. In the beginning of the sixteenth century one of the books of the *Responsa* dealt with this problem and concluded, "We believe in it—we don't publicize it."

Q.   What puzzles me is that man, even if he has to find his own way, is still involved in a process of unifying contrary and opposite elements throughout his life. For example, in the table of the *sefirot* again, we have the idea of *Yichud*, binding or unifying, and I understand this is used as a meditation practice in combining different names of God or in experiencing the unification of two opposite *sefirot*. I understand that the highest level of the soul is also call *Yechidah* from the same root.

Steinsaltz.   Well, *Yechidah* means the unique one. There is a certain point at which all souls are really one, and this is called *Yechidah*. The higher one gets, the more one sees the unity, until there is one point at which all souls become one. The lower one descends from that point, the more differences appear. In regard to this we must remember that man, with all his weaknesses, is a many-sided being. Man is not just one instrument, he is an orchestra. Because of this, we are not all alike—we are all different combinations. In a certain way each man is all the world. It is written that when the Lord said, "Let us make man in our image," it was something that he said to the whole universe. "Let *us* make man." Each being contributed, and that is man. He has something of everything. All of us are combinations, and the difference between us is that some of us are more lions and some of us are more foxes, but all of us are combinations of everything. The problem is to have this universe of beings, which is our being, work together. How to make the orchestra play together. It is done in so many different ways, and each way is unique. I cannot pass my way on to someone else because his way is slightly different, even when we seem to be alike.

Q.   Many people feel that there are two different tales of the creation of man and the universe. The first creation is sometimes even interpreted in Hebrew legend as concerning an androgynous man-woman. Do you believe that these narratives concern the creation of a man of different levels—Adam, Ish, Enosh?

Steinsaltz.   I surely think they are representing three different levels of being. The androgenic, the hermaphrodite form—again one of those things that needs to be made complete—seems to be a primeval one. So the three stories tell of the first idea of man in a primeval state and how it becomes more and more detailed as it goes on and becomes closer to our world. The story of Genesis describes the way from the abstract, from things that are very general, to the more and more concrete. In the first creation of man he is just an image; in the second, man has the problem of good and evil, of pairing, parents, family, blood, and so on; the third is man in history. So I would say there are at least three stages of man described in Genesis—from a basic image to a more and more detailed and down-to-earth one.

Q.   Since man is allegedly the image of God, we seem to have the same problem with God. *Ain Sof,* the endless God of Jewish tradition, is an abstract deity of whom images cannot be made. At the same time, throughout the Bible and rabbinic mystic literature we have anthropomorphisms. How do you interpret the concrete personal nature of this impersonal, spiritual God?

Steinsaltz.   To do it properly, we don't have the time, perhaps not even the space. To do it improperly, we could begin with what I consider to be one of the highest paradoxes. The *Maharal* of Prague (Rabbi Judah Loew) was the first to define it in clear terms. He said something like this: "Something that is really transcendental, which is beyond any limit, cannot be limited even to the point of being something abstract." There is a biblical saying that also relates to this. "The Lord is higher above the nations, on heaven is his glory." That is my translation, a very bad one. I'm sure the King James does it better.

Now the second verse is "The one who is sitting higher up, that looks down on heaven and earth." The interpretation of this saying is something like this: The nations do believe that the Lord is transcendental; He is in heaven; we do believe He is even *higher* up, therefore He looks down at heaven and earth. Even heaven, even the abstract, even what we call and understand as the infinite is really a kind of putting borders, order, and limits. When we say that He is even higher up, then the difference between heaven and earth disappears.

One of the basic explanations for the Jewish preoccupation with material things comes from the idea that the spiritual is not more important and nearer to the divine than the material. To the *Ain Sof,* a galaxy is not greater than, say, a virus. If the Lord cares for the galaxy, he cares also for what the virus will do in the next moment. Any way that we try results in describing Him as a chairman of the board who says he has no time to deal with the small people. This kind of greatness is also a limit, but when we speak of the real limitless greatness, it contains the details, the smallness; it contains the image, as it were, as well as it contains the thing that has no image.

Q.   What is it that man returns to in *teshuvah* [repentance, return] and in *tikun* [restoration]? I wonder if you'd tell us a little more about whether these two words both refer to different levels of the same process. Does repentance emphasize the rejection of man's ordinary level, and restoration emphasize the world as it should be? Or is repentance a process of feeling and sensing both worlds?

Steinsaltz.   In essence, it's all. I rather don't like the word "repentance." Repentance seems to have a restrictive, puritan meaning, while *teshuvah* has so many more connotations. At any rate, the basic idea of *teshuvah*, which is not exactly repentance, is a return, a going back to the basic form. That is *teshuvah*. Now, the need to come back, to revert to the real basic form, means that one has left many things behind, good and bad things. *Tikun* is another step. There is a saying that a person who never sins can do *teshuvah*; even a complete person can return to his basic form, which is on a higher level. But *tikun* means changing things and making them complete. It is always connected with the world, with deeds, with life. If I am doing any kind of *tikun*, correction, then I have to be connected with myself, with my past, with the world. It is not a process done in isolation.

   Teshuvah is a much more solitary activity, in which a person turns in a certain way. He may repent or not—in some cases there is no need for repentance. There is a very profound saying that a person has to make *teshuvah*—and this is, by the way, one of the hardest cases—to make *teshuvah* not only on his sins, but on his virtues. And it seems to be much harder to reunderstand the good things that he did, to make them more complete. In *teshuvah*, I am not so much involved with the world, but in *tikun* there is always involvement.

Q.   The term *Hitbodedut* in Chasidism, I understand, refers to solitude and is associated with meditation.

Steinsaltz. It is one form of meditation, certainly.

Q. There are various kinds of meditation in Judaism. There is a meditation on the names of God that many people are familiar with, and we have read about breathing exercises that accompany some kinds of meditation. Could you tell us something about the role of meditation in Judaism?

Steinsaltz. First of all, you are quite correct, there are many ways. Some of them are really esoteric because the systems that supported these ways have not survived to our times. It is very clear, for example, that the prophets had schools. There were schools for prophets, and they had their own ways of meditation. For one thing, their meditation seemed always to be accompanied by music, which is a way that has almost entirely disappeared today, though it still exists in some forms. In the Chasidic section from which my ancestors come, the rabbi would sing with others for a while and there would then follow a long period of silent meditation. There were times when my ancestors would do this for six hours; this combination of music and meditation was one way.

But many of the forms really disappeared. We know, for example, that there were certain postures people took while meditating—in order not to fall asleep as well as for other reasons! The *Hitbodedut* type of meditation was developed among the Bratzlaver Chasidim and is an attempt for a personal feeling of communion and conversation with God. *Chabad* meditation is entirely different. This is a form in which one takes a certain idea and thinks about it during a certain time of prayer; sometimes for as long as six or seven hours. There are still some people who practice this way, silently meditating on a preset problem, a very fine point in Kabbalah or in a book.

The *Kotzk* meditation is the one perhaps nearest to Zen meditation. The point of this form is to discard external images, to get rid of empty words, and to reach a point where you are able to say exactly what you mean. After a very long period of silent meditation, one tries to be absolutely true to the words he says. It is a terribly tiring process. You find that this or that is not what you mean and so you have to go further on. And so it goes, on and on for hours until a person has a feeling that he can say something properly. There is a very famous story about one of the great rabbis who spent his last years in Israel. He said, "When I was young I used to pray to have the grace to say one prayer properly. Now I have come to Israel, and it is said that the air of Israel makes one wiser. I now pray to be able to say one word properly."

There are other mystical forms of meditation that are practiced but not aired very much—and there are many reasons for this. One of the reasons is that at one time, people were not interested in it seriously and those who did it were terribly concerned about the practice being true and proper. When it becomes a plaything, when it becomes a fad, there is something wrong about it. One of the ideas of the sacred is that it is not a plaything. There is a feeling of distance, and one should not play with it. And if one cannot, one should perhaps stay out. This is one of the reasons why for years these forms were not publicized.

Q. I'd like to ask something about the idea of the sacred in regard to sacrifice. In Genesis, it's indicated that one cannot consume the blood of an animal because it is his life, and his life belongs to God. How do you interpret this return of the blood, which is life, to God?

Steinsaltz. It can be taken on so many different levels. But the first thing to keep in mind is that any sacrifice is outwardly a symbolic act. The act in itself is a ritual, and the ritual points to the ideal sacrifice of giving. It is not the only one, because sacrifice also means denying something that I want from myself. It is not the same thing. This giving that is spoken about is a giving of the soul, of the essence, and the most obvious representation of the essence of life in any form is the blood. This is repeated in so many different ways. It is stated partially in Genesis and repeated and emphasized in Leviticus: blood symbolizes life. Blood cannot be used because it belongs to the Creator. But this is at the same time clearly a symbolic form. For example, the blood of some animals such as fishes is consumed. It is not a magic idea about the quality of blood as blood. The animal sacrifices are a symbolic giving of a part of the soul, and the ritual sacrifice of blood is an essential part of it.

Q. Does this have something to do with the fact that God breathed the breath of life into man and that the breath of life only stays with man a limited number of years and returns to God?

Steinsaltz. Let's say that is a beautiful way to put it. There is another way to say it that emphasizes it: that the world is made by a word which is external breath, but that the soul of man is made by breathing into him, giving the innermost into him. While the world is a more outward manifestation of the power of creativity, the soul of man is the innermost giving of life. The idea of life—blood-life, breath-life—is connected on a symbolic level. It is not a mythical level. There is a difference. One doesn't think that blood in itself is intrinsically holy, that breath in itself is something holy. When it is used, it is understood as a symbolic form, not as a concrete one.

Q. I believe in Judaism there are at least two different kinds of sacrifices: communion in a peace offering and purification or atonement in a sin offering that was totally consumed by fire.

Steinsaltz. The peace offering is a communion, the feeling of peaceful connection and thanksgiving in which everyone participates: the person who sacrifices, the priests, and God, whose symbol is the altar. The sin offering is also made as a form of communion, but the sinner does not participate. And the sin offering is not entirely consumed by the fire—the priest partakes of a part of it. The third kind of offering is the one that is burnt entirely and understood as a pure gift. The sacrifice has so many different meanings. One of them is this whole-hearted offering, which is not a thanksgiving but what I would call a pure sacrifice.

Q. Is there any substantial difference in the inner state of man in regard to these various sacrifices?

Steinsaltz. Certainly, they refer to three entirely different levels and meanings of the word "sacrifice." But every sacrifice basically means coming to yourself. The aim of every sacrifice is to create a link. The idea is that a link is created by a process of interchange, of giving and taking. The process of taking from the Lord is much easier than giving to Him, so I have to find ways to symbolize and structure the act.

Q.   You mentioned before that in denying something in myself I sacrifice as well as when I give something.

Steinsaltz.   The point is that in a sacrifice, I am giving up something of myself, of my property. Fasting, for example, is a sacrifice because it has the same effect. There is a beautiful part of the prayer book which says that because we no longer have any sacrifices in the temple I give my blood and my fat and glands by way of fasting. This is what I call the denial.

Q.   Is it necessary to create this link in some way?

Steinsaltz.   In a certain way, I am always in the middle of a process: I am living, I am breathing, I am doing, I have something. The link exists already—the bounty, the power, is being given to me at every moment. Life is being given to me and I try to do something to make the link mutual. There is a very important idea that is stated in many different ways: that while receiving creates a link, giving makes a deeper link—psychologically and in many other ways. In a very broad way, every commandment is a small form of sacrifice because it contains this: at a certain point I don't do exactly what I want. So what is sacrifice? In a small way, if I want to tell a joke and I don't tell it, that is a sacrifice: I don't do exactly what I want. It becomes a sacrifice when it is oriented in this way.

Q.   Could this have anything to do with the transmutation of the material body? Legends regard Adam and Eve as having a body of light before the fall, and there are talmudic references to our spiritual body. Do you think there is anything in the Jewish tradition regarding the transformation of the material body, or do these examples refer to one of the higher levels of the soul?

Steinsaltz.   While there are references to the nonmaterial body in kabbalistic literature, it is not the main line of Kabbalah. One of the reasons for this, I think, is that the way of Jewish mysticism is not so much the *gnostic*, knowing experience but the participation and work experience. There are many things that can be known, but in Judaism, they are often regarded as useless things. There was once a person who attained a certain stage of spiritual development and found that there were many supernatural powers attached to this stage. He prayed for these powers to be taken from him. As he expressed it: "If I cannot worship with these powers, what does it matter if I know what someone is doing a hundred miles from here?" There are many authentic stories of this kind. It always brought a struggle, because you cannot play with people, you should not play games with these powers. If you cannot worship truly with them, they are useless.

Q. I understand that the synagogue prayer book contains remnants of the ancient temple ritual of sacrifice before its destruction. Doesn't the survival of this ritual as prayer demonstrate that sacrifice was essentially a dedication to a higher level, and only incidentally the killing of an animal?

Steinsaltz. First of all, remember that I'm not a reactionary. But I rather dislike spiritual people, spiritual things. And I don't agree entirely with the concept that prayer is a higher level. I spoke a while ago about the idea of the material and the spiritual, and I think perhaps one may say that the thing that is wrong with Christianity is its preoccupation with the spiritual. I think it is the beginning of every corruption. You can also see it in Hinduism and in Hindu politics. In the spirituality and the allegory of these religions, there is a corruption. I don't believe that the Lord is nearer to the spiritual realm than He is to the material realm. I think to make Him a spiritual being is to belittle Him. The common concept that prayer is a higher form of sacrifice is very clearly refuted in the prayerbook.

Something not generally known is that there were synagogues at the time of the temple. After the morning sacrifice at the temple, the people went to the synagogue to pray. This dispels the concept of prayer as a higher and later development. Prayer can contain a memory of sacrifice, but I don't believe that sacrifice is any lower. I rather think that it is a higher level. Of course, it entails the slaughter of animals. Had we been spiritual beings there would be no need for sacrifice, but as long as we are rather crude animals ourselves, we are connected to the material world. This animal nature is at least fifty percent of our being—in some cases ninety-nine percent—and animal sacrifice touched us very deeply.

This is a matter for a much longer discussion, but to put it briefly, while sacrifices are not nice to watch, they are not made for watching. Almost every human experience that has any depth and real involvement has within it the ambivalent feelings of attraction and disgust—the sexual act, birth, and so on. The observer is not always the best person to be the judge, and our own involvement is deeper by far when it has a physical form than when it doesn't. I think the prayerbook is not a higher level but a substitute—a spiritualization of something that, unfortunately, cannot be done.

I have the same opinion about the difference between the circumcision of the heart in Christianity and another kind of circumcision in Judaism. Circumcision is felt and understood as a sacrifice. The person who holds the baby is called the altar, and he is the most important person involved. In it there is very strongly the idea of the sacrifice and the blood. I repeat, if you are not involved in it, it is not a nice thing to watch. It is not made for watching.

Q.   Does not prayer move the upper levels of the universe in Judaism?

Steinsaltz.   Yes, it does, but not in a magic way, because everything moves all the worlds. It moves them in one way or another. Prayer is what I call a directed way of doing things, but it is not the only way. If someone spits in your face, perhaps more worlds are moved in a very real sense. There is a saying that you can laugh at someone and destroy your own soul so entirely and completely that one hundred prayers won't mend it.

29

The Vertical Adventure

Q. It says in the Zohar, "The Holy One, blessed be He, created man in the likeness of the All." Does this mean that the wholeness possible for man is on the scale of the universe?

Steinsaltz. It is said that God created man in his own image. The only way that can be understood is that man was created on the same scale and on the same level. The same idea is expressed when it is said that God turned to all of creation and said, "Let us create man." Let *us* create man. He turned to the whole universe and said, "Let us all participate," and each of the parts of the whole gave something of itself to create man.

Q. But the whole universe—what does it mean? We are taught that there are worlds within worlds.

Steinsaltz. One of the stories is that Adam was created tall—that he reached from earth to heaven. And God put his hand on him and

------

Conversation with Jean Sulzberger, *Parabola* 10(1):80–85.

squashed him to a certain size. We do believe that a human being is a multileveled being, a being that is made of, so to say, several stories, one above the other. The highest one is really identical with the Godhead: the highest one. But there is a point of the self, and the point of the self is the point on a column that goes from earth to the highest heaven. I would say that self-consciousness and self-image are at a certain level of this column. Perhaps very small children are almost entirely on the physical level. Later on, perhaps a person may move slightly higher into something that is less corporeal or not entirely corporeal. The column itself can become higher and higher still, which means that the self can reach to higher and higher levels.

Now, when the self is on a particular level, a man can understand only that one level. The words and the notions he can speak about are connected solely with the images and notions of that level. Because humanity as a whole is usually on more or less the same level, one of the problems of every kind of prophet is that even when he sees, he cannot tell. There are no words to describe what he perceives. These perceptions don't have words, so they have to be translated into images that are symbolic.

Q. Would you describe a whole man as one who can see, indeed *be*, in more than one world?

Steinsaltz. Every human being lives in more than one world. We are living in the world of emotion, the world of thought, and so on. In some ways we are always living in more than one world, almost by definition. More than that, some of us at least have a grasp, to a greater or lesser extent, of some existence that is beyond the purely mental plane of existence, and occasionally find a way to a world or worlds above us. But usually for most people, existence is just the "amphibian" state between the purely material and the mental-emotional. There are people who can achieve a state beyond this more perfectly, but it is perhaps only once in a generation that someone like this may appear. It is as though he doesn't really belong to this existence—not that he doesn't have a physical body, but his physical body is just what it should be: only a small part of his whole being. As it is, it's as though I inherited a skyscraper and I'm living only on the first story, or sometimes even below, in the basement.

Q. Are you saying that most men have only physical bodies?

Steinsaltz. I think each of us inherited the whole building. Most people stay in the basement, some people climb to the first story, some go higher still. We know that even climbing a mountain in a quite ordinary way requires a great deal of hard work. And in relation to the climb we are speaking of, even though the potential is inborn, it needs a huge amount of training. In another kind of example, human beings seem to have the inborn ability to learn to read and write—a very abstract and complicated ability, but every human being possesses it to some degree. Still, there is a necessary period of turning this potential into practical ability, even though there is the capability inherent that makes it possible.

Q. Can a person move from the basement to the next story through his own efforts, or does he need a guide, a teacher?

Steinsaltz. A teacher is always a great help. We should have to say that this climb is theoretically possible almost independently, because it is the individual's heritage, but practically speaking, for most people it is impossible without help. Some people have living teachers, some have dead teachers, but they still have teachers. How many people learn to read and write on their own?

Q. So most of us need a guide.

Steinsaltz. We need someone who has gone a part of the way and who can show how it is to be done and what can be done. There are people who have an inborn aptitude for this climb; for others it is necessary to work harder. Though there are guidelines that may be more or less true for everyone, each person has an individual form of growth. We are not identical—unless we would reach the highest point of our being, in which, possibly, we are entirely identical.

Q. What is the Jewish method for moving up in the building? There are many Jews who search but who can't find a method. So many

Jews go into Zen Buddhism or Sufism because there seems to be no one within our own tradition to tell us how we can grow.

Steinsaltz. There are two reasons for this. The first is practical and historical. For many years, the number of people wishing for this was very limited. Most people, if they want adventure, want horizontal adventures. Those who had a deep desire were always very few. The many disruptions in the history of the Jews caused many of the teachers and their pupils to disappear along with many other things. So this is historical. And it is also true that there are always places where such teachers exist, but you cannot find them listed in a telephone directory.

The second reason is far deeper. The major part of Jewish tradition holds that while there are methods to achieve many great and even holy powers on many levels, the question is, what use is it? Clairvoyance, levitation, "second sight"—it was a firm belief that all these are possible on a certain path of development. The question is, should there be what is called a systematic, well-taught way of spiritual growth per se? What is the aim? Let's say that I grow twice or three or ten times bigger in a spiritual way. The only thing that makes this worthwhile is the worship of God and not spiritual growth. The spiritual growth may be an outcome.

Q. Worship doesn't seem to be enough. We can worship to the end of our days and say the Psalms to the end of our days and come no closer to God.

Steinsaltz. We reach here a basic theological point. We believe that God is infinite in such a way that the human being of whatever size and whatever growth can never reach Him. The greatest, highest human soul is still separated from God by an impassable gap. There is an impassable gap between the Creator and the created. Now, this impassable gap can only be passed on one side, on God's side. He can, so to say, give a hand to the people on the other side, to pass, to cross. I can grow as tall as I want and I am still almost at the same distance away: unless He gives me a hand I will never be able—because whatever I become, I am still a creature. Even the highest man stands on the brink of an impassable gap.

The main question therefore becomes, how do I jump over? From that point of view, whatever I am as a person becomes only a personal query, because the real question is, how do I make this jump? And the size I have achieved is not always entirely helpful at this point. It has been said many times that you cannot have growth only in one direction. It is as certain as Newton's law of reaction. There is always some kind of danger with growth—they go together. The higher a person aspires, the stronger the forces below draw him. For every move in the direction of good, there is a natural balancing power that reacts and drives toward evil in one form or another.

One of the sages of the last century put it in a very beautiful way. He said, "In a diamond, you have what is called the diamond part and the plain stone, which is the carrier of the diamond." Now, if you have a huge diamond, it is bigger as a diamond, but the stone is also much bigger. That is why there are stories in all literature about the simple, the ignorant, the innocent sometimes making this jump while higher people who had really great souls could not overcome their own problems, the problems that come, I would say, from the size of their own personalities. So the question is, what can we do to achieve the one, the only great achievement?

Q.   The jump is a process, isn't it?

Steinsaltz.   It is, but in a very real sense it is irrational—it is above any type of reasoning process. Because of that we have to do it, we have to do it every day—possibly every minute. It is almost impossible for a person who did it not to achieve greatness as a kind of by-product. But some people are using their whole powers without knowing what they are doing, while others who have far more knowledge of it never manage to do it. It comes back to the separation at the beginning. You can be of the highest size, you can be made in the image of God, but you are not immune to sin.

Q.   The mystery is still how. To be whole we must begin with a kind of unity in ourselves. And if one sees that the mind is going in one direction and the body is going in another and the emotions in yet another, then how to bring them together? It's a work, isn't it?

Steinsaltz. Oh, that's a work. Here is one of the basic differences among spiritual formulas, or paths. Many of the Far East traditions, for example Zen Buddhism that you mentioned, one may call a kind of secular spiritualism, because they are so very much interested in the growth of man, in the enlightenment of man. There are very many similarities, but one of the basic differences is that it represents a kind of anthropocentric spirituality. In Judaism some of the great masters put far more stress on the basic man–God relationship than on what man is. As I have said, it has been a debate whether a systematic form and method of growth will end in something more than just the growth of the human being.

Q. Sitting here listening to you, I feel a little more collected, as though my head and body were not so separated. With that comes more of a feeling of presence. What is that process?

Steinsaltz. These two parts are not basically enemies. We speak about them as the informed and uninformed parts, and one of the problems is, how do you inform someone that is in a way stupid? The body—and not only the body, the simple animal spirit—and the soul have the problem of coming to a mutual understanding. The example of riding a dumb animal has been used many times. At first there may be no communication—not enmity, but lack of understanding. Later, rider and animal can become so very close that they begin to understand one another. With a good horseman, the horse does not have to be beaten—they have become, so to say, almost a unit. When the soul and the body and every part of it become a unit, then they in fact help each other. The rider will never achieve the same thing without a horse. The soul needs the body because the body has tremendous powers that reinforce it. If we take the parable of the building again, the body is the foundation, and it is very powerful because it has to support the whole structure.

Q. What is man's part? It is God who has to bring down His hand, you said. What is our part?

Steinsaltz. First of all, one of the first conditions is to listen. He is speaking all the time. The Baal Shem said, "The voice inside me never stopped speaking." The voice doesn't stop; we just stopped hearing it. It isn't a phenomenon in time, but a phenomenon in eternity. It is our work to be ready to do the listening.

There are moments when a person is given a gift. Sometimes it is for a minute, sometimes it can last for a day or for months. Usually it is not a permanent change—just a gift, so to say, a loan. To use entirely different symbols: it is like giving someone a million-dollar check on the condition that it be returned after a certain time. The real question is, what use can he make of it in the meantime? Sometimes we get such a big "check" and it will have to be returned.

Sometimes there is a beginner's gift. At that stage I told one of my teachers about my experiences and he said, "Well, you have to know that these things will only last a certain time—you don't know how much time, but they will pass. The only significant thing you can do is make use of them. If you don't make use of them, they will disappear and leave you in the same position that you were before." So many times as a beginner you receive so much more than you do after you work for years, and sometimes you wish again for the days when you could achieve things so much more easily.

We don't know why or when a person is given such a gift, but again, it is only a loan, which is given for a certain period of time. On a different level, Maimonides speaks about the prophets. He says, "Humanity should be seen as a group of people being in the darkest night. From time to time there is a flash of lightning, and then you get your bearings and you see everything, but it disappears after a moment. That is prophecy." That is his symbol of prophecy. On a lesser level, almost everyone gets such a gift. Sometimes it's once in a lifetime, sometimes it is far more frequent—but that is something exceptional. There is no way of ensuring that it will ever come, or come again, and sometimes it is very disappointing. One is waiting and preparing for that . . .

Q.   Is the most important thing, then, just to try to be open?

Steinsaltz.   It helps up to a certain point, but whether it comes or it doesn't come—there are many Jewish ways, as one called it, of becoming a "vessel." Another called it becoming a violin that can be played upon. I have to do all the tuning of the violin and only then will it be fit to play. What can one get from an imperfectly prepared instrument? Some people say that the whole of what Judaism is about is a way of preparing body and soul for having this ability.

Some things are repeated again and again, in our tradition as well as in others. One that is very much stressed is that the biggest and most terrible danger is thinking about oneself. This is considered almost a definition of evil, being self-centered. In a practical and spiritual way, the less I am motivated by my ego in every way, in every form, the more I am able to become a receptacle, a vessel, for receiving what is there. It is there. It is something in the air. I have to have an instrument that can pick it up. We have a soul—we have it *all* in us. We make too much noise. If I am always listening to myself, I cannot listen to any other thing that passes through me. That is a part of it, and part of it is the relation of the individual and others.

More than that, sometimes I may be doing something that in itself is good, but it is not a thing that *I* should do. Sometimes I am trying very hard to do something that is not necessary for me, while neglecting to do something that is necessary. I am speaking about instruments. You see one person is a violin, another is a cello.

Q. What has the perfected man attained?

Steinsaltz. I would say he has attained his whole stature. That means he is able to move on all the scales of all the worlds that correspond to his soul, to all the levels of his soul. The idea of the perfect man is that he can move on this ladder—in his lifetime, during his existence—that he can move from the physical to the highest heaven, that he can understand every level with his own images, with his own ideas. He is going from one heaven to another, or from earth to heaven, and he is at home in all of them. He has a consciousness that attains, I would say, in theory, the whole universe—not just the horizontal. Perfection is not just attaining a certain level, say, the level of an angel. It is the ability to have a double, treble, five or tenfold mode of existence, of understanding. It's a multilayered existence.

It won't do any harm to tell a story. It is told about two great men, a father and a son. They were great leaders, both of them, and the father was possibly one of the outstanding people of his time. He was passing through his son's home one day and he heard a baby cry-ing. He looked and found the baby and his son, who was sitting near the cradle, immersed in meditation. The father soothed the baby and then he shook his son and said to him, "My son, I didn't know you had such a little mind, because even when I am in the deepest medita-tion, I can still hear a fly moving about."

Q.   Does God need perfection from us? Is God in search of man? In a time when everything seems to be going downhill, is there at this moment—which could almost be called the "end of days"—a need for conscious men? A cosmic need?

Steinsaltz.   A definition of our times is complex. In one way, things are becoming worse; in another, many more people are conscious about it. What's more, it seems that they used to say that each period has different souls, different sizes of souls, that behave in a different way in each period. It seems that we are living in a time in which there is a possibility for extreme changes. The extreme changes we can see from one direction to another didn't seem possible thirty or forty years ago. People moved in these directions much more slowly. So it seems that the movement—or the ability—has become accelerated.

The search for man is constant. God is searching for man—the saints and the evildoers alike. The need vis-à-vis God is the same as it ever was; the need in the world is perhaps greater. There were times when it seemed that humanity was distributed in a more even way. Now there seems to be great diversity of levels, and great complexity.

There is certainly a need for the teachers to be greater. In an enlightened age you don't need such a great teacher, even though it seems just the opposite. As I said, perfection is the ability to operate on many different levels. Now, we are living in a time in which there are souls scattered from every level one can imagine. They are inter-connected not only socially, because an age is not just a random min-gling of people who happen to be together, who were born together by some mischance. They are interconnected, and in complicated times like these, a teacher must be very great.

A teacher needs two things—perhaps three things. He should understand the subject that he wants to teach. He should know methods of teaching it. And he should understand the level and understanding of the pupil. If he is not able to do any of these things, or all of them, he is no good.

Q. Could it be said that we must first know ourselves as we are? Would that be a first step?

Steinsaltz. I sometimes say that the first step is to acknowledge our yearning toward something; it is far below having a desire, but to acknowledge that there is something in ourselves, just to acknowledge it.

I had a friend who passed away many years ago. He wasn't troubled in a personal way, but he was troubled about his spirit. We used to meet many times for years, off and on, and I once asked him, what was it that made him go on, because it was obvious he was a person who was troubled for years, surely more than twenty years. He said that there was a sentence in the Book of Job that was the key sentence for his life. Job is speaking to the Lord and saying, "You are yearning for your handiwork." And my friend said, "If God is yearning for me, how can I say no?" And that was pursuing him, as I say, for twenty very troubled years, and possibly toward the end of his life that was the main point . . .

Q. What is the mark of a real teacher?

Steinsaltz. One thing that is always a clear mark and true of every real teacher is humility. The reason is a very simple one. It is not a moral reason. It is because the greater a person is, the greater he feels his insignificance and his lack. By definition, a great teacher will have great humility. Another mark of a real teacher is the feeling of responsibility. It is essential for a teacher and is also a mark of the personality. Sometimes you can look at two teachers and you don't see the difference. Outside they may look very much alike. One of the ways to find out is when you look at their disciples, and then you see what was in the teacher. It appears in the disciples in a far more marked way and so it is a good way of assessing the kind of person the teacher is.

Q. At the same time, what can a teacher really transmit? Can unity be transmitted? Can consciousness or will be transmitted?

Steinsaltz. Seemingly, partially it can. Partially. Sometimes you feel in the presence of someone that something is transmitted beyond whatever was said, something very definite. But the main work of a teacher is as a teacher. Quite a number of people are capable, to one degree or another, of giving somebody else a push. But the real demand on a teacher is that the pupil doesn't want only to be pushed. Sometimes a person can become just a puppet. Whatever he has is the handiwork of someone else. The person becomes a kind of implant, or transplant. You can transplant something in a person, but it really isn't his. It works, but it isn't his and he can't do anything with it.

What a teacher has to transmit, if he is really a teacher, is how I can utilize myself. They are giving a map. I have my own road to walk on and nobody can walk it for me. What I really need is for someone to show me the way. There are very few mystical descriptions in the Talmud—it is traditionally a hidden literature—but in one place Rabbi Akiva, the oldest of a certain group, says, "When you come to a certain place, don't say so and so." That is the work of a teacher. You come to a certain pathway, you have a right turn or a left turn, one way of doing things and another way. Someone can tell you the right direction and then you have to walk on. He can't walk instead of you. You walk on. Then you get to something else.

Q. What do you think is the real question about wholeness?

Steinsaltz. I would say that the big question about it is the question of defining it. The basic question is that wholeness, completeness, may mean so many different things, and can be understood in so many partial ways—and misleading ways. Sometimes achievement is taken for it, or attainment, or talent, or even fame. These things may be good things or not, but they are different from wholeness.

Q. Doesn't the definition depend on the level on which it is being defined?

Steinsaltz.   The problem is that the best definitions are the least useful. The best definition is that man is made in the image of God: that image is wholeness; that image is perfection. I'm saying that is the best definition. It is also the least useful one. It is the least useful one because there is the same danger of being misled, and perhaps in an even worse way. A definition closer to the measurable world would be a harmonious relationship between the different parts. That is not on the same level—it is a far lower level—but one can deal with it better. I think that wholeness is a kind of standard by which almost everything can be judged. The degree to which something is whole can help evaluate it—not how big it is but how far it has become harmonious and proportioned. This is true whether it is an apple, a glass, or a human being. A blemish, by this standard, would mean that there is something lacking, or something out of proportion, inharmonious. In many cases, a lack is indicated by the fact that there is something that could function perfectly that is not functioning.

Here we come to one of the problems of a person who has achieved what could be called this perfection. Actually it is not a problem for them so much as for others. Such people sometimes do not want to be moved, do not want to disturb their harmony. Sometimes they don't care for others. Caring for others is the problem of every great teacher, because when he gets in contact with other people, he is destroying his own balance. You see, if you make a connection with someone else, then you become, at least for the time being, a unit with that person. But this new unit is not balanced, and to try to balance this new unit requires a very, very different effort on the part of the person who is, by himself and on his own, a balanced person. That is why so many people, including most of the prophets, did not want to be teachers—not because they were blemished, but because they did not want to destroy their balance. The story of Moses and the Burning Bush, his repeated refusal to be the Redeemer, is not just caused by humility. He is being asked to take an interest in other people, to be involved with people, some of whom are perhaps, so to say, nasty people. And you cannot work with a person or speak with a person without having contact and having at least his image imprinted on you. So there is a great sacrifice involved for the harmonious person to agree to be connected with others.

So as I said, this wholeness requires harmony, and other people entering disturb it constantly. The deeper his connection with others, the more his balance has to become a kind of moving balance. If he succeeds, of course, he gains—he is able to incorporate all the others into a greater wholeness. So he is growing enormously. This is true of a figure such as Moses, of any true and real leader of the people: everything is magnified a hundredfold, a thousandfold. The individual becomes like a powerful lens in which forces from below are focused and transformed.

═ 30 ═

Becoming Unstable

Q. We live in an egalitarian moment in which it is considered that everyone is equal and everyone is free, and the idea of hierarchy is perceived as an arbitrary imposition on the freedom of man. I wonder how realistic this conception is from your point of view.

Steinsaltz. My point of view is almost the opposite. Egalitarian ideas are not supported by any evidence. The inequality of man is blatantly apparent. The only way one can find any support for the idea of equality is in a very difficult religious concept: the concept that people are born in the image of the Lord and are therefore equal. There is no other argument that I have heard that serves any purpose. All egalitarian movements are an outcome of Judeo-Christian ideas that contain within them the notion of receiving a divine soul that for everyone is more or less the same.

We can speak, in a way, of the equality of souls mostly because we can't see them. But it is very hard to speak about equality in any

Conversation with William and Louise Welch, *Parabola* 9(1):8–15.

other way. All forces everywhere, within and without, work against equality. People are so inherently different—not only different, but unequal—that it requires a constant struggle to accept the notion of some kind of equality. The only justification for the idea is what you may call a mystical one; even though people don't appear to be equal, there is something equal in them. From this point of view, whether it is a good thing or not such a good thing, hierarchy seems to me to be a given element, inherent in creation and in nature. This is nature—everything else is an attempt to change nature.

Q. The evidence of hierarchy in the physiological organization of man is quite clear: from above downward, with semi-independent functions, each with a certain autonomy but subject to control from above. Might there be a relationship between the higher and lower in our psyche and some corresponding potential, if not actual, authority?

Steinsaltz. The physiological model has the advantage of stressing that hierarchy involves interdependence. For instance, the mind is far superior to the legs—anyone would prefer to have his leg cut off rather than to have his head cut off. On the other hand, there are functions that the legs perform that the head cannot. Recently I taught some ancient texts that spoke about inner spiritual hierarchy—for hierarchy exists not only as an outer biological and social structure, but also as an inner one. There are higher and lower forces within our world, within our souls, and within our concepts. And even there, hierarchy is interdependent. There are lower elements—clearly lower by every definition—that have a basic power that makes them not only worthwhile, but in certain situations far more important than higher ones.

There are many discussions in Jewish mystical tradition about interrelationships between mind, or intellect, and emotion. In our view, in the hierarchy of the soul emotions are below mind, because mind gives meaning and direction to emotions. The powers of conceptualization and of thinking are called the father and mother; the emotions are called the children. It is a common way of describing them; but even so, we know that in the working of the soul there are instances when the mind cannot do anything. The intellect is powerless to achieve things. That which emotions can achieve, the mind cannot, but the emotions cannot operate without some kind of subject–object relationship. Emotions, dependent on information and direction supplied by the mind, can only work within that context. The mind works as a watcher, or censor, of things without and within.

It has often been noted that the strength of emotional and intellectual ties is very unequal. Whether we like it or not, emotionally we get attached to things and aren't able to change our attachment with the intellect.

Q.   Isn't there also a hierarchy within the realms of thinking and feeling?

Steinsaltz.   There is an internal hierarchy, and another hierarchy of different sets of things, one above the other. There are also complete cycles that go one into another.

Q.   Where do you place the sense of values? I think different levels exist in what we value, and how we value it.

Steinsaltz.   We consider the sense of values as something that comes before, or hierarchically above, conscious mind. We believe there are powers within every framework that give direction. I am speaking now not about mystical experiences but in a practical context: on one level my mind is made up about whether it wants to be for or against something. Then it creates the network and the building blocks for my basic attitude. Later, some kind of appropriate emotion arises. Because emotion is secondary, in order to develop, it needs something to build upon. If I don't have any picture of whatever it is, I cannot have any emotion—love or hatred—

Q.   Or reverence.

Steinsaltz.   Or even reverence. I have to have a point of view; and to have a feeling of awe, of facing the unknown, on an emotional basis, one has to have a very deep intellectual background. In the Middle Ages people said that the peak of knowledge is "I don't know." The question is: If that is so, what is the difference between the person who has no knowledge whatever and the person who knows? The difference is that the person who knows, knows that he doesn't know. The person who does not know, doesn't even have knowledge of his ignorance.

So the feeling of reverence is enhanced by knowing the distance. Even if I think that something is far beyond me, I need to know the gap in order to have the feeling of reverence and awe. If I don't know about the gap, the distance doesn't make any sense to me. To know that I don't know is more than just making a statement; to be emotionally involved in it, I have to have an idea of what the meaning of it is. Newton supposedly said that he felt like a small child playing with pebbles on the shore of the sea of knowledge. To feel that really and truly, you have to know as much as Newton did. Those who don't know may say it, but they don't feel it emotionally.

Emotional life is hierarchically dependent on conceptual life; conceptual life makes it possible to have emotional life. And conceptual life is hierarchically below a value system that makes things desirable or undesirable. I have given lectures concerning what philosophers say about the nature of proof. Philosophy has no real way of defining proof, except what is said by some conservative philosophers: the proof that something is true is that it clicks. That is the only way I know something is true—that I have proved it: there is some kind of click. That is possibly the highest hierarchy in our conscious minds—that which says one relationship is true, and another is not.

So we are, in fact, judging things, and we say: that fits and that doesn't fit. Now, we cannot explain the way something fits together, because explanation itself comes back to the same question: does it click? If it does, the explanation makes sense. The nature of proof is something that, within the soul, is above anything in the conscious mind—even above the power of pure reason. Above pure reason stands something—we don't know what it is—but it convinces us that something *is*.

Q. Is the vision of hierarchy essential, then, for the movement upwards of the sense of values, and the spiritual search?

Steinsaltz. There is something that has to be achieved. If there is no hierarchy, nothing can be achieved by moving from one point to another. When there is a difference, movement makes sense; when there is no difference, movement does not make sense. If one goes into it further, one gets into very complex concepts of movement and what movement means; we would be speaking about the theory of relativity. In the abstract, when there is no interrelation, movement or size doesn't make any sense. Without a scale, there is no movement; to advance or retreat depends on having a direction—a beginning and an end.

Q.   One has the sense that along with the force of emotion, and the polarity of like and dislike, there can be at times an intelligence of feeling that has its own quality. You place the mind above emotion, but where do you place this intelligence of the emotions?

Steinsaltz.   People say that the heart has its own reason. We believe that every emotion is made, roughly speaking, of three parts, as mind is made up of the same three parts. There is the intelligence of the emotion, the emotions of the emotion, and the mechanics of emotion (getting it expressed). So the intelligence, or mind of the emotion, does exist. We believe that the intellectual powers are also made like this. There is intellectual thought and emotional thought, because intellect has in it an emotional part. That is one reason why the process of thinking sometimes becomes enjoyable per se. Intelligence is not pure; it also has a part that is emotion. The reason of the emotion works in a different way, on a different level; that is the inner hierarchy. Emotion has its own way of conceptualizing, not intellectually but by creating images.

Q.   Is there a concept in Judaism that this model within the individual is a reflection of an order that exists on another level? Do the same elements exist on a cosmic scale?

Steinsaltz.   Given the creation by God of a complete universe, it is a basic assumption that everything is interconnected. One can see something like that by looking at drops of water. One sees reflections, smaller ones and bigger ones, like in a house of mirrors—the same thing, the same nature, reflected in different ways. It follows that if I would know perfectly, completely, entirely, one part, than I would know the whole.

It is a beautiful thing; when God says, "Let us make man," He is calling the whole universe—"Let *us* make man." And each contributes something: the foxes and the lions, the monkeys and the angels, all give something! So we are the result of everything that is. The idea is that we contain (and this point is considered essential) the mind–body point of connection; the same hierarchy that exists in the body exists in the mind.

One of the ways to explain the basic concept of our religion is to say that because we are men, we have to correct. We have free will, and we have the ability to repair. Because we have free will, we are also the only ones who have the ability to distort. One of our problems is that of choice. There is an attempt to become better; it is like making corrections for a lens. The lens became for some reason not right, so it distorts whatever is seen through it. We believe the main duty, the chief work of man is to make corrections until it is possible to transmit the right picture.

Q. The question in my mind, before you said that, is that there is an order evident in our bodies and in all nature; everything is perfect—except me. If I am a reflection of this perfect order, why am I not perfect?

Steinsaltz. Free will is an element of disorder. It is also the only element of advancement. Any kind of movement is a way of destroying a system of order. Walking, for example, is *becoming unstable*. Running is becoming even more unstable. Flying in a plane creates a different kind of instability; the plane becomes less and less stable until it takes off, and then it restabilizes and gains equilibrium. Movement destroys equilibrium all the time; the power to move is also the power to destroy order.

The imperfection is inherent, because I am the only creature that has independent volition, and the only creature in the universe that can distort. These distortions are part of our common human work for coming to a higher point, because other creatures, seemingly, cannot move of their own volition, and we can. And being able to move means that we can move in different directions. We don't have the same biological point of view as other creatures; we are free of instinct—not entirely, but to a very great degree. That is our power, and that is our downfall.

Q.   You almost say *choice*, don't you?

Steinsaltz.   Yes, I am always saying *choice*. Animals and plants don't have that element of choice. It used to be a habit of mine, when I felt angry or discontented, to go to the zoo and watch the animals; animals have a certain type of perfection that we don't. In a way, it's the same thing that makes babies beautiful. Sometimes you wonder why so many babies are born wise and beautiful, and why when they become adults, they lose both those qualities! It is because babies are innocent; they reflect the power of relation and choice. They reflect something we call the great order of things. The bigger they become, the more they are able to move. There are some people who, as they grow older, clearly become wiser—not just more knowledgeable (there is a great difference between the two)—and also more beautiful. Their choice, their achievement of consciousness, was a growing from one set of relationships to another, a bigger one, a better one, which is what all this is about. On the other hand, there are some people who make the choice of distorting, and they become less wise and less beautiful, everything less. So as I say, this difficulty of mankind—being the one creature that is not in order—is my strength and my weakness.

Q.   You are speaking of levels of order, aren't you? Because doesn't a human being then choose to live according to another, higher order?

Steinsaltz.   That is what I am saying. We are in movement. In every set of circumstances, every level of hierarchy, there is stability of some kind. Movement is a disturbing element, and also rather dangerous. Between one step of a ladder and another, there is a void; the void is necessary because it makes the difference between the levels. But if I want to move from the first rung to the second or the third, I have to take the risk of passing though this void, of abandoning my foothold in one place in order to get to another, and in between I may fall down. It often happens.

So our process of growing, from the physical to the spiritual, is getting from one set of ways of behavior, and so on, to a different one, which we hope is a higher one. It is not necessarily so, but it is a movement into a different order in which things, after some time, again become more or less stabilized. In any process of inner growth or evolution, there is the same problem of getting from one point to another. Being born is in a way ceasing to exist in one set, one type of order, and getting into a different type of order in which almost all the rules are changed. As a fetus, I don't breathe, and my life system is entirely different. Being born is the shock of transfer to a set of circumstances in which almost everything is done in a different way, in which there is an order of a different kind. Dying is doing the same thing—again, in a different way, perhaps coming to a point where I discard certain things about my being. The shock there is clearly that of transferring from one set of circumstances to another.

Our notion of people going to hell has to do with this transfer. I might be magnificently suited to survive in this world, but now I have to go into another world with other rules, whether I want to or not. And the things that equipped me to be, for instance, a financial success in this world will send me to hell in a different world! If a person doesn't grow through adaptation to a certain order and then move into another one, he is unable to deal with it. It is like the tadpole and the frog. We see this all the time: men who were wonderful as boys in schools are not necessarily wonderful as adults out of school. Because a change creates a necessity for a different order.

Q.   The transformation of a tadpole to a frog, or from one set of conditions in life to another in death, is something that happens automatically; but isn't there another possibility of transformation for human beings, an intentional one?

Steinsaltz.   Oh, that is what it *should* be! That is what I meant about a person going to heaven or hell; the process of learning, of education, determines which way one takes. It is a process of knowing the direction consciously and following it consciously to a different state, so that one is not thrown into the workings, so to say, but is preparing consciously to go into them. I would call any type of school or learning preparation for entering into a different order—a conscious preparation. The tadpole doesn't learn to become a frog; but for man, as we know, it is very hard work. What I said about emotional hell refers to when a person is kicked into a different set without being prepared. Imagine: all your desires, images, ways of thinking are tied to a very particular set of values and notions. If you are put into a place where none of this applies, then you don't need devils to torment you; you will be as miserable as anybody can imagine, because of your inability to deal with something you are not equipped for.

As a human being, I have some ability to change consciously to a different order, but actually, we set our hearts on a certain place and don't want to get any higher. There is an old Russian story about a simple soldier who rescued the Czar from some danger. The Czar told him he could ask for whatever he wanted, and the soldier said, "Please, change my commanding officer!" Instead of moving upward in the hierarchy, I just want to shift into a more comfortable position on the same level.

Q. What is the difference between mechanical and conscious equilibrium?

Steinsaltz. Conscious equilibrium is not a stationary stability, but rather a constant readjustment. If I consciously want to remain in equilibrium, in quiet, in peace, it means I have to work very hard, to adjust all the time. In a mechanical equilibrium, forces are more or less in balance, they can go on in the same way until something changes. In a conscious equilibrium, I have to work very hard to stay in the same place. What Alice said is a very good definition of conscious equilibrium: to run very fast in order to stay in the same place.

Some people seem to have such equanimity that they do not mind anything, but this may come from two very different ways of being: one, in which the person does not care about anything, and the other, in which he cares very much but is able to make constant adjustments in order not to get angry or sad or overjoyed. This sort of conscious equilibrium is very, very hard work. You have to work all the time. It's like what a pilot does in a plane. You can't fall asleep.

If someone makes me angry or does something I don't like, then I may say something or think about something that is just the opposite. But I don't only want to learn, as every adult person learns, not to *show* a reaction—I wish to learn how not to be overwhelmed by the reaction. If I just escape the situation, nothing really happens. When events occur that I don't like and I'm not prepared for—there is the test.

I would say that hierarchy is an infinite number of orders of laws, one above the other. Each order has within it an inner order; and with this interdependence, all in all, the whole hierarchical situation is a complete set in which different parts are working. So there is a context in which we are all equal, in which existence is equal in this eternal interdependence.

Q. What you have said raises the question, What is equality? Are you saying that authority is determined by the degree of consciousness?

Steinsaltz. I am a part of something. Authority is the rule of the higher over the lower. I think that, as you say, possibly hierarchy is defined by greater consciousness. Julian Huxley seems an unlikely source to quote, but in speaking about evolution he says that only in this sense of growing consciousness can we make sense of evolution as a progressive line. Advance is not in terms of "fitness"; if evolution is simply a matter of the survival of the fittest, it would have stopped with the cockroach. But there is a different striving, for more consciousness; and in this way, we may say we have something above the cockroach.

So power or authority is connected with the level of consciousness, on every level, to every degree. It determines what is bigger, what is smaller; the bigger is bigger because it can encompass the smaller. In every hierarchy, the one who knows where to put the others is the one who is in charge. The highest in the hierarchy is the one who can put all the parts in some kind of complete order. Otherwise, whatever the official, apparent order may be, it is a false hierarchy. In a real hierarchy, the one who is most conscious about what is happening is the higher. Other people may perhaps be more powerful, but they are not higher.

One of the things that makes life so complicated is that there is not one type of hierarchy, but many. And because there are conflicting hierarchies, we get confused. There is the hierarchy of the good, the hierarchy of the wise, the hierarchy of the powerful. Each is different. I would say that all designs somehow end up at the infinite, at a convergent point; but in our world they are not convergent. The problem of existence is that different hierarchies are not aligned, not compatible with each other. It has been said before that in this world we have the clever and the good—and they are usually not the same people. A world in which they would become more and more identical would be a better world.

So our problem is not lack of hierarchy, but too many hierarchies. Our problem is to make order among them, to arrange the different hierarchies in a hierarchical formation. We have different types of ladders, and when they are not arranged among themselves, they don't lead anywhere. We have the feeling that we have lots of ability and can climb higher. What we need is a way of attaching the separate ladders into one that becomes far bigger. But every group has its own ladder and doesn't want to share it, and because of this we come to the point where no one in his separate way can go any higher. So we divide and come to a sort of compromise that says: because we don't agree on which is better, let us assume that nothing is better; because we don't agree on who should be on top, nobody should be there.

Q.   What authority will we all accept?

Steinsaltz.   We all accept that there is a certain ladder; what we dispute about is which one. The ladders seem incompatible; they don't meet. We are dealing in different areas. The difference between us— for instance, between the believing man and the knowledgeable man— often take precedence over something that is more urgent: Which ladder is the more important one.

Q.   Is it finally a matter of agreement or decision? Or is there one that simply is more important? It seems there would have to be, if there is real hierarchy.

Steinsaltz. I would say there definitely is one; that we don't agree about it doesn't mean anything. All of us agree that what is most positive should be at the head. The question is not so much about hierarchy as about what hierarchy to adopt. Almost every religion tries to give some way of measuring things, some kind of scale. We need a way of bringing different things to some kind of common scale, some common value into which they can all be translated. That is what we are in search of.